The Way of Love

Joseph of Arimathea
*tells the True Story behind
the Message of Jesus*

Recorded Channelings
Compiled by Peter Wheeler

The important objective.

*The Master has stated that the
purpose of books such as this is to
motivate people to think, to work
things out for themselves and not
to rely on explanations from others
every step of the way. So it is hoped
that this book will give the reader
new knowledge, and through
experience and gleaning
information from many other
works which perhaps otherwise
would never have been thought of,
will give rise to further knowledge.
If that is so, this work will have
achieved its spiritual objective.*

Publisher/Distributor: The Leaders Partnership
Copyright © The Leaders Partnership
Box 16457, London, SE 14 5WH, England
Fax 0171 652 6467

First edition 1996, printed in the U.K.
ISBN: 90-75635-01-X
NUGI: 626 Esoteric

In the beginning

was the Word

and so shall it be again,

and the Word

is the Law,

and the Law

is Love.

A Leaders of the Way Book

Acknowledgments:

To Ursula Wheeler without whose help and guidance the text would not have such clarity.
To Sylvia Joyce for her suggestions, particularly concerning presentation and to E.J. for proof reading.

The Way of Love

The source of the Revelations

On a cold wet day in the summer of 1970 the mother of an English woman died. At the time this woman was unaware how this event would slowly but inevitably completely change her life. The death of her mother created an overwhelming desire to prove to herself that her mother was not dead, but continued to live in another dimension. Of course this desire is not uncommon in the recently bereaved but few pursue it with such dedication.

Some two years after her mother's death while convalescing in a nursing home she met a spiritualist healer who introduced her to the idea of spiritual healing. Soon after that for the first time she entered a spiritualist church. After receiving healing she decided to attend the service. This proved an enjoyable experience up to the moment when the clairvoyance part began. Then with a mixture of apprehension and fear she sat through the spiritual messages (none for her) resisting with great difficulty the desire to get up and run away. However she continued to attend services and eventually proved (at least to her satisfaction) that her mother continued to exist in another dimension.

Much later she was given the opportunity to join a psychic development circle in that church. However the leader of that particular group was adamant that she had no talent as a medium and in any case there was no place available in that class! A month or two later she was however approached again by the leader who now had a vacancy and surprisingly now considered her to be suitable. She found the work arduous, the discipline difficult to sustain and was unsure whether the messages she gave were channelled by guides or her own imagination. Occasionally she also gave what was considered an inspirational talk on a given symbol or subject. Months passed and then one day she began to feel hazy, not exactly going to sleep, but drifting as though every-thing going on around her was not real. As her eyes closed, colours drifted by, voices became jumbled and she thought that she was speaking, but after some time regained normal consciousness. Just by chance the leader that evening had brought a tape recorder and when she saw what was happening she turned it on. Our medium had arrived. However what was said was not very complimentary to the person opposite her and she had to apologise!

She persevered and in 1976 she began to channel a voice which was unemotional and none too pleasant to listen to for any great period of time. This voice wished to be known as 'The Master'. Besides Sunday evening attendances at spiritualist churches, where she was occasionally the visiting medium, she found that there was a demand for healing. At this time she had major surgery and during a difficult six months' convalescence all spiritual activities ceased. It would seem that during this period her vocal channelling was changed for the voice became strong, clear and capable of emotion.

People who now heard the Master asked that a group be formed specifically to hear his teachings and ask him questions. Such a group was formed and still continues to meet regularly, of course as often happens over the years the composition of the group changed. As is the way of Spirit, different people from all over the world were guided to the group, initially with the desire for spiritual development and to share an inner awareness of a contact which is difficult to express and to understand.

2000 Years ago.
One day our medium was told that the Master had revealed to one of the group a past life at the time of Christ and its karmic implications in the present life. During the next few months this occurred many times in different trances and soon she had a collection of these lives. Then it became apparent that many of the family of Joseph of Arimathea had reincarnated in modern times. In the teachings given to the group the Master now began to talk about the life of Jesus, or Yeshua as he was called, in great detail together with His teachings, which the Master called 'The Teachings of the Way'. Some two years ago the Master asked that these details of the life of Christ, the teachings and some of the past lives be collated and published. The result is this book.

These sessions were, and still are, very practical - about life as it is today, and how the understanding of past events can often influence the future for the good of all. All trances are recorded on cassettes then transcribed and there is enough material for a book solely on the teachings; this is in preparation.

How mediums receive their information.
There are several different ways that spiritual communication can be effected, mainly through mediums or by inspired or automatic writing.

By far the most common method is for the medium to be fully conscious and receive the information in the form of pictures or words which she or he interpret. This can result in the information received from spirit not being truly presented. The so-called deep trance medium is virtually unconscious during the trance and thus her thoughts cannot influence what is being said; also after regaining consciousness the medium is unaware of what has been said. Unfortunately there are those who profess to remain partly unconscious but are not so.

The true deep trance medium attunes to spirit through the right side of the brain. The greater the separation of the two sides of the brain during a trance the purer the knowledge received. The Master explained this as follows - "When we speak (through her) she is encased in many colours, each colour being an energy that is needed at the time to keep her still and quiet. She is aware of sound, but not aware that the sound contains words and only after slowly returning to consciousness do both sides of her brain coordinate so that once again she hears and speaks normally." It is worth reporting that this medium voluntarily undertook a number of scientific tests which showed that during trance her normal blood pressure of 140/90 falls very much lower, the heart beat from 70 to 40 and the alpha and beta rhythms show the two sides of the brain are working independently.

In 1979 she had severe laryngitis with almost complete loss of voice but surprisingly the Master's voice was loud, clear and normal. Several years later she had an X-ray involving the larynx. The consultant said that the X-ray was not at all clear, would have to be repeated and added that if he did not know better he would say that she had two sets of vocal cords. The second X-ray was the same as the first - she has in fact two sets of vocal cords!

A test on the Master's recorded voice using an oscilloscope show that 'his' voice tracings are predominately male whereas hers are female. During trances questions have been answered about which the medium has absolutely no information. For example she has no scientific knowledge yet has answered questions on atomic physics. Incidentally she has no memory of what is being said during trances. In fact her own guidance from the Master has to be obtained by a friend reading out her prepared questions while she is in trance.

These findings are very important to the information presented in this book for they show that the material is from a genuine deep trance medium given through direct voice.

Who is the Master?

It was not until 1987 that the Master revealed that in his last life he was Joseph of Arimathea, the Biblical figure reported in all four Gospels as the one who obtained the body of Jesus after the crucifixion. Independent references speak of Joseph's association with Glastonbury in Somerset.

The Master is the spokesman for a group of souls who help and guide people on earth who are experiencing difficulties in their personal and spiritual lives. Where necessary this is achieved by referring to a past life. The Master teaches that out of the thousands of lives on earth (reincarnation) which we have all experienced each individual life is complete within itself. The lessons of life do not change. For example, hopefully in each life we all learn in greater depth the lesson of tolerance. At least we are assured that we never go backwards for whatever we achieve in a life is ours to build upon in the next life. There are a limited number of purely spiritual lives which involve searching, giving and being less aware of the needs of the self than of the needs of others.

The past life that is revealed by the Master usually has a direct bearing on the problems in this life and its karmic lessons. (Karma is the cause and effect of our actions. Every action of ours interacts with the actions of others and it is necessary to make amends for the misdeeds that we commit against others - 'As ye sow so shall ye reap'. Not necessarily in the next life, but at some time in a future life we must pay back the karmic debt we owe to others. Therefore the same group of souls tends to reincarnate at the same time - of course not all karma is bad.) The initial interview with the Master unlocks the awareness of the person's soul to its intended pathway and usually leads to further consultations for guidance as changes take place and spiritual consciousness grows.

How the soul remembers.

Each individual soul consists of numerous parts (known as aspects or segments) within the whole and there are as many aspects as there are cells in the human body! A different aspect comes back to earth (incarnates) in each life time and when that life is finished it returns to spirit and rejoins the total soul which is known as the Higher Self. The knowledge gained from that life is shared among all the other aspects and thus enriches the whole soul. Therefore all that happens in each life is known to the soul and that is how we can relate to a past life. However, at the time of birth knowledge of the past is concealed, although from time to time throughout the life certain events may be recalled if they are able to help the personality advance and spirituality develop. One of the ways this may be done is through meditation.

Because this concept of soul is not easy to understand the Master has explained this with an analogy. "Fill a cup from a bucket of water and add to that cup of water some ingredient, for example salt, then return it to the bucket. Although diluted, the entire contents of that bucket now contain that special ingredient. So it is with the soul, for all that has taken place in a life is re-absorbed, and when another segment is born all the knowledge is within." Yet another way to explain is by computer language. The Higher-Self could be regarded as a computer data bank and the particle of soul on earth can access this data at all times. After death the aspect of soul returning to spirit has little interest in the progress of earthly matters but inputs its spiritual attainments into the data bank (the Higher Self), which consequently grows in stature. The little voice inside ourselves that we call our conscience is in fact our Higher Self to whom we are always linked. Apparently we do not always make our own decisions for sometimes an aspect of our Higher Self will do that, for the Higher Self always seeks to guide. It follows that the more advanced the soul the larger the data bank it can call on and the more advanced will be the segment of soul on earth.

The Master speaks on two levels. "To the soul within, reminding it of its purpose and to the conscious mind or personality which has its own awareness and ability to judge. It is the latter which often needs to change so the soul may express its purpose more dramatically allowing it to develop early in the life."

The Book.

The following extracts are taken from the Master: "The purpose of this book is not to re-write history nor to bring a new Gospel into being - the very opposite - it is to bring clarification to many who do not understand how creeds and dogmas have become such a prison to mankind. It will take two or more hundred years before all dogma has been rejected but even that length of time, in the way that we perceive it, is not very long. During your lifetime you will see great changes such as a lessening of dogma and a willingness of different faiths to meet and share. The true teaching was not called Christianity, this is a word given many years after the death of Christ. He called it the way, the truth and the life, for Jesus brought a way of life based on Essenic teachings, an indication of the spiritual advancement which can be gained through knowledge. His disciples were committed to this teaching and none turned away from the commitment. For centuries The Teachings of the Way passed to others through word of mouth . However many took those teachings, turned them into their own way of living and began to demand that others should follow their example. They presented the Truth as a creed and many of those who could not accept the doctrine perished. That which we teach are the simple words of the Master Christ: 'Love one another'. How can there be any other teaching?

"Christ endeavoured to show people that life after death was a certainty for all mankind, not just for those who followed Him but for people of all faiths. Alas His teaching has been distorted and we set this record straight whenever we are able. Ever since St. Augustine, great teachers and writers, Popes, Archbishops and clergy have marched down the Ages proclaiming to the flock who listen to their doctrine 'believe or perish'. We say - believe and live."

The scrolls.

"The whole of the life of Christ could not be encapsulated in a few verses written many years after His death by some of who if not illiterate were humble men who used scribes to record their words. It was many years before Christ's life was recorded. Even that which is in the scriptures is not a true recording of His words. It has always been assumed that those were in fact the words that He uttered. It was also assumed that because He was a great orator He spoke in parables, but this was not always so.

"Most was eventually written upon scrolls, a long and arduous task, and over the years before they were rediscovered and reproduced by other means much was lost by erosion. Scrolls and many other writings produced throughout the centuries have been hidden and have yet to be found. Some that have been found have not been fully released because of the nature of the contents. Hundreds of years ago it was decided what should be included in the scriptures for Man to read and understand, and what should be withheld. Anything that was thought to conflict with the basic tenet, of love one another, was omitted. This is why Christianity has become so narrow. In the Koran and in the teachings of Judaism there is more fundamental Truth; it is Christianity which is dogmatic. To understand this one must realise the dilemma of the Church.

The Christian Church.

"The teachings of the church are ancient, indeed much is based upon what St. Augustine decreed would be the dogma and the creed of this new church. To endeavour to change these teachings - this discipline - could create havoc, for mankind would have no direction and would not know whom to follow. For many hundred of years the vast majority of mankind had no schooling, though a few had a classical education passed on again by the church. It is only relatively recently that children in large parts of the world have been allowed to learn how to read and write and initially this was largely under the direction of the Church. Many of you would say quite correctly this was a rule of fear and it has been stated that Christianity was born through violence. If once the hold of the Church over the people slipped there would be no discipline and they would not know what to believe.

"In addition It is thought that the nature of the revelations would bring great fear to many ignorant of the truth of life. Only the light of understanding can bring forth peace, enlightenment and love in the world, but there are many who do not desire peace but power at any cost. While such men continue to live in the world it will be very difficult to gain and maintain harmony. However it is mainly the Church that is withholding this. Their desire for power is as great as any dictator, Pharaoh or minister. They rule largely by fear. If they released all the teachings man would realise how free his faith and understanding make him, and then the churches would have little power. Some churches are manifestly rich and they would no longer have this wealth if men were free - so the Truth must be hidden. The power of the Church is very great, for they have the power of fear and where mankind fears, they will submit."

The Vatican.

"You can be assured that the Popes throughout the ages have been well aware of the true teaching and how little of it is revealed either in the Gospels or in other spiritual doctrines. A few facts are allowed to satisfy the curiosity of those who search deeply and insist upon revealing them, but the Truth which Jesus brought is still hidden within the Church archives. They are important for they would bring spiritual freedom to everyone. If men were able to share in these writings they would be released from the concept of original sin, or from believing that only certain sects will go to a place in spirit where the soul lives. This is believed by many who would also cease to believe so implicitly in the different areas of spirit which encompass people of different beliefs. But this is nonsense for the soul only knows life. As soon as it leaves the body and understands that it has been released from the earth, enlightenment comes. Often those who on Earth have been the most dogmatic about certain doctrines are the first to rejoice in the freedom and love found in the spirit spheres!

The objectives of this book.

"By means of this book we wish to give a greater understanding of the opposition that such a man as Jesus met in endeavouring to speak out in a land that was occupied, by a force that was pagan and felt threatened by any talk of a supreme power. We have spoken to many people of their past lives and these give a scenario of life at that time which should show readers a fairly vivid picture of the way that ordinary people, as well as those of noble birth, behaved. This is important if one is to understand that particular age. The inclusion of the members of Joseph of Arimathea's family, who played an important role, helps to show what kind of man Jesus was. Above all we wish to show that the teaching of Jesus was especially that of the Essenes, but contained much of the strict understanding of the Jewish community. We have therefore enlarged on the Gospels and changed some of the occasions where the records are inaccurate.

"This book is intended to widen the horizons of the Gospels and to show that nothing magical or mystical took place that could not occur now. Much of what is revealed in the Gospels is largely true, but mankind has been left with illusions. They imagine many things taking place which are not only illogical but fantastic. The events which took place around the Christ do not mean that He was above science, which is fact, and linked to Universal Law. Also we show that within the heart and soul of every human being there can be this link to the total soul - the Higher Self. Some of the phrases and verses in the Gospels can be altered simply by changing one or two words and indeed in some of the verses the content is wrong. Very little is recorded regarding Jesus' life but He was indeed the Christ consciousness in person, a great and gentle man. He brought the message of love but very few understood it.

"Eventually we hope that the Gospels will be revised, possibly by popular request, and that the information in various scrolls will be released and incorporated. When the original teachings are released and are published in full it will be seen that there is a relationship between the Master's message and the scrolls and then there will be a greater acceptance of this book. Until that time it is to be hoped that some who read this will go to the Heads of Churches and Heads of States and demand that The Truth, so long withheld should be shared. In any event even if many remain in the Church which continues to hold on to its power, as Mankind accepts the Truth, the Children of Light will eventually become teachers and supersede those who hold back the Light. There are of course many in the priesthood who have no knowledge of the Truth for they too walk in darkness."

The revelations in this book are more than the Gospel story seen through the eyes of Joseph the Arimathean. The source of the knowledge comes from a group of souls which includes some of the Apostles and other major figures in those remarkable events of 2000 years ago, revealed through a deep trance medium.

This book is therefore for all who seek the Truth and the Light be they Christian, Jewish, Moslem or those with no religious faith.

Note: The term Children of Light referred to above also appears several times in other chapters and has a specific meaning. At the present time thousands and thousands of children are being born all over the world who have souls which are spiritually fulfilled. They do not actually need to reincarnate upon the Earth. The oldest of these children are about 15 years old (1994). The Master describes these children as follows: "Their intelligence far surpasses anything that Mankind has ever known. These children will not fall by the wayside of materialism but will save the world from the destruction which Man is so intent on creating. Because of their knowledge they will not take kindly to dictatorship, to authority. They will distribute harmony within the world and will have little to do with things that are negative. Of course they are still children and until they grow and eventually raise similar children there can be no true changes in the world. Most of them will be leaders of men. They will have their own way of sharing and will become part of the governments of the world, the universities and the schools. They will be everywhere, but all this will take time and there will not be any significant changes for the next fifty years."

Compiler's Note.

The medium wishes to remain anonymous. There is indeed no particular point in knowing her identity, for the value of this book lies in the words and the truths which are revealed.

This book has been compiled mainly from transcribed notes received over the last five years but also includes some information collected over a twelve year period.

The past lives are from a wide spectrum of people, trades and professions. Although the identity of these people is not revealed it is considered important that the reader appreciates they are not from some Hippy culture but from all walks of life. They include one or more of the following - Accountant, Computer specialist, Secretary, Musician, Healer, Psychotherapist, Sculptor, Business Executive, House-wife, Plumber, Physiotherapist, Writer, Taxi-Driver, Yogi Teacher, and Marriage Guidance Counsellor. Some of these people work for the European Union and NATO, and one is a musician with a National Orchestra. Their nationalities encompass - American, Anglo-Indian, Austrian, Belgian, Brazilian, Colombian, Danish, English, French, Irish, Scottish, South African, Swiss, and West Indian. They include people from the Jewish and Christian religions and those who profess no faith. Their ages range from 17 to 80.

The following terms are defined as they may not be familiar to every reader.

Aura.

The aura is a three dimensional electromagnetic field surrounding the body of a living person. It is like a candle flame. Around the wick is a bluish form surrounded by a dark area that is bluish grey. Surrounding this is an oval shape of a golden or yellowish colour within which are layers of varying degrees of colour. Beyond the flame itself is a subtler oval shaped field of energy, a sort of dissipating glow. The human aura, like the candle flame, is made up of progressively more subtle levels of density and may extend as far as 4,5 to 6 metres beyond the body, though on an average it is from 1,5 to 2 metres. The aura has seven layers, the closest to the body reflects its health. The next reflects the emotional state of the individual and this continually fluctuates. The colours of the aura change constantly according to one's mood. The soul is also portrayed in the aura and the colours reflect the personality of the owner. Each aura is as individual to each person as his fingerprints. As one comes to the end of life changes occur in the auric structure; it begins to move away from the body. When death takes place the aura is completely removed and forms the etheric body in which the soul dwells when it lives in the spirit realms.

Alchemy.

There are a number of reference in this book to alchemy and they have a very specific meaning. Originally the word was used to convey the way man could use his mind to influence matter. This was done by thought and the use of certain incantations. Some early men were very advanced spiritually and some of these - very, very few - could conjure up material things from thin air. Today they would be called magicians except that there was no trick involved it was genuinely a case of mind over matter; it might also be called a miracle. The power of man's mind is strong enough to control everything and anything but he cannot imagine that this is so, for he feels weak compared with nature and therefore he is so. Jesus was so spiritually developed that He could control anything by the power of thought. A good example is when He stilled the storm on the Lake of Galilee. Another example is in Chapter 5 of this book when Jesus continually poured out wine from an empty jug.

The use of the word alchemy in this book should not be confused with its normal use today which concerns the chemistry of the Middle Ages (and 16th century) that is the pursuit of the transmutation of baser metals into gold.

The Ages.

The Earth's rotation on its axis gives rise to our solar day, while the Earth's orbit around the sun gives rise to the year. The position of the Earth's precession with the sun and the twelve stellar constellations of the Zodiac - (beyond our solar system but within the Milky Way galaxy) - Pisces, Aquarius, Capricorn etc. give rise to the Ages. For example the Age of Aquarius.

It takes 25,868 years for the Earth's poles to accomplish a full cycle around the celestial poles. This is divided into Ages according to the twelve Zodiacal constellations and so each Age lasts about 2000 years. There is no sudden change from one Age to another, it is a slow transition and the Ages overlap each other. The age just completed was called the Age of Pisces when Man learned to discipline himself. It was a great Age, one of great scientific discoveries with spiritual advancement in abeyance. It was an Age where Man's greed and hatred of fellow Man destroyed much of the Earth and nearly destroyed himself. For the last one to two hundred years or so the energies of the Age of Aquarius have slowly moved across the world bringing an influence of fulfilment. During the new Age Man will slowly become more understanding of the needs of others. The differences between the Ages is simply one of different energies.

Sanhedrin.

This was the Jewish ruling council in Jerusalem. It met in the Temple and possessed administrative, judicial and quasi-legislative powers. There are references in the Gospels to the Sanhedrin at the time of Jesus' trial. "the chief priests and the whole council" (Sanhedrin) conducted a formal trial of Jesus on the night following His arrest. And again "the chief priests with the Elders and scribes and the whole council" (Sanhedrin) reconvened the following morning.

Torah.

The teaching of the Law for the Jews. It consists of the first five books of the Bible - The Pentateuch - and became known as the Torah.

Note: When Christ spoke of God the Father he did not mean His own personal father the way mankind looks upon a parent but the father of the Universe. God is within plant life and animal life as well as in mankind, so let us relinquish that word 'God'. Let us look upon it as 'The Absolute' which is the yogi word for God - Absolute Truth, Absolute Spirit, Absolute Life.

Part I

The Master Jesus

Chapter 1

The birth of Jesus

Every Christmas the traditional nativity scene is visible in most churches and the story is acted by young children in many schools but are we really sure it happened just like that? At Christmas 1993 there was quite a fierce controversy when a senior Churchman suggested, among other things, that probably there were no three wise men. There is a mystery surrounding the birth of Jesus. Where was He actually born? Where was His home? The Gospels are even uncertain about the place of Jesus' birth. Only two mention Bethlehem and one of them considers Bethlehem as the parents' original home which they changed quite quickly to Nazareth and were in Bethlehem only temporarily because they had to register at the family's place of origin. In June 1993 a questioner asked the following:

"Master, you have already said that the birth was on the road to Nazareth and of course in the Gospels it is always reported as Bethlehem. Is this one of the examples of where the place names are wrong?"

The Nativity

Master: "Many of the records are incomplete, either through the nature of their recording or the lapse of time between the occasion and the recording. That particular event came after the ritual of reporting in Bethlehem, when all registered their dates of birth and marriage. This had been done and they were then returning via Nazareth to see the progress of the house, for they intended to dwell there once the child had been born."

"So was the child born early - born on the road so to speak; is that where the stable comes into the story?"

Master: "He was born slightly before the time anticipated, mainly we feel because of the method of travel, the arduousness of the journey and the movement of the animal upon which Mary rode. They stopped at an inn - that was quite correct. She needed privacy and there was none because there were so many people seeking shelter within that inn, so she was given the only private place possible, which was in an outer building where the animals fed and spent the night. In that area, she with her handmaidens were able to procure the birth, in peace, quietness and with respect. In the noisy inn this would not have been possible. It was a very beautiful birth. The outer building itself was partly open to the starlit sky and for the mother, newly recovering from labour, to be able to see the darkness of the night and the moon as it rose and the sharp outline of the stars, produced total peace and harmony within her. There were two handmaidens who had travelled with her to make the registration. One was her faithful servant of many, many years who devoted her complete life to Yeshua and Mary. The other had been with Mary since her own childhood, had been present at her birth and loved her very dearly as a mother might. These two handmaidens were constantly with her."

"You have said that (page 24) 'The story (of the birth) most of you know well; we do not propose to repeat it', but were there really three wise men? Did they really bring gifts and if so what was the significance of these events?"

Master: "There were three travellers of some notability in their part of the world who were staying in the inn for that night. On hearing that a child had been born in those circumstances and with their knowledge of planetary configurations they realised that this baby could be the Messiah they were seeking. Learning that the parents were indeed Essenes of a high order, which confirmed the prophecy, they wished to present themselves to mother and child. They had with them gifts which were for the King and some of these ritual gifts were presented to Mary for Jeshua so that this beautiful young baby should be treated as the king that He could possibly be. As for shepherds, it was a part of the country where sheep were in abundance. Some indeed were being nursed within that stable. Lambs born prematurely, and which their mothers had rejected, were cared for by the people at the inn and the families of the shepherds. All these thing have natural sources and are all part of the normal human life both of that time and of countless times in history, but many who recorded the Holy Scriptures were so enamoured with the story that much of it has become a legend."

Were the Holy Family poor?

Were Jesus' parents really poor? Joseph is mentioned as 'a carpenter' does this mean he was a skilled craftsman and possibly an employer? There are so many other questions and so many gaps in the knowledge of the events at that time. The following is part of an answer to a question asked by a group in London in February 1992 about the poverty which supposedly surrounded Jesus' birth.

Master: "Jesus was a little more blessed than many upon the Earth at that time, since He came from a family who enjoyed great wealth. It has been assumed that His parents were poor but it is important to remember that both Joseph and Mary were of the the line of David and those who followed in the footsteps of a great and noble king often inherited great wealth. Although His father is recorded simply as a carpenter this does not mean that he simply carved and fashioned wood for there were great buildings of wonderful beauty which were planned, designed and partly decorated through his talent. His two elder sons by a previous marriage inherited his gift and one of them helped him greatly in his work. It was hoped at first that the child Jesus would also be interested in this work which entailed design and required imagination and dexterity, but He was not inclined to follow that path. His parents owned a beautiful house in Bethlehem and one in Nazareth and initially it was in Bethlehem that they lived and worked, for Mary helped Joseph with his beautiful designs, particularly those for interiors. After they had registered themselves they were, as already stated, indeed travelling to Nazareth at the time of Jesus' birth to see if the preparation for their house had been completed so that when the child was born, there would be a second home in pleasing surroundings."

A tenuous contact with Jesus?

The following past life was given to a West Indian.

Master: "You have been aware of the soul of Joseph of Arimathea both when he was that personality and during other lives when he was the High Priest in Egypt and again a monk in Tibet. Many who knew him at that time know him now and respect both the knowledge and the healing that came from him in those lives and the present teaching he gives them now.

"Your past life that we wish to give was at the time of the Christ and you were travelling in the Holy Land. You were already a grown man but not yet fully mature. In that life you were born in India and with a group of pilgrims you travelled to different places endeavouring to learn spiritually as you endeavour similarly to learn in this life. But at that time you were a wanderer, you enjoyed experiencing different countries with their culture, their ways of life, their different forms of food - these things delighted you. When you arrived in the Holy Land it was at the time of rejoicing at the birth of Jesus. Many understood His birth to be more than that of a newly-born child in a loving family, who were committed to caring and bringing up their children. Those who lived in His neighbourhood were aware that this child would grow to be special and yet they did not really understand in what manner it would be.

"You yourself entered the town of Nazareth seeking food and a place to sleep. It was in the heat of the summer months and you were exhausted and dehydrated for you had travelled with the hot sun beating down upon you and no shelter. The springs that normally carried water had dried in the long drought and you were indeed near to death when at last you came upon this town where you hoped to gain succour. Going from house to house you looked, as you were, a weary traveller who had not been able to refresh himself. You looked like a beggar. Your mouth was so dry and parched you could barely speak and door after door was closed in your face. And then you came to a house which stood apart, which was larger and better built than the others. It looked like the house of a nobleman and yet a nobleman's house would have been more majestic, there would have been pillars and perhaps a large garden but certainly it was a house where those who dwelt would be richer than those in the small white abodes clustered together where you had tried to gain entry. By now you were desperate, your head was reeling with pain and you could barely see. You went to the front of the house and later you hardly remembered knocking at the door. It was opened by a servant and you collapsed and lost consciousness.

"When you awoke you were in a cool outer chamber. The floor was of marble and you were laid on it, upon a mat. Near you there was a cool fountain which played within the dwelling. One side of this room opened on to a garden and another fountain played there. Dusk had already fallen and It was very still and very peaceful. You became conscious that there was someone within this large half-open room who had sponged and cooled you and was busy refreshing you, for you were hot with fever. Seeing you awaken she summoned a servant who brought fresh liquid for you to drink and very slowly you began to recover. When you felt more awake, you were invited to sit in the courtyard in the cool of the evening, next to the fountain. The woman who had attended to you had with her a baby, no more than one year of age in a crib. You asked who he was and she explained that she was his nursemaid. She then brought the master and mistress of the house to you. He was an old man with white hair and a flowing white beard. He had been very tall but was stooped and seemed to be in pain. The woman with him was young, barely beyond childhood and she was both beautiful and serene. They greeted you and asked what your business was. You explained that you were a traveller, a seeker after the truth and that many forms of belief interested you, also you showed interest in them and the young child. The three of you talked far into the night and then you were left to sleep. The next day after breakfast you bade them farewell with many thanks and set forth once more on your travels.

"Your next call was to Jerusalem. You desired very greatly to see the Temple which was reported to be of great beauty and importance. You went inside only to be challenged by two men who sat on either side of the large entrance. They asked your business and you told them. They said that upon that day it was not possible to enter as it was a day of counselling, that there were those within who would counsel people who had problems and especially those who were unable to pay for this help. However you were permitted to look inside. Groups of people were gathered round those who were there to advise. The Elders of the Temple were dressed in robes of different colours and styles and the door-keeper explained to you that according to the attire of the Elder, those who desired certain information or help would know whom to approach. You became aware of one who had only two people sitting before him, you asked who he was and were told that he was an aspiring Elder of the Temple, one Joseph of Arimathea who helped those who were sick, or troubled, or bereaved, and also would explain the Talmud - the words of the Jewish faith. This could only be read by those who had been taught Hebrew and Sanskrit but most of the population could neither read nor write. Articles of the law would also be explained by this elder who was dressed in purple and gold and looked magnificent.

"At that moment the door-keeper was called away and seizing your opportunity you went and stood before the Arimathean. When he had finished with those he was helping he turned to you and asked what you desired. You explained who you were and why you were present and your interest in the Temple. This was your first encounter with one who could truly explain the meaning of the Jewish faith to you. He was also aware of the faith the Indian culture portrayed and had been to India in his youth. Until another sought his attention you spoke together and then you departed and went on your way. Before you left however you told him of the kindness of the people in the large white house in Nazareth and how you might well not be alive had it not been for their aid and commitment to a stranger who at that time must have looked very wild and dishevelled and more like a thief or beggar than a member of a high Indian household. The Arimathean smiled and said that he knew these people, that the mother of the child was his own niece and that her husband, also named Joseph, was his own cousin and like him from the house of David. The child you had seen was the young Jesus, or Yeshua as He was known.

"From there you went to another house where you knew that you could obtain refuge for that night. There were many there who had travelled from different parts of the Holy Land for the next day was a feast day and they desired to be present. There was one woman who sat apart and alone. She also had been to Nazareth and was speaking of it to someone from another group. You made yourself known and said that you too had been there the previous day. It appeared that she also was a relative by marriage to the Holy Family. Her husband, Lazarus, was their cousin. She herself was of dark skin, although not from India, for she was a Nubian from Egypt. You spoke for some time and supped together but when you woke up next day she and many others had left to join in the festivities in Jerusalem. Although you looked for her having found her speech interesting and her knowledge to your taste you did not see her though you remembered her intelligence and love for the child Jesus.

"You returned after this to your own country. From time to time you heard of the young Jesus until He also came to India to obtain knowledge from the gurus there and from those who had the wisdom of the ancient ones whose task it was to teach Him the mystical rites for which He became renowned. At that time He was a grown man and you were crippled with age. So twice in your life you met Him - once when you were young and He was still a baby and the second time when he had matured and was about to start His ministry and you were about to leave life and return to spirit.

"You may feel it was a tenuous contact and yet it remained within your conscious mind throughout your life. It was as though you knew that this family, linked as they were in their love for such a young child, had great purpose at that time within the world and it has been shown throughout the two thousand years which have followed that this was indeed so. At some time we will speak of other lives, but we wished you to know that this Nubian woman whom you met at the feast day was indeed the soul of the woman who in this life is your friend and teacher. This is why the memory arises and the knowledge is there. She in this life has also great inner memory which she uses to help others in their spiritual advancement and their purpose in life."

The significance of Christmas.
Master: "It comes to mind at this season of the year that there are many among you who doubtless wonder at its true significance and ask whether it is a festival which has been created by Man for Man, or whether it is truly a spiritual time. The true festival of Christmas takes place at the time of the winter solstice. All the special times of the year - the equinox and solstice - have their purpose. A time of gathering together of like-minded souls communing with nature, being linked by the spirituality within and the links that the soul has with creative light and energy. Because Christmas time is usually very close to that of the solstice it has become a time to celebrate. The actual birth of the Christ took place during the summer months but very few people in the world are particularly concerned as to when a birth, or even a death took place, once they are thousands of years away from the event. The Christian calendar is different from the Jewish calendar and also dates, times and places vary with Mohammedanism, Buddhism and all the other faiths, but the winter solstice and Christmas have become synonymous with festivity.

"What is the significance of Christmas? A birth is being celebrated but at the time of that birth the Child was virtually unknown. Where He was, who He was, was of no interest except to His parents and the encircling family, but an important event was anticipated and had been for many years. Those who studied the grouping of the planets were aware that a special occasion was imminent. Those who studied spiritual matters (for the spirit is not only for Christians, it is for all people who have a sense of unity and oneness within themselves), those who worshipped one God, were also aware that a momentous event would take place. The story most of you know well; we do not propose to repeat it - but that Child was of world-wide significance not because of His birth, not because He was to be Christed in manhood, but because He was the Son of God.

"During the Age of Pisces we seem to have moved away from the understanding of that significance. We know that we are all children of God, we all emanate from the one source. But He was different from the rest of mankind and different from other teachers, for both the Yogi and the spiritual teacher watch over the needs of humanity attempting to guide and direct mankind both spiritually and materially. Being part God and part Man they are able to transform themselves and to produce miracles every bit as wonderful as those of Jesus. He was called the Son of God because He was descended directly from the God essence and did not need to come through the path of reincarnation. There are many hypotheses as to whether He had been Moses or perhaps an aspect of His soul had been Abraham; again, surely the Buddha had a Christ essence within him. Could that be yet another incarnation? And since then there have been others with deep spiritual understanding who have been called the Christ of the Second Coming. That Second Coming has been imminent for some nineteen hundred years and it continues to be so, but as yet there is no other Christ within the world and there can never be that particular Master and Teacher again.

"The Christos is universal within Man; but it is only those who accept total personal responsibility for their lives who truly use this, those who are aware of the spirit and soul within them. They do not fear death for they know they will enter another life. They value their lives and care for themselves but also care for and uplift others who are in a less fortunate position. They are not perfectionists, but they have a love of humanity and a true awareness of the meaning of compassion. All these experience and share the Christos.

"This describes Jesus, or Yeshua totally. He was an extraordinary child Who was aware from an early age of mysticism and had the ability to raise animals and birds from the dead. These things were born within

Him and He experienced them. As a young child He had a near death experience and it was only the love and understanding of those close to Him that brought Him through the Valley of the Shadow of Death. However there are many others who have shared this experience and have grown spiritually because of it.

"As He grew into manhood He had the same fears as many others - fears for His powers, fear that they might be taken from Him or misused and an even greater fear of His own depth of knowledge. Many fear the knowledge within them wondering from where it comes and whether they should refute or acknowledge it. But he Had one quality which made Him shine among men. Once He grew from childhood, through adolescence into manhood He wore the mantle of Humility (see note at end of chapter). He was truly beautiful in His nature and appearance.

"His parents rejoiced at His birth, and when they returned to their home in Nazareth, so did His older brothers and sisters by His father's first marriage - which had ended in the death of their mother. However Joseph of Arimathea realised that this child would be special and he celebrated that birth in his own way. He often went into the desert for peace and meditation, for he had a busy life, often a life of turmoil, a life of service and of teaching others - a not altogether safe life. Very often he would go quietly to the desert and commune with God, from whom he received his reserve of energy and purpose and while he was there he had a vision.

"Much is said of the Angel Gabriel visiting Mary but there is nothing in the Holy book that tells of his also visiting her uncle. Joseph of Arimathea sat under the starry sky in the desert, his shawl around him against the cold of the night and the Angel Gabriel appeared before Him. He was told that his great-nephew had a special power within Him, that He had descended straight from the cosmic God and understood the will of God as no other man had before or would in the future. The light that shone within Him was pure; His understanding was total. Then Joseph was told of Jesus' passing and in what manner and he was also told that he must keep these utterances to himself, that he could not change this karma, but that he could help it to be as easy and free of pain as possible. And do not you, my children, also often have to accept a responsibility which you would rather lay aside, such as acknowledging that another would be better laid to rest and the life extinguished than to remain alive, unable to understand the true meaning of life? An yet you know within you that person's soul had chosen that life in order to learn a very important lesson and no man has the right to take away the chance of that soul to express its karmic need.

"Joseph wished to return to Nazareth to share with his niece and cousin that knowledge which he had received. Instead he spent another night in the desert, then returned to Jerusalem and went about his daily work. For more than forty years (See chapter 7) he kept that secret within him until the time was right and that which the Son of God was born to experience had taken place.

" Many who are born unaware of what lies ahead might wish not to continue with their lives if they learned how they would end. The young Child knew His purpose at a very early age for He too was visited by a messenger from God and was told His purpose, but He was guided each step of the way forward in each phase of His life from childhood into manhood. He was guided by the deeper Consciousness of the Self and by the Higher Self - the total Soul; so also are you my children. This is the true reality of being spiritual, the awareness of the Higher Self with all its knowledge, with its ability as the voice of conscience to guide you forward, to avoid the pitfalls of life, to be able to appreciate that which is full of beauty and wonder and to live through whatever karma your soul has decided to experience within your particular life. All karma is to be recognised and appreciated, then overcome and transformed. You achieve nothing by turning your back on that which is difficult, for achievement comes through recognising the difficulty and working out the right way to approach it. Accept help from others if they are prepared to uplift and help but always to look within - in meditation, for the guidance so readily given and shared by God."

The above was given to a group which met in Gloucestershire in December 1991.

An immaculate conception?
The following was given to a group which met in London in December 1991.

Questioner: "I would like to ask a question about my religion which is Roman Catholic. We are led to believe that when the Mother Mary had Jesus it was an Immaculate Conception. Is this true and if not, who was the father of Jesus and where does Mary stand in Spiritualism - what level is she on?"

Master: "Firstly there was no Immaculate Conception. The father, the earthly father of Jesus, or Yeshua as He was known, was Joseph who was betrothed to Mary. The light which shone around Mary was great and she realised that her son would have within Him a light known as the Christos. It is a truth, a knowledge, which has come down since the creation and which is achieved only by those adepts (one who is highly skilled) who have obtained the power to create things, for example the creation of wine in an empty jug (see chapter 5). Alchemy is part of this, as well as being able to achieve within that ray of light great teachings to help Mankind to a different level of understanding of themselves and of Creation. It is an encircling of spirit within an individual. The aura which surrounds each individual man is far greater in the adept. It is of the Causal Plane - the plane of the mind and is seldom seen in individual man. It is known as the Flame of Light and Yeshua had that bestowed upon Him at the time of His baptism. He then opened Himself to this radiance and all knowledge dwelt within Him to be released as and when it was needed. His mother understood the nature of her Son. The visitation of the Angel was an inner manifestation of Truth given by way of a dream. Many in mankind have such visitations, but not all remember them or are aware of the teaching and Truth within them. Mary was a young woman barely into puberty. She had knowledge, she came from a line of wise forebears - the line of David - but she was very young, she barely understood what was encircling her, let alone an Archangel who visited and talked to her. She is worshipped by those within the religion you mention, but it must be born in mind that religions arise from ignorance not from Truth. It is those who set themselves apart from the dogma and creed of religions who know the most. It is they who work through the knowledge of God, through that light manifested through truth, without desiring to change the ideas of others, but simply to allow self-expression and self-knowledge to arise from within.

"Yeshua had a remarkable personality. As a child He was wilful because of His great knowledge. He had to learn to stem the tide of knowledge, to place it in perspective as He gradually grew from youth to manhood. His mother was a gentle woman. Her capacity for love was great and she remained loyal to her family and to her children amid great suffering. All mothers who adhere strictly to the love of their calling deserve a similar form of worship.

"We have spoken quite extensively at different times of the work of the Holy Family, of their lineage and of the part that was played by mankind at that time, for it had its place. It is unfortunate that so many individual branches of religion have stemmed from one simple truth, but eventually all that will be laid aside. You ask 'What part does Mary play in Spiritualism?' Unfortunately Spiritualism has also become a rather set dogma. Whereas at first it was more of spirit and enlightenment, they seem now to have developed their own creed as to what should be believed and what disregarded. Eventually it is better that Man remains aside, removes all labels and simply worships God."

A note on humility.

"When we speak of humility we are not speaking of a person who cringes and whines and begs forgiveness for every action at each step of the way. That cannot be called humility. Humility comes and is born from total knowledge, accepting that the Truth within is the only Truth which needs to be expressed to show that life is pure and to be lived to the full and that the recognition of that fullness of life will help others to learn and grow through their experience and through sharing."

Chapter 2

The Boyhood of Jesus

Nothing precisely is known about Jesus' youth, the sole narrative in the Gospels is in Luke - the incident in the Temple. The following answers and two past lives given by the Master give great insight into Jesus' boyhood.

Master: "Jesus as a child followed implicitly the guidance of the Rabbis and the teachers in the Sanhedrin. It was important for Him, as it is for all youth, to be able to relate to a truth that would guide Him and help Him into young adulthood. It is quite wrong to suppose that He had greater knowledge than other children of His age. He had greater ability, but this had to be disciplined so that He would understand the importance of obedience and self-discipline. Like other young people He had a strong will and showed it. If others spoke against His beliefs He would immediately be incensed, He would try to teach them the same precepts that His family for centuries past had believed in so implicitly. Often he would visit His uncle, Joseph of Arimathea, in some distress, because He felt on considering parts of the Law that it was not possible to believe entirely in the Torah. He also felt that there were many other beliefs which He could study and find great Truths. He could see no reason why a gentile friend should not consider his own belief to be true and often would discuss with great knowledge and at great lengths the intricacies of these beliefs. His parents, quite naturally, would become annoyed with His independence of thought. The Jewish faith supports each member of the greater family and very often they defend each other with their lives. To find that the youth who had been blessed in a particular way, before and after His birth, should be so free in His thinking caused them great anxiety. Also, in His own way He was a moralist. He could not bear it if others lied. That part of Himself which could always be believed for its total honesty shamed others if they withheld the Truth, however slightly. Instantly, with His clarity of vision, He would then show them to be untruthful, would say quite boldly that they were not true to their own principles and to their own life. When an adult merited such reproof, it was not easy for a child to continue to have respect for the law. Those who loved Him and cared for Him had difficulty in understanding His logic, which He would try to explain with limited language when very young, but very eloquently and easily as He grew older.

"His touch was miraculous. Anybody who felt unwell would long to be near Him. The slightest brush of His hand anywhere upon their body brought instant relief. He accepted this and was surprised it did not occur when others touched, for He felt that this healing ability should be shared by all mankind. After He had spent years travelling in India His awareness of instantaneous healing developed even more and He endeavoured to share this ability.

"It is not easy to share a conviction. Proof is only in the eye of the beholder. Those who do heal others have strong conviction as to where the energy comes from and their part within it, but others who are onlookers will either tend to worship those who can heal, which is wrong, or have great doubts and then the healing energy does not work as strongly as otherwise it might. So belief plays a very strong part in total healing."

The above was given to a group which met in London in May 1992.

Further details of Jesus' Childhood.
Master: "Jesus was educated as many other children were and had the added advantage that His uncle Joseph of Arimathea was a teacher within the temple walls, an Elder of the Sanhedrin, who desired above all things to be a bringer of glad tidings, to teach the Jewish faith and draw together mankind to one God, one Love and cease all division.

"After the visitation by the angel Gabriel, Joseph was both elated and saddened by what he heard. He realised there would be an arduous life for his nephew but he would play a very important part in the guidance and upliftment of His soul throughout that period of years. He also played a large part in helping Him with money. Like all young men Jesus desired many things and did not always have sufficient to pay for what he needed. He was also open handed and gave much money to different causes - to the poor, to the deprived, to those who had been beaten that they might receive attention for their wounds. He always upheld those who had suffered greatly because of their beliefs and their desires within the world and He knew that His uncle would always be prepared to help. He and Joseph were very close, almost like father and son, far more than His own father and Himself. His own father was old at the time of His birth and very soon became disabled and unable to fulfil his role as father and guide to his son. Jesus had very strong self-will and was determined to succeed in that which He desired to do. You will find it is the same in the Children of Light, as they grow and mature, they have the same intensity and the same aims and goals as He. Jesus often stayed in the home of Joseph of Arimathea. He too enjoyed wearing beautiful robes and would often in His childhood delight, as all children do, in dressing in the robes of His contemporaries, as well as of His elders - beautiful silks, exotic cottons. The 'coat of many colours' was not invented by Joseph in the Old Testament to no avail. Children for generations subsequent to that would delight in similar robes and would often wear them together and rejoice in the beauty of the colour. It was not until He became more mature that He realised He must truly study in order to understand his mission. It was His uncle who presented that mission to Him, instigated His journey throughout India where He sat at the feet of the teachers and learned to be truly spiritual, to lay aside earthly matters, to concentrate upon healing, to become an initiated Being of Light, so that he could return to His country and His people and enlighten them also in God's ways. It was then that He took the oath of poverty and wore a simple robe and walked barefoot and ate that which was given and not purchased, but even so when entertained by the rich He enjoyed it to the full for He believed that life was for the living and not for the dead."

The above is part of an answer to a question asked by a group which met in London in February 1992.

A Close Friend of the Family.
The following life was given to a Belgian woman in April 1991.

"Could you tell me where I was when Christ lived and what my life was like?"
Master: "We can answer your question. You were in Nazareth when the boy Jesus, or Yeshua as we called him, was growing toward manhood. The family returned from Bethlehem to their house in Nazareth, this was a small town and yet it was a hive of industry. The father of Jesus had two sons by his first wife and as they grew into manhood they

helped him in his work. Mary, the mother of Jesus, was his second wife. As she grew up she had become a friend of the whole family and Joseph had great fondness for her. Mary tended his wife in those last hours before she passed to spirit and then he turned to her for comfort and eventually made her his second wife.

"Jesus was a boy of great spiritual understanding, but He was also wayward - He could be as frivolous and as pleasure seeking as many other children. It is much the same with the Children of Light, for although they have spiritual understanding and total acceptance of life in its full reality, they find it difficult to conform to the rules and regulations of life or to be obedient.

" Mary, Jesus' mother, was a gentle woman. She found it hard to be strong and firm and He was beginning to show wilfulness. This saddened Joseph the father, who felt that his son was very special but was also aware that this wilfulness might lead to disappointment and even great punishment as He grew older. Joseph was a great though unrecognised visionary. His knowledge went beyond that of mere book learning of which he had little.

"You lived in Nazareth and your name was Sarah. Within that life a woman, as within this, you had grown to womanhood and had been married. You had no children and your husband had died. There were no others you could turn to for comfort and you were very much alone in that place, your home town being a great distance away in Samaria.

"You would comfort Mary, the mother, at times of sadness, especially concerning the wilfulness of her son Jesus - Yeshua - and you were brought into the home to help, to give Him discipline, for you were a strong woman. You had found discipline within your life through hardship. You also had great love and yearning within you for the child you had never borne. The friendship with Mary and the child grew.

"There came a time when the young Yeshua was taken from the home and travelled with his uncle, Joseph of Arimathea, through Palestine and into Egypt. Joseph travelled greatly through his work and the family business and he felt that the boy would learn discipline through this travelling and seeing other parts of the land and learning in that manner. And Joseph himself, was a man of learning, a man who was in the Sanhedrin, an elder much respected and admired. He felt that his great nephew could also learn from him scholastically and this indeed took place.

"When He returned, it was on the eve of His father's death. As we have already said Joseph the Carpenter, was much older than Mary and therefore had reached the peak of his years quite sometime before. He fell ill and after a short illness was laid to rest and Mary mourned greatly. She had depended greatly upon her husband whom she loved very deeply. Yeshua tried to comfort her but it was a woman's touch and love that she needed and she turned to her friend, Sarah, for this.

"At that time, you had a call to return to Samaria where members of your family lived and whom you had left behind many years before in order to accompany your husband. So you returned to the home town of your birth. There you remained for the rest of your life, not returning for the trial and the crucifixion, although you heard by word of mouth of the terrible things which were occurring to the child whom you had helped to tame and discipline in His youth. You knew well His fiery nature, His dedication to truth, His great desire to hold mankind in the majesty of understanding which was His and how His people had been driven to great poverty, sadness and even degradation by the alien forces which ruled their land.

"He had mellowed as He grew older and His great love for mankind shone forth. But He was still the fiery youth, the dedicated change - provoking man He had always been. His truth, His teachings, His wisdom we seek to re-establish within the spiritual world, that thinking man may understand the changes that have been wrought throughout the Piscean Age, not all of them good, not all of them true. The perception of Wisdom can be changed and must be. The truth not only of the life of that time surrounding the Master Christ, but also the truth of the reality of Spirit and God's teachings will gradually be re-established throughout the world. As more and more reach out, (away from the dogma of the individual religions which have been fostered by man) and within to the inner soul and the heart beating with love, this will fashion changes to make the Earth a better and calmer place to live in.

"So you see that which you have felt within you, that sharing, that yearning, that feeling of oneness with the great Spirit of Truth has its foundations in the past, and it comes about that when it is right to learn then it is given. Each phase of life, as life continues throughout your spiral, will have new meaning, will have new understanding. Truth cannot be buried. Truth must be given expansion, room in which to grow, and that is the right of the individual as it is of nations."

A Childhood Companion of Jesus.

The following life was given to a woman in London in October 1991.

Master: "Virtually all those who have been drawn to come and speak with us have been aware of the influence of Christ during one incarnation of their lives and you are no different from those others. But naturally, not all were able to be close to Him, within His circle of relationships or friends. But there were many who passed His way throughout life. Your awareness of Him was as children, for he grew as other children grew. He had to learn and the lesson that He found most difficult to learn was that of patience. He was a talented child but also wilful. And He found that there were things that He was capable of doing which many other children were not. If a small animal was brought to Him that was injured, the great love that was within His heart for it would bring forth healing. And this could disturb both himself and other children.

"You would play with Him as you would with any other young child. He had no greater wisdom than yourself, except His ability to listen, to retain and thereby to learn. And He would sit on the edge of a gathering and listen to the wise men as they spoke to those who desired to learn. Young children were often discouraged from doing this because it was felt they should be about the process of growing and learning to be adults within themselves. And many times those who were with the young Yeshua as He grew would try to draw His attention away from this form of learning. Book-learning was virtually unknown except to those parents who had influence or riches. His family had both and He was allowed to enter the temple where the elders of the Sanhedrin, would give their classes to the young members of influential families. He was permitted to attend although often He found the lessons unstimulating and He would try to avoid them, to go down to the river to fish, or to swim, or just to commune with nature.

"In that life you were a male child and you enjoyed the same activities together. And if He healed a bird or small animal with a broken wing or a broken leg you would try to do the same but not always with the same effect, for you did not have that deep awareness of love that was to develop in Him as he grew to manhood. And you were still quite young when He left Palestine and was taken to India and also to Egypt to complete His education. But you were present at the time of His death. You travelled from Bethlehem where you lived with your family in order to see the spectacle of death, to try and be aware of the young Yeshua that you had known so many years before. And you were aware of the heart-breaking decision that He had to make to fulfil His destiny. For there were times, even as a very young child, when He would prophecy His future and you, along with your companions, would try to laugh and tell Him not to think of manhood and death but to enjoy His boyhood, to make the life before Him one of interest. It may sound trite but there were many at that time who were visionaries, not just He. And yet to have vision of the future is always frightening for it presents the possibility that change cannot be affected by thought and action and yet it can be. He could have evaded that fate, but he knew His destiny more clearly than most and the profound effect it would have upon all of mankind."

Chapter 3

Jesus as a young man

Apart from the account of the boy Jesus in the Temple, (Luke 2:40-52) which showed His abnormal aptitude for religious debate, absolutely nothing is precisely known about His early life.

The Master illuminates the obscurity of Jesus as a young man with family details as well as His visit to Egypt and, the most important part of His education, the years he spent in India.

Visit to Egypt

Questioner: "Did Jesus travel to Egypt?"

Master: "He did in His younger days. Joseph of Arimathea himself accompanied Him. They went to some pyramids built long before the ones that you are aware of today. These pyramids were not nearly so high and in many cases have been destroyed, either by natural means or by those who in acts of warfare and desecration sought to disturb the graves of the Almighty Ones as they were known. Some of the Pharaohs' remains were removed and when it was again safe were reinterred in other areas, but there was one pyramid where a great teacher had lived and reigned for a very long time. He was a Nubian and he had loved his people greatly and given his life for them. When he was buried a pyramid was erected over his tomb. It is still in part within the land of Egypt. Over it has been built another pyramid and it is within this one that many of the truths of life are engraved - scrolls that have been written both by the Nubian Pharaoh, or by scribes who were faithful to him. At the time when Yeshua and Joseph travelled there they entered by an entrance which is now unknown to mankind. They looked upon the tomb and the face of the Pharaoh. Yeshua read the scrolls and because of His phenomenal memory and His ability to read but once and remember for always certain teachings that were given to Him, He knew immediately many of the things that would occur within the world long, long after His own passing. Those prophecies were indeed true and have been coming to pass and will continue so to do. It is our belief that there will come a time when there will be a great earthquake in that region. The secrets of the grave will then be given up, but only those that have vision, those that have great knowledge will be able to interpret the writings, so ancient are they. The Children of Light, in whom there is so much hope at this time, will be able to interpret and understand those scrolls. It may not be in the lifetime of some of you, while others may be aware of it at the close of their lives, but come it will. These Children, and those that are born from them, will have great power when they begin to use it. The time has come when more knowledge is needed throughout the world to enable the world to survive the holocaust.

"Yeshua spent a long time in Egypt and when they returned again to Palestine He made a vow that He would not speak of these things, other than with those whom had accompanied Him. Because of His integrity, He kept that vow."

The above was given to a group which met in London in May 1992.

In June 1993 the Master was asked to give more details of the particular pyramids that Jesus and he visited.

Master: "Constantly throughout the times of the Pharaohs these edifices were being built in pyramid shape, some were for worship - for magical rites and others for burial. The ones that we referred to, where these scrolls are indeed buried in secret chambers, are where the Arimathean, Yeshua and a companion discovered the secrets of life and decided that if this documentation should be made public knowledge it could lead to the seeking of power and mass destruction It was therefore sealed in a chamber. There were two pyramidal structures. One still contains the questions regarding eternity and the meaning of life and in the other the answers were placed. This was done deliberately for if one was found and not the other it would not then immediately lead to the understanding of the conundrum. It was also placed in such a way that the ancient language used would defy any form of translation. The children of light, as we have indicated, will be able to decipher the hieroglyphics and understand the very ancient language in which it is couched. Now those particular pyramidal structures are not the ones that are the famous ones in Egypt. They are among others. Every two or three hundred years a new structure was completed, some indeed not very large now scarcely protruding above ground level after all these years of erosion and subsidence. Is this easier to understand?

"Yes, thank you."

"The famous Pyramids of which you are thinking were not used for this purpose, they were not consecrated and no rites of any consequence took place within them and the secret scrolls are not there."

The visit to India

Questioner: "Recently you commented on Jesus' long visit to India. Could you tell us more about why He actually went and how long he was there."

Master: "Certain events were taking place in Palestine at the time of Joseph of Arimathea's decision to travel to India with his nephew as part of His greater education. Also he was aware of Jesus' purpose in life and what would transpire and had taken Him to Egypt, a place of great historical importance where He could enter the tombs and the temples and commune with the spirits of those in whom His own incarnation pattern had taken place. (See chapter 7). At some future time we will speak more upon this theme. Upon the return to Jerusalem there was awareness, even several years before His ministry, that He was being sought by the authorities. There were those who realised during His extreme youth that he was an unusual child, and we have ourselves mentioned His wilfulness. Often His parents, as well as His uncle, tried to silence Him and to make Him conform. He had special schooling because he was a brilliant scholar (this refers to the individual teaching that was given to Him by His uncle Joseph) and did not adapt easily to the usual pattern of teaching. There was much He knew within Himself which arose to the surface though but a matter of a few words. He easily lost patience with others' slowness and would play truant from His lessons in order to do other things. His teachers needed great patience. He enjoyed His sojourn in Egypt but on returning He was again restless. At that time it was not possible for Joseph to accompany him elsewhere. During his own absence there had been trials and tribulations in his own domestic life. He needed to be present, but there were others within the Sanhedrin, Elders in whom Joseph had great confidence. They communed together and the son of one of these offered to accompany Yeshua to India. There He might perhaps extend His spiritual education by speaking with those who had through long ages of communication, learned especial ways of magic, transformation and similar arts, as well as their form of Yoga teaching and breathing; this interested Jeshua greatly. Therefore He was accompanied by this friend during a long journey which lasted several years. In fact He did not return to Jerusalem and to His family until he heard that His father, already a very old man, was near to death. There was a great closeness in the family. There were several children; two step-brothers, and another brother who became a Disciple. There was also a cousin whom

He loved as a brother and another younger brother (Timothy) who does not feature in the Bible, or in any other story regarding Jeshua because he died young. It was when He returned from India His ministry began."

The above was given to a group which met in London in November 1991.

The Visit to India in detail

Master: "We wish this evening to speak in some detail of Yeshua's early adulthood and particularly of his travels throughout the Indian continent as we feel so little record of this remains and only brief glimpses have been relayed to those who have come and spoken with us, and who remember that they themselves took part in some of His travels and activities.

"He would have been in His very early twenties when he was allowed to travel. It was a sad time for His parents. His father was quite old and infirm although his other sons worked in his business which allowed him to rest a great deal and to oversee in a capacity which did not demand too much energy. It was this younger son whom he truly loved and desired to have with him. He felt so much better when Yeshua was present, for His energy radiated throughout the entire home. He had only to enter the room and touch His father gently upon the shoulder for the energy to flow through him and revitalise him for the remainder of the day. His mother also feared His leaving knowing that much of that wonderful energy which belonged to her son was virtually keeping her beloved husband alive, but she had to bow to the inevitable as did the remainder of the family knowing by this time much of His purpose.

"So a friend, the son of one of Joseph's colleagues in the Temple accompanied Him. They were all eager and excited to be on their travels, none of them truly realising the hardship that would ensue. We have already said in the past that language was no hindrance to Yeshua. Even if He did not totally understand and speak the languages of the countries through which He travelled, He was still able to communicate and to largely understand that which was divulged to Him, especially by the Indian teachers.

"Some of the journeys were indeed arduous. He had not been on the continent of India very long before He realised that He had to embark upon a special journey. At the end of that journey there would be a teacher, one who could unveil to Him many of the truths that He had only the merest inkling of in His childhood teaching and learning in the Temple. When He contemplated the many days of travel involved which would be preceded by a fast (which was an essential part of His learning) and knowing He would be travelling to great heights where the air would become ever thinner and rarer and where there would be little to drink and nothing at all to eat, He passed a night which should have been spent in sleep in praying to God for strength - not strength for Himself but for those accompanying Him. When the dawn came He found not only His own friends, but others who had joined the encampment and were eager to go with Him. Again he was afraid for them, afraid that if they should fall by the wayside there would be no help, and they might die. His own companions would not be able to accompany them back to the foot of the mountains and they would have to remain where they fell. He felt that the whole responsibility for this expedition lay upon Him, and with this fear they began their arduous trek.

"On the first day they walked up the mountain very slowly by its narrower and less arduous slope, but soon realised at nightfall that this would take far longer than their strength would allow. As a tiny dot at the top of the mountain they saw a small temple and in this temple there was a man of great knowledge and great age with whom Yeshua could speak. They were burdened with the amount of food and refreshment that they were taking for this scribe for the only way that he would eat and refresh himself was when those bearing food would seek him. Often for many weeks he would fast, but such was his great understanding of life and the lives that lie beyond that, he could conserve his energy and could spend his time in reverie and meditation; but he was human and his body needed food. They carried this food upon their backs and they realised that they must climb the craggy peaks in order to get there as soon as possible.

"Before the sun had risen, Yeshua spurred the others to life and led the way. Always He was several yards before them. They followed faithfully in the prints that He made unerringly as He found footholds and handholds and led them onwards towards the peak. When at last the figure of the man became very clear as he sat under his canopy, Yeshua bade the others sit and rest. They were all greatly fatigued and extremely hungry and many were unable to think logically because of the thinness of the air, but Yeshua went forward, made His obeisance in front of the scribe, offered the food and waited patiently while some of it was consumed. Toward nightfall the scribe began to speak. For three days, without sleep, without pause, he taught. Yeshua sat enraptured by the wonderful Truths that fell from the lips of this man. It had been said that he had reincarnated several times while still within that part of the world, but he had not returned as a child, but as a middle-aged man and when he had grown old he then allowed his body the sleep of death and would awaken again rejuvenated, many years younger. Jeshua desired much to be able to do this. He felt He had so much ahead of Him that to complete His life while still quite young was a hateful thought and He asked how he could survive death and still be alive, speak with others and be able to teach with such beauty. It was here that He learned of the etheric. He learned that when the body closes itself in death, the etheric body then houses the soul and returns to the spirit sphere. He also learnt that the very wise ones were able to use that etheric body to continue the teaching. In all respects it looked and felt like a body of flesh and could be used for as long as necessary for the teaching to continue.

"Fascinated, he questioned more and more. The scribe who knew who he had before him, also desired to kneel in obeisance and yet he knew that on this occasion he must teach and the young man listen. At the end of the third day he offered a repast to Jeshua. At that moment the young man felt intensely tired, that He could no longer stay awake. The whole atmosphere of that place seemed to be charged with electricity, but still He thought of His friends and other companions, and began to be afraid for them, as they had also spent those three days and nights without eating. He refused that which was offered to Him, except for a little fruit and went down part of the mountain to where they slept, exhausted and near death. He aroused them. He laid His hands upon them and with the renewed strength of what He had learnt, He healed them totally and they followed Him to the summit. There, all had an audience with the scribe and all ate of the fruit and drank of the wine. There was even rejoicing among them for what they had achieved and had indeed been able to learn, however little, and to watch a scribe and his pupil eat of the fruit of knowledge. Saying farewell to this ancient man they then went down the mountain until they reached again the valley. They slept for many days and yet still

Yeshua sat gazing above Him at the silent sky, reliving the words that had been spoken and feeling elated at the attainment of knowledge which He knew had only just begun.

"He was many years on the continent of India. His companions came and went, some following Him for months, others for hours. He gained His strength from them and they from Him. He entered many monasteries and He learnt many things, but if He had been asked what meant the most to Him of all the knowledge that He had gained he would say it was with that great teacher who had lived for hundreds of years and had taught those who had the strength and the energy to overcome all problems on the way and reach him.

"Yeshua often spoke in parables. In this true story that we have just related to you, there is one of the greatest parables of all. All of you have your burdens, all of you have to travel the steep and agonising way of life overcoming often terrible indecisions, not only for yourselves but for those who depend upon you and your wisdom. If you look ever forward to the wisdom that pours from the ancient ones, you will find that your burdens are lighter, for you can lay them there at their feet. This will nourish them and lighten the burden that you have borne. Remember these words for you will find them increasingly important as you realise that your way is also the way of Yeshua and the way of God. No one can evade their responsibility, each one must accept it and in so doing gain immeasurably of the Truth of Life."

The above was given to a group which met in London in May 1992.

The following questions were then asked.
First questioner: "All the people who accompanied Jesus up the mountain eventually ate of the fruit of knowledge. Is this the "forbidden fruit" that is referred to in the Bible and if so why had they chosen it?"

Master: "We are aware that it is called that within the scriptures, but indeed it was never forbidden. There are so many anomalies in the written word, especially when most of it had until then been conveyed orally. So few that encircled Yeshua at that time were literate. Mostly they did not even have a good memory, which became very apparent when he tried to teach them some simple truths so that they could continue with His teaching and philosophies after His passing. This was why he returned in His etheric body several times to speak with them. He realised that they had not truly listened when they were with Him and is this not often so? When a loved one has passed away, do we not then remember so many questions that we should have asked and did not and then find that they are no longer there to satisfy our curiosity and although it is still possible that we can hear them and be with them, there are very few upon the earth who subscribe to that knowledge and therefore it does not occur. But Yeshua was able to use that etheric body as he wished and for a while He returned and continued to teach until those who could accept the truths which before they had rejected went forth to share them with others. Among them were scribes and they wrote much upon scrolls which were hidden. Gradually they are being found and, as we have already said, up to the present time they are not being shared

"It was not the fruit of forbidden knowledge, it was the fruit of knowledge which is difficult for the ignorant to understand because their intelligence, especially at that time was not as sharp and as great as in the present time. The opportunities were less for there was no education except for the rich and for those with power, so how could the average citizen understand some of the great teachings? But no knowledge is ever forbidden as such - some of it is withheld as Yeshua had to withhold some of the teachings from the scribes and also from the scrolls that He read in the pyramid of the dead Pharaoh, but when the time is right others remember and then it is shared."

Second questioner: "Why did Jesus' travels to India not feature at all in the religious scriptures we have today?"
Master: "Because it is among the knowledge that is withheld. It was considered, but if it were known that He led such a full life, that He travelled so much, those who seek to worship Him as a god, as an anointed one and as a descendant of David's line, would think less of Him because He was a man."

Encounters with Christ in India.
The following records the same meeting with the holy man on the mountain, but as seen through the eyes of two of the followers.

The following life was given to a Belgian woman in March 1992.

"Is there anything you can tell me of my life at the time of Christ?"
Master: "As you are no doubt aware, many who are in the World at this time, in fact, the great majority of Mankind, did live 2000 years

ago during the time when Christ was on Earth but mostly without any awareness at all of his presence. That was not necessary. It was the atmosphere, the energy within the World that He brought with Him, which was important for Man to experience and in the last 2000 years that energy, that force field of love and understanding has become stronger.

"The Souls who are born at a specific time of revelation desire to return together when another spiritual revelation is about to take place. And we feel that in a few years from now another teacher will be born and grow, ready to express the needs of Mankind as they are within this particular age. Those who were born in Palestine or at least within the Holy Land 2000 years ago were expressing a need of their Souls to be aware of this energy.

"You were not born in Palestine; you were born in India very close to the border with Tibet. Your parents were ordinary humble people working in the fields, content with their lives together and helping their children to grow strong and with purpose in their lives. You could say that those parents had spirituality within them. Spirituality and religion are many miles apart. To have spirituality is to be able to grow inwardly toward the true purpose of existence, while religions are often very narrow and even prevent that advancement and progress. Within that life you were a male child with a deep sense of wonder at nature. Often in your extreme youth you would cause concern by wandering away from home sometimes for many days, immersed in the nature that surrounded you and in your own thoughts and meditation. At first your parents looked for you, afraid some harm had befallen you, but as you grew older they recognised this need within you for solitude.

"As soon as you were able, you took leave of your parents having decided to travel to Tibet where you knew there were teachers. There were places of sanctuary along the way where you could rest safely and receive nourishment. But you wanted to meet the chief spiritual teacher of that time. He was reported to be partly man and partly of the gods of the past, with great wisdom - great love of Mankind. It was rumoured that he had lived for hundreds of years, that he renewed his strength and energy and was reborn as a man again and again without going through the process of birth and childhood. You wanted to see him and speak with him. The journey was long. At one place of refuge you were very weary and unwell and were allowed to stay for several days. There were other travellers also seeking refuge. There was one, a man becoming mature and yet with the fire of a zealot within his eyes, a great passion for living, for sharing, for loving. A man who had come from Palestine who had a very clear complexion, blazing blue eyes and reddish gold hair. He would sit all night speaking of the wonders of the afterworld and how they could be brought into the World of the present time and of the changes that He visualised. And those others who were with him would sit at His feet enraptured as He spoke. As you yourself began to feel stronger, you asked permission to sit with them and listen to Him. His words inspired you in a way you had never dreamed of, and you grew to love Him as did the others who travelled with Him.

"When it was time for all to leave, you found that they too were travelling in the same direction as yourself, also desirous to meet the great Lama. So you all travelled together. The journey became more arduous as time went by, steeper, with more sheer rocky faces to be climbed. Yet always this beautiful young man strode before leading the way, finding those parts upon the path which were easiest upon the feet. Although you had a rough form of footwear, and so did the others, He did not. He walked with bare feet, and yet his feet never showed signs of blistering or soreness. His energy always flowed and that energy was absorbed by all who were with Him.

"Eventually, the place was found where the great man held audience. The young man was given permission to speak with him first. And as the days went by the two could be seen sitting together in an open space, shielded only by a construction to keep the heat of the sun off their heads. It seemed impossible that they could go so long without sleep and talk so deeply. Exhausted you and your companions would sleep by night and watch them by day until eventually the young man bade farewell and walked toward you and said now you should go and speak with this wonderful man. He separated Himself from the others and sat meditating in the shade, not seeming to need sleep or food for He had such visions of the wisdom that had been imparted to Him.

"When all had spoken with the great Lama, you began again to go down the steep craggy mountains toward the valleys below. You all felt uplifted, and full of spiritual energy from this encounter. But this young man, who you have rightly supposed was Jesus, still led the way rejoicing at the wisdom within Him and with a great outpouring of energy which kept all upon their feet. A life such as this, inspires the Soul and the Higher Self throughout the remainder of the incarnations that the Soul seeks and desires. In each life the culmination shares the wisdom equally with the Higher Self. Therefore, that which is born subsequently is enriched by the knowledge and the wonder of what has gone before.

"Be aware always of His wisdom, His love, nurtured within you by the knowledge of His presence, and this will lead you forward and enable you to ensure that your purpose upon the Earth is fulfilled and completed both in the way your Soul desires and your consciousness also."

The following life was given to an Irish woman in July 1992.

Master: "You were born in Palestine of Jewish parents at the time when many children were in fear of their lives because a Christ light had been cast on that part of the world and caused great fear to Herod who became aware that he could easily be dethroned. We are sure that you are familiar with the story. So at the time when the Christ child was taken to Egypt in order to escape certain death, your parents because you were a boy also fled the country so that you and your brother and sister would be safe. Your father was a physician and many valued his help and advice. Within the primitive frame of medicine of that time the hope that he gave others was profound. But he remained humble and mixed with the people and did not seek in any way to become famous.

"While in Egypt another child was born who was hopelessly crippled. Indeed if it had not been for the skill of your father she would not have survived the trauma of birth. It may seem that when a child is born in this manner it is kinder to allow death to spread its gentle wings and allow the soul to return to its spiritual home. But if karma provokes such things then it is intended that the soul should survive to learn a lesson and the life force is stronger than the body's desire to return to spirit. Your sister survived for two years. You yourself were but a year older and you spent much time at your mother's knee watching the lack of progress in this tiny child. You observed also the love that your mother gave to her, endeavouring to create a response, to bring happiness and contentment to such a small being who had no awareness and a general paralysis of the limbs due to lack of oxygenation at the time of birth. It made a profound impression upon you and when she was wrapped in cloth and laid aside at the time of death you could not believe that the quiet stillness was death and not that total relaxation and peace with which you were familiar.

You went to the place where she lay, a tallow candle was burning and young as you were you waited for a sign of breathing. When this was not apparent you unwound the cloth around the tiny body. At that moment there appeared to be a bonding for it seemed that the soul hovered so near that child on its return journey to Spirit, that it bonded with the soul within you creating a knowledge far beyond your years. Just then your father arrived and suggested the rebinding of the child and explained to you the state of being dead and also what life held for a growing child and the importance of allowing the soul a time of peace to adjust to the state of death before being interred. You listened with great attention and the words flowered within you. As you grew and returned to the land of your birth those very words and others like them you held closely within you to allow the knowledge to continue to grow and mature. Then you followed in your father's footsteps and became a physician.

"You were also aware that one called Jesus of whom you often heard stories was able to raise the dead and to bring about total cures. Before Jesus left for India he called His family and friends together. There was one friend who agreed to guard Him and keep His feet upon the trail of knowledge for though Yeshua desired to learn He felt that knowledge was already powerful within Him and that He did not need to learn from the sages and from those who had spent all their lives in the pursuit of knowledge. By this time you, who were also of a similar age had sought and found His companionship. You returned to your family requesting that you be allowed leave of absence from your studies so you could accompany Yeshua to learn spiritually all that was possible in this far off land. Your father was disappointed. He had reached that stage in life where he felt that life was being held on to and must soon be released, above all he wished to see his son fully fledged and be able to take over his own simple practice. But he saw the pleading in the eyes, the great desire to do this, to accomplish what he himself had been unable to do in his youth and to learn from a physician perhaps even greater than recognised at that time. So he granted permission and you were given sufficient money for your needs.

"The journey began and there came a time, about which we have spoken, when Yeshua reached a place in India where he knew a great sage would be able to give Him the law of life and death, of continuing existence, of reincarnation and also of using the etheric body to maintain life. It was in the Himalayas and the great Yogi sat on a plateau high up the mountainside."

Here follows details about this man and the journey up the mountain as already told in the preceding life.

Master: "With this mission came a great deal of understanding of the way of the pilgrim, to fast and even be without water, though few could achieve this. As you reached the rarefied air of the mountain your memory became fragmented and you felt that you were no longer progressing along the rocky path but you were back again as a young child viewing the corpse of your sister and almost willing it into life. You lay there in a delirium, your mouth so dry your tongue clung to the roof. You heard the voice of your sister, unheard in life because of her infancy, beseeching you to hold on and to allow your soul to experience that which would never again be presented in life. You saw her as a personality, felt her body as she sat beside you, felt the dew from a damp cloth enter your parched lips and its coolness upon your forehead.

"The time passed pleasantly while Yeshua talked to the Yogi. You did not realise that they spoke for three days and three nights. The one that was with you had passed to spirit, and his body had been covered, while further down the plateau there were those that rested in the shade waiting Yeshua's return. When He came back you awoke from the dream-like state where your sister had been maintaining your life and you accompanied Him to this great being. You also learned about the power of the etheric life before returning with Yeshua to the lower plateau and exchanging that which you were permitted to share with the others.

"After this experience you returned with a light heart to your home and devoted yourself fully to learning all the medical knowledge of that time. Within you however there was also a greater knowledge, not the power over life and death, but the power to sustain life, to be able to overcome the beckoning of the Angel of Death in those to whom karma still meant much and who needed to continue their life to overcome some painful aspect and to learn from it.

"At the time you knew Yeshua you were His physician upon that journey. You had understanding of the needs of the body and you recognised that there was great suffering going on, not only in Himself in His desire to prove Himself worthy, but also in others who accompanied you. It is not easy to deprive a body of the nourishment that is essential to life and to survive. It was only through great power - through the mysticism that was His as an Essene that allowed Yeshua to live for many days and nights with neither food nor water.

"Your life was long but not arduous, for always there was interest and the desire to share with others the great knowledge you possessed. You did not meet Yeshua again and you were not present at the Crucifixion but you heard of the Resurrection and in the secret place in your mind you smiled within, knowing from whom He had learned this and why it was that the intention to learn from this powerful being had been instilled in Him. It was therefore no surprise to you that the Christ continued His ministry for a time in His etheric self. You felt His presence because of the friendship but never again did you feel the touch and the love of your sister until the time came for the release of your soul as you embarked once more upon the passage of the inner plains.

"You have returned in more than one personality that you might continue the ministry of learning and sharing and being aware. Your life is indeed one of service, one of allowing others to experience what you yourself have found invaluable - the gift of words and of memory - and if you desire to seek knowledge from the far past or even from the future it can be made yours if you ask for it."

A Friend of Christ in India.
The following life was given to an English woman in 1991.

"Was I with Christ?"
Master: "You were indeed quite close, and this is why in many ways you turned from a vocation which you felt to be untrue. It was while He sought experience in India.

"When Jesus had reached puberty, in order to extend His education so that He could realise that there was a world outside His own rather limited awareness of that which lay before Him - and remember He had not at that time received the baptism of Light whereby the Christos entered and the fulfilment of what was to pass would enter His conscious mind - His uncle, Joseph arranged a visit to India. We will not enter into the description of those things that took place as he listened to the different teachers, as he walked through the land and participated in the life of the people and in that which they believed, but there was one who had left her home in Jerusalem and had some years before passed to that continent and entered into a form of marriage with an Indian. She was indeed driven from her town by those that felt that she had married outside her people. With great humility she followed her husband to his country and her new home. The soul within that women was a facet of your Higher Self.

"For some years it was with great difficulty that this woman tried to be part of the life that her husband had chosen. Several children were born and died from disease. On one occasion she wanted to take her life. She missed her family, was lonely and no longer had love nor desire for her spouse. He had already taken other women whom he also called his wives and had lost interest in the original woman who was beginning to age, who no longer had the sparkle and the desire within her that had attracted him on his wanderings throughout Palestine.

"At this time the young Jesus and His friend came to a nearby town. They were following the teachers who had gone before, to allow the understanding of similar young people to reach a far higher knowledge than that presented to them by their Judaism. Already Jesus had turned from His race. He was beginning to understand that other peoples also held truths which were profound and which raised their intellect to a new height, but He Himself was confused. All that had been taught to Him in the temples seemed unreal and that example which he had within His home was so far away. In His confusion He had tried to meditate, to draw sustenance from a Higher Self which was becoming more and more detached and remote in its preparation for the Ultimate Truth which would enter within Him at the appropriate time when He returned to his country.

"You were one of those that waited upon the teachers. They shared your home for a brief while and so also did those that followed them. You looked upon this young man in His youth and His beauty and you thought of the children that you had borne and who had died and you longed that one of them should have been as He - innocent with all things before Him, all desire, and yet within His breast was this deep love for that which had not yet arisen within Him and yet as a mother you felt profoundly. You came upon Him as He shed bitter tears of loneliness and a desire for His own mother and his kin. Already His soul was calling Him to return and that which He desired above all else to know was unassuaged - the reality of life, the importance of being and acknowledging that being. And you were there, and you comforted Him and you allowed Him to weep in the way that others would not allow, for they expected Him to be strong, they did not expect His purpose to weaken and at that moment He had an insight as to what would be. It was, He felt, his mother's arms that encircled Him and stroked His head and murmured words of love and comfort.

"Next day he had left, but you felt released, no longer were you in slavery bound to a man who did not respect you, who had neither shown love, nor that respect for a long while. You knew that the young man could not have travelled far. Leaving behind all that you had gained in those years, you left your home and you followed Him. For many days you all travelled, until you became too weak to continue. There was another, His friend, who had become ill and was desperate with fever. You all sought refuge within the home of one who understood the plight of travellers and opened the door to them, and you stayed to nurse the friend while Yeshua moved on, returning ultimately to Palestine and then to Jerusalem.

"You did not see Him again, but had the memory of the young man, so steadfast, so true to His purpose, so unflinching in where he was led, despite the lack of knowledge, despite the desire to learn being withheld from Him until that moment of blessing. And as He went into the distance your heart travelled with Him.

"You did not return to your home, you remained in that place, nursing the friend until he too followed - too late to help Yeshua in His hour of need, but love does not always need to be present, love is beyond the power of thought, it is universal, it is within everything that exists.

"Allow the memories to arise, for they will help you and eventually you will indeed receive the peace you seek."

Chapter 4

The Baptism of Jesus

All the Gospels report the baptism of Jesus by John the Baptist as the event which marked the beginning of Jesus' ministry. In this chapter the Master describes the origin of baptism and in great detail what actually happened at that beautiful ceremony when John baptised Jesus. Also discussed is the significance of baptism today and the nature of the baptismal spirit that entered Jesus. Finally a personal profile of John the Baptist and some details about the Essenes.

John and the origin of baptism.

Master: "Very soon after the birth of Yeshua and John the Baptist, Herod announced that he desired to make a register of all male children born at that time. Certain members of the Temple and synagogues realised the significance of this and felt that the lives of these children were at risk for Herod feared that his position would be jeopardised through the rumours of the birth of a king - the Messiah of the Jews. Word therefore went forth that all children in danger should leave the country by night and should travel across the border to an area where they were not under the jurisdiction of Herod or any who could threaten their safety. Among these were many members of families known to Joseph of Arimathea and his contemporaries and among them also were Yeshua and John the Baptist. Their parents joined together to travel in secret so that if they were captured this would not threaten friends and relations who might well suffer at the hands of authority.

"They successfully completed their journey and remained in Egypt until the death of Herod when they could return home without fear of reprisal. During that time John and his cousin Yeshua were much together. Other friendships of course were made but the Jews in Egypt kept much together so as to protect themselves and their values. It was at this very early period of his life that John felt deeply the difference between himself and many others. His open approach to life and the value that he placed on education was different from that of many orthodox Jewish people, and both he and Yeshua realised that the spiritual values of Egyptians were of as great an importance to themselves as Judaism to the Jews. He felt also that to understand other languages, beliefs and traditions was important. Joseph of Arimathea who had through his family line many friends and close associates who lived in different countries both in the east and the far east and parts of Europe, also felt the importance of this form of education for the young boys and he encouraged their interests and helped them to gain knowledge.

"When the time came for them to return again to Palestine each family returned at different times. Yeshua with His parents Joseph and Mary went under the protection of Joseph of Arimathea to Bethlehem. At this time, John was beginning to understand the difference between himself and other more orthodox Jews and he felt very keenly about separation from many who had rank and nobility. His family was wealthy enough to be considered among the most powerful of the time, but he desired none of this for he felt that he should prove his own worth.

"When his parents returned to Palestine John travelled first to India and then to other Eastern Countries before returning to his home. So during the time that Yeshua was in India learning things that would be of importance to Him for His own Ministry John also travelled, but in different areas to learn different things. He had a Tibetan teacher who taught him much. His strict orthodox views lessened and he accepted many of the Tibetan ideas including the washing away of sins in a similar way to the Essenes. As soon as Essene children reached puberty, not only did they follow the adult procedure regarding their religious rites but also a form of baptism. They were totally immersed in the waters that were close to one of the main Essene centres, that of Qumran. It was not without its own hazard. Total immersion at that time was not a brief immersion and then a rising again barely having taken breath. It was an endurance test where the body was laid under the water for quite a few moments and there were times when those that were so immersed did not recover. It was thought that this was because they were not worthy of life. Those that survived were considered cleansed of all sin. So John knew of this form of Essene baptism and he was aware of its doctrine and history.

"In Tibet there was a similar ritual, but this ritual also assured those who undertook it that a certain ray of light would enter the body stirring the soul into acceptance and understanding of the purpose of life. The tradition of reincarnation was already firmly established, the acceptance that the soul lived many times in order to learn the ways of life and to accept also the guidance and the love of the Higher Self - the total soul. Comparing these two very similar spiritual understandings

John felt they should be taken to many places and established as a way of life, so that cleansing could purify those who had sinned, not only against the authority of the time, but against tradition and against God. He received baptism from his Tibetan guru, and survived the initiations which followed, which are in essence secret, and cannot be divulged, and was even more determined to follow the way of truth and light.

"Word of the ministry of his cousin also reached him from time to time. it is not to our knowledge recorded that John had entered into a form of marriage but he had. We say advisedly 'a form of marriage' because it was not into the traditional Jewish faith, but with a Tibetan woman more advanced in years than himself, (as his own mother had been during her lifetime). He wanted to have a son and yet it was not in his way of thinking that man and woman should be tied to one another for all their life nor yet through the ties that bind from babyhood as was the way of Judaism at that time. (Joseph of Arimathea had similar beliefs regarding his own family.)

"John entered into this relationship with this Tibetan woman whose name was Yansing. He did not in any way truly love her but he respected her values, her traditions and she taught him a great deal of the way of the country and life within the home that they briefly shared together. It was here that he continued his lessons with the Tibetan priest who had agreed to oversee his education. There were many who would come to this home to receive teaching and direction and be aware of this illumination - this cleansing, which took place as a rite at the end of the time these people were under the guidance and teaching of John. A girl was born to Yangsing and John was disappointed that it was not a son. Already his wife had been considered too old to bear a child and it had been her prayers and certain rites that took place that she felt had permitted her to conceive. Great was her fear that John would so regret the birth of a girl child that he might indeed turn away from both of them, but he did not. He recognised that this was indeed his child and therefore did his duty toward her. She lived to maturity and was herself given in marriage to a Tibetan to propagate the line. The son that he had so longed for was born, but lived only briefly. This was part of John's reason for deciding that he would return again to his country of birth and continue his teaching there. He left his partner Yansing in the care of others who were deeply committed to the path that they had been baptised into, knowing that he would not see her again, but aware that part of the prophecies of the ancient ones had been fulfilled by his earthly presence in that part of the world.

"When he returned to Palestine he realised that his cousin had begun His work but was waiting also for the fulfilment of His task to be ordained by baptism. This took place according to the Essene rites. Baptism for them was also a commitment to a way of life, commitment to the teachings as in priesthood. It was important that Yeshua should undergo this rite before being fully committed to His task.

"It was at this time that John became aware that many were rising against Roman authority and were fighting pitiful battles. Many young men were being killed and many had abandoned their homes, families and their way of life, and were virtual outcasts. This disturbed him deeply. He made a refuge in the hills that could shelter many of these young men to whom he might impart his values. He went from that refuge, which he left in the care of those who well understood the needs of the young, and journeyed into the desert. There, several times he was aware of the presence of Joseph of Arimathea and others who realised that the time had come to stand firm against Roman rule. The refuge there was built with his own hands and those of many of his followers who were eventually to become known as the Zealots. Many meetings were held in secret to discuss how best the Jews could again become all-powerful within their own country. Unfortunately John's way of life was not revolutionary enough for the Zealots. One by one they deserted him and his desire to uphold them and bring them back into the fold of belief. Their last stand at Masada* is recalled and recorded sufficiently."

The above was given in answer to a personal question, London -1993.

* Masada is the ancient mountaintop fortress in south east Israel, the site of the Jews' last stand against the Romans.

The baptism of Jesus.
Questioner: "Would you please give us some instances where the recorded history of Jesus is wrong."

Master: "Occasionally places have been named within the Gospels which were not correct. Is that a good example? We believe it has been suggested that John the Baptist baptised in the river Jordan. Those of you present at that time in the world would have realised the impossibility of baptising anyone in the Jordan. It just would not have been expedient, and no-one would have put up with it. Most of the rivers and sea coasts were as relatively polluted as they are at this time, and do remember that there were no adequate sanitary facilities at all in that part of the world. Therefore many of the rivers, inlets, sea outlets etc., were used actively as latrines, and those who lived nearby would make their daily trips down to the water. Would you wish to be baptised in such water? We understand your mirth. But there were some places which were different. Some inlets were very beautiful. The water would be clear and sparkling and many would bathe for the sheer beauty of bathing and being cleansed by the coldness and the beauty of the water itself.

"John the Baptist, as he was known, travelled to many places. At the time when we remember him most clearly he was still a very young man and very enthusiastic. He was a man who had great purpose within his being - a fiery man in every sense of the word. He was tall and his hair was brilliant red. He scorned clothes and wore rags most of the time in order that those he endeavoured to reach and to enlighten could recognise within him someone akin to themselves, in spite of his noble lineage. Like his cousin Yeshua, he did not conform readily and willingly to authority. Many times he had to flee for his life. There were times he was imprisoned and during those times he was severely beaten. His body bore the marks of the lash where it had bitten deep into his very sparse flesh for he was a thin and angular man. He lived mostly in caves or slept out in the open but he had a great love of water. He would sit on a lonely stretch of shore gazing into the distance at the horizon and he loved to see the sun set and rise again at dawn. He felt that this was his time of communication with spirit and where his greatest inspiration would come. He too realised while still a child the duties that would come as he grew older. His mother, already old at the time of his birth, tended her son very gently in his youth, for she too realised his purpose and the part that he would play in paving the way for his cousin Yeshua, to bring what enlightenment would be received willingly by the members of the community where he lived. When he actively began the baptism for which he is famed, he did indeed baptise in some areas of Galilee. There was at that time a small inlet and an island which was not far from the shore. At certain times of the day you could walk across to it, although a boat was needed when the tide was in. He would choose a time when the little group of people he wished to teach and to immerse in the water could walk to the island, and there they would sit and commune together and pray and when they were ready to release their tensions and fears and accept what to John was the truth of life, he would lead them into the water. Many would have experiences akin to drowning when he laid them beneath the surface for they were not just dipped in quickly and then stood up. Some were nearly dead when he lifted them out and laid them upon the shore. He felt that this near death experience was necessary for them to release their sins, to be reborn - the nearest that he could bring these people to the awareness of renewed life and purpose. (The near death experiences which many were aware of through holding their breath for quite a while beneath the water caused the mind to reach out beyond the self of the body requirements and move into the etheric. In this way a communion - or communication - would take place and the person would feel the extreme closeness of the God force and of the world which lies beyond the Earth.) John became extremely skilled at this and although there were some of frail, elderly, or weak disposition who perhaps would succumb, the great majority survived. This was his favourite place and he would always seek one where the water was as pure as possible and where people would submit to baptism without fear of pollution.

"It was to this inlet and small island that Yeshua went with John. The way it is depicted again is not completely true for it is inferred that John did not recognise his cousin. This was not so for they had indeed been in India together for a while, and John himself had learnt, with Yeshua, at the feet of some of the yogi there. He had returned at the death of his father and begun his ministry to pave the way for his cousin. At a prearranged time they met together and communed and supped, and then John took his cousin to this island. They were alone together. Others waited on the far shore, those that Yeshua had already called to His service and they waited quietly, knowing it was an important time for their Master. John and Yeshua talked together into the night, into the day and the following night again. They ceased to eat or drink, so much they had to share; and then John asked that Yeshua baptise him, but Yeshua refused until He himself had been refreshed within the water and after He had received His communion*.

* The word 'communion' is used here in the sense of 'communication'. The communication with the water is purely symbolic.

He then communed with John. They still had to wait till the tide went down. There was a vessel waiting to bring them back but they rejected it for they desired to walk together to the shore and to share their experiences and inspirations, with those who had waited for them so patiently and with such tolerance. All were famished, but first they talked and shared, then they returned to a prearranged place where all supped together, sharing bread and wine.

"Why this was not recounted in the Gospels, none can say, for there were those present who helped to write them and yet perhaps that moment was so private, so beautiful, that they did not truly wish the whole world to share their secret."

The above was given to a group which met in London in November 1991.

Note: The reader may wonder why the Sea of Galilee, which is of course an enormous lake and not a sea, had tides at that time. The Master explained that because of inclines on the sea bed there were in fact three movements of the water - three tides. The land between the little island and the mainland was never completely dry, the water would come up almost to the knee, but it did allow people to walk to and from the mainland. During the last 2000 years in every part of the world there have been many changes in the topography of the land and this area is not discernible today.

The Christ essence.
The following question was asked during a group meeting in London in February 1992.

"At what age did the Christ essence enter the soul of Jesus and was His Higher Self within the Astral plane as it is for ordinary human beings?"

Master: "Let us speak of this last part of your question first. The Higher Self of the vast majority of mankind dwells within several planes. It begins initially in the plane which is still part of the Earth but of a slightly higher vibration and it moves through to the Astral and the Causal, it can even go beyond. Much depends upon the spirituality and the learning and developing process of the soul throughout many lives. The Higher Self of the Christ performed in the same way, but. it was more radiant, there was more growth within it and it extended vastly beyond that of average souls.

"You asked at what time Yeshua received these particular lessons. First, he had to be baptised. Who better to choose than His cousin and we have already spoken of this, but once He had been baptised He felt that He had been cleansed from any sins, for He was a man and though celibate and having made vows to Himself quite early in His life, He was still prone to temptation, to lustful thoughts and desires. Many of these things were released from Him in His journeys throughout the Indian continent and of course He did become an adept and was able to sublimate these very earthly feelings in higher spiritual attainment. It was when He returned from this journey that He again met John and received the Baptism. Within quite a short while after that time He began to gather together the chosen ones, as they were known, and this anointing took place. He Himself had a very special aura. It was one which could be seen from afar. It often looked as though the sun was rising or setting behind Him and many when they looked upon Him could not see the man but only saw the beauty of His auric self. Few have attained such an aura."

Supplementary question asked in June 1993.

"If Jesus had this bright aura around Him why was it necessary for Judas Iscariot to identify Him to the Roman soldiers."
    Master: "Not everyone could see the very wide aura around His head. Certainly most of the Romans could not see it and therefore He did not, shall we say, 'stand-out' in a crowd."

Baptism today.
Later during the meeting in February 1992 the following supplementary question was asked.

"As Jesus did not receive the Christ essence until after He had been baptised - cleansed in His physical being from all impurities - is it important for us to do something similar?"
    Master: "In essence yes, but this can take place in many ways. It does not need the immersing of the body with a ministering cleric performing the task. It can be done by commitment to the path of spirit, by such rituals as took place recently when some who were present made their declarations to work for and with spirit. Little groups of like-minded people, restoring within themselves this commitment, first initially and then perhaps occasionally if they feel that the power is waning does help replenishment of spirituality. The cleansing of the body itself is but a symbol. What took place at that baptism was far deeper. It was the ability of the soul to reach out with total clarity and understanding of its purpose, which rushed in as would

a great wind. This total knowledge for many could be so overpowering that the intelligence, the brain, might even fail to work rationally and normally again. Indeed in some instances if there is too much spiritual energy and learning taking place and it is not interspersed with the normal rituals of daily life - entertainment, laughter, happiness and family life - this can indeed occur. Yeshua was fortunate that He had so many around Him who were very ordinary and basic people. Many had been brought up not only without education but also little idea or understanding of any social graces. They improved as they set about their tasks. They mixed with many people and learned from example and this is important in every avenue of life. Children learn from the example of those who teach them, who bring them into the world and who love them. It is invaluable; a lesson that if not learnt can destroy the intellect as well as part of the soul itself. But this outer cleansing, this symbolism of purity, can take place whenever a person desires to release the taint which may have been drawn to him, perhaps by being established in a pattern of work or habitat which is distasteful. The daily ritual of cleansing which did not take place within those lands at that time, but which mankind today follows, is important also. It can be turned into a little ritual of giving the self once more to the love of spirit, can it not? The Christ within, more aptly named the Christos, is available to all, but few accept it and its responsibilities. There are few within the world worthy of that spirit of annunciation, but those that have it, serve it well."

The nature of the Baptismal Spirit.
During a meeting in London in July 1988 a question was asked concerning the nature of the spirit of God which entered the Christ at His baptism.

The Master replied as follows: "That of which you speak is an essence of light, the divine light of knowledge which entered at the time of baptism and was not present before. Jesus was as others, but when that spark of great light entered the awareness of the Soul and allowed it to spring to action then there was a difference between the Christ and many others. But this was not unique; throughout the Ages others at different times of their childhood have received this form of spirit. It is sometimes depicted as a dove which bears the light and at other times as a bolt of light throughout the Universe, but in essence it is intellect, knowledge and understanding in a pure form of energy which again comes with the breath and is accelerated by the acceptance of the Soul - the Soul's awakening."

John the Baptist - a personal profile.
In April 1993 the following details emerged about John the Baptist and the Essene community.

Master: "John the Baptist was two years older than Yeshua (the Master commented that this was another example where the Gospels are incorrect) and they knew each other from infancy. It was difficult to become close to John for as we have said he was a fiery man of fierce independence, a man who chose his own path and would not be deterred from it by another, however great their principles or learning might be. John was indeed a man who would not be restricted by rules of any kind for he had fixed ideas on many subjects. He could be brilliant and he could be obtuse. Many followed him because of the light that shone from him but others feared him, for those that followed his path often walked in the path of death. The very brilliance of his eyes could hypnotise while the brilliance of the eyes of Yeshua brought about an inner weeping because of the beauty and the compassion that was within them.

"John greatly resented the occupation of his country by the Romans and he brought together a group of young men who eventually became known as the Zealots. Although he was an Essene he did not practice their rites and their beliefs to any great extent, but believed very strongly in his purpose in life as the forerunner of the Christ, although he did not realise for many years that his own cousin was He who would be Christed. John had received a vision when young, as also had his father, as to his work and purpose.

"The Essenes were a spiritual body and those that joined were very carefully chosen. The whole of the Holy Family were associated with them. Joseph the father was one of the Elders within their group and Jesus therefore attended the meetings when young, but went from choice when he grew older.

"Both Yeshua and John did indeed study together in the dwelling of the Essenes at Qumran but their life together was stormy. They were both men of vision from quite an early age. Because of the difficult conditions that were prevalent in Palestine at that time Yeshua was concerned that this would restrict His education and opportunities. After their journey to Egypt Joseph - the Arimathean - together with the faithful ones undertook to bring them into Palestine under the shadow of darkness. They were taken directly to the Essene brotherhood where they were concealed for several years; at that time they had not yet reached manhood.

"The Essenes were left quite alone by the Roman authorities who had a certain fear of them because of their reputed power. Some of the teachers were reincarnated from the Atlantean's who had waited many centuries to be reborn, others had been reborn in Egypt establishing themselves there in their own right before travelling to Palestine and establishing the Essene community outside Jerusalem. Initially it was like a fortress, but that was long before the time of which we speak and gradually the fortifications had crumbled or had been taken away as respect for them and their life grew. Certainly they had powers and those powers were used for protection and advancement when it was found necessary. Those that studied there were taken under the auspices of teachers who bestowed upon them the secrets of the universe for there were many who were the scientists of that age, others were alchemists and many versed in astronomy. They had invented a machine by which they could study the stars and planetary configurations and thereby foretell the future. It was a very complex machine which occupied a very large area and most of the students were taught how to operate and maintain it. Many ideas concerning the planets and stars which are acceptable today were initiated by the Essenes two thousand years ago and it was their calculations that foretold the birth of Jesus, its connotations and many other divine omens. But John and Yeshua were not interested in these things. It was the pure teaching of life that fascinated them and linked them together, but not as brothers as many have said. Many years after they graduated from that school they went their separate ways. John eventually returned to begin his own community which was run partly in the same way as the Essene community and partly following his own ideas. After Yeshua returned from the further education and teaching that He received in India He commenced His work in Palestine and in the surrounding areas and they met again to fulfil the prophecy of the Christing through the initiation of baptism which both had learned in the Essene community. John baptised those who believed they were cured by this - their faith had made them whole - and taught them. He practised a form of baptism that truly cleansed the entire being of any evil or wrong beliefs. It was, as we have already said, total submersion. He did in fact hold under the water those he was baptising until they struggled, believing that unless the self was tortured to a certain point the spirit would not break free and understand its ultimate purpose upon the life on earth.

"Perhaps to a limited extent this could be regarded as madness. Many who have great vision, and cannot see the practicalities of what is under their feet have been called madmen and to a certain extent they are, for great vision does raise the consciousness away from the practicalities, thus bringing the more prosaic among mankind to doubt their own beliefs and authenticity and no one likes to feel this about their understanding of life."

Note: The Essenes had a wonderful capacity for knowledge and only those that were considered to be of the highest mental calibre were accepted as disciples. They believed that woman also should learn and in Qumran, unlike most Jewish establishments, there was no segregation for it was considered that men and women were equal in the eyes of God. It was from these teachings that Joseph, as one of their number, desired that the life of his own family should be as integrated and as free as possible. (In later chapters it is revealed that this was to have a very profound effect upon Joseph's family.)

Chapter 5

The Last Supper

The disciple Peter rented a large upper room in a humble dwelling in a remote area of Jerusalem. Today this would be called a 'safe house' for it was away from that part of the city where Roman Officials would come looking for those they were seeking. Jesus, the Disciples and the women who served Jesus met there often and it was here that the last supper took place.

The following past life was given in April 1991 to an Englishman.

The man from Samaria.

Master: "We will tell this in the form of a narrative so that your soul may accept it and your consciousness also. There came a man from Samaria who was stricken with epilepsy and the ague, which had tormented him all his life, and there had been loss of consciousness and awareness. People turned from him as from one who was beleaguered by devils for this form of illness was not understood. He was a lonely man and he lived like a hermit in the hills. He heard that there was one who was baptising, ridding the body of evil and tormenting spirits, so he travelled the great distance to Galilee. John, the cousin of Jesus, was performing baptism in the lake, for the waters at that time had great healing properties and they were well chosen. On the third day after his arrival it was his turn to be immersed and John turned to him and blessed him in the name of God. As this man was laid beneath the water he lost consciousness and his whole life swam before his eyes. He relived each moment of pain, but then his eyes opened and he looked into the face of the man who had given him new life and he went on his way rejoicing. He was a man no longer in the first flush of his youth and he could have returned to his lonely path but he no longer felt the desire for solitude.

"He stayed within that area and did many tasks to help his fellow men. No one who lived in that part of the land had any knowledge of his past and no longer did he suffer from epilepsy nor the ague. He was as other men, but he felt empty when the first exhilaration of the healing had passed away. He felt a great desire within him to fulfil a hidden purpose which the newly awakened soul now urgently desired. When the soul is awakened it is as a baptism - the urgency, the desire to progress, to bring truth into the lives of those who have little, is beyond all other desires and this is gradually being understood by those whom we teach.

"And then Jesus returned to the Holy Land. He had been travelling with those who taught Him and had been to many lands. He returned to fulfil His destiny and knew it would not be long before that time faced Him.

"Almost as soon as He began His teaching and healing, the persecution began. There was no place that He, nor yet His disciples, the followers and friends that He had chosen could meet - could talk - could discuss the teachings among themselves.

"This man from Samaria by now had a house and those that passed his door who were weary found shelter. On the lower floor there was a wooden table and always upon it a jug of wine and bread. There was a large room above that was not used. He desired greatly to find a companion who would share his life and then the room would be used for the wedding feast and until that time it was not to be used.

"He who is now known as Saint Peter approached this man knowing of this empty room and asked if it could be used for these meetings. At first the man from Samaria was hesitant for he was afraid of the authorities who would look carefully through houses and if there was a sign of activity that was outside the law then those who participated went through great torment - great physical torture - for the Romans had no respect for the Jews. But he looked into the eyes of Peter and he loved him.

"From that time forward this group of men met within that place which has become known as the Upper Room. It was greatly blessed. There was a simple wooden structure on which were cushions filled with the hair of horses and camels - and a flagon of wine upon the trestle to relieve their thirst. It was there that those who attended upon the Master Jesus would come and show their appreciation and their love. It was there that His feet were bathed when weary from long journeys through the barren land.

"Then came the time before the trial for It was known when it would take place. Jesus had told His followers and those He loved of that time but they did not believe Him. He bade them all come together in the Upper Room. The man from Samaria brought them a flagon; he had not known that they would come that night and he was ill prepared. There was little left within his store and no time to prepare more but Jesus bade him leave what there was, for it would be replenished and he need not fear.

"Consumed by curiosity he reascended the stairs when the throng were deep in meditation and hid himself, he thought unseen, behind bales of cloth and watched to see what would happen. There was wine for but a few, but Jesus placed His hand over the neck of the flagon and then poured again until all the cups were full. The communion took place. When all was finished and the tears spent Jesus said "We now rejoice, we now celebrate that which will be the outcome of the suffering". And the man from Samaria knew that the flagon was empty, but the wine flowed constantly for it was always full.

"Until that time he had not been sure of the identity of those who came, except Peter who came often and talked quietly with him, coins passing between them to buy food and drink but now his eyes were opened and he knew who his guest was. First there was fear, fear that he would be discovered and all he had taken from him and then came a great sense of wonder that he had been chosen.

"No man knows how and when and where he will be chosen, not only by Jesus but by any holy man who comes along the way and bids the person follow, leaving behind that which they treasure, to change their lives and to give of the truth.

"There is always suffering in life, it cannot be avoided; it is the acceptance of the suffering as a lesson, the understanding that once it is truly accepted the burden will be lifted. You feel you accept but you do not - when you do you will be whole.

"We do not need to speak more on that which we have already said. This man and yourself are aspects of the same soul. Many of your memories are there. Dwell upon this and understand that the task ahead is incomplete and will therefore continue.

"All who have drawn near in the few years when we have spoken more openly have their tasks. Each one will be individually told of this if they have not already been so instructed. The importance of the understanding of truth is high upon the agenda of teaching. All who listen will gain. There will be an inner response in all those who were present at that which took place 2000 years ago."

The following questions were asked by the Englishman also in 1991.

"Was I acquainted with you during the life that you described to me as 'The Man from Samaria', or any other past life?"

Master: "Joseph of Arimathea visited the house on more than one occasion as he was also a disciple of the Christ and would take a repast there. It was not just the Last Supper that took place. The house was a place of relaxation, a place where those who delighted in the teaching and the love of their Master would come together to hear of his travels, to receive even more enlightenment than He could give them collectively - and certainly he who speaks with you was there on many occasions as also were some of the women. Those who waited upon their men both with victuals and with care, were not excluded from these particular gatherings. They were of great importance. Yeshua loved them very deeply and valued them for their support and their care. They would often tend His weary body with lotions which were very soothing and peaceful especially to His feet. And the aroma of the herbal preparations that they would prepare, also relaxed Him and allowed Him to sleep. There were many, not always the same ones, who would enter that place and find harmony and peace."

"Was it just a house or an inn?"

Master: "It progressed throughout the time that you lived there. At first it was a very simple structure with only two rooms, one above and one below. But as your life continued and you found the woman that you could love and who could love you and give birth to your children, you built on to that dwelling other rooms that could be used apart from the larger rooms which were hired, you may say, by the disciple Peter for the work and the use that we have described. As time went on the larger room on the ground floor was used as a form of tavern. The dwelling was quite isolated which made it excellent for spiritual purposes. None would pass the door without intent, so there were no Roman officials who would come looking for those they were seeking. However often a traveller weary from many days of travel, without food, or water, would find your house. Such as these would enter and would receive kindness from those that dwelt there. As it became known that the Master Christ had been there and found such service others would seek it out and so the lower room became almost a tavern. Always you kept refreshment there and it was a place where the weary traveller could rest and be revitalised before continuing along his or her way. We could say the dwelling was a tavern but it was still a home, it was still a place where as a family you enjoyed your life and had your purpose. If someone arrived on an ass there was a place where it could be tethered and well fed. You served humanity.

"In this life also you have served humanity but in a different manner, and that part of your soul which was present 2000 years ago was absorbed into your total soul allowing the aspect within you in this life to experience, to understand and to value service. Your name was Mathias Ben Ahab."

The following question was asked by a group which met in Brussels in April 1991.

"At the so-called Last Supper, Jesus is reported to have broken bread and said: "Do this in remembrance of me". If He did say this what did He mean? Did He really mean us to celebrate the Last Supper in the way it is done in the Christian Church?"

Master: "That was not the intention, but it does not matter in what way an object is achieved as long as it is achieved. A wedding does not bring two souls together for life unless there is love. Just as the ring that is exchanged between the man and woman is not perfect in its circular shape - for no ring ever made is quite perfect - so no marriage will ever approach perfection unless the two have real love in their hearts, and so it is with any form of ritual, for ritual it is. Bread was broken and wine was drunk in no way differently from other occasions when they were all gathered together to receive teaching - to be given direction as to how they were to continue the teaching, the Truth, after Christ had risen. It was a simple union. The Master Christ broke the bread and handed it to each of His beloved brethren. When each had received a piece of bread, together in unison they ate it. Many of these ideas come from a passionate desire to remember, to anticipate once more that act of union, when all were as one and when the beloved Teacher was present among them. Many were ignorant, they did not truly understand the spoken word, each had dialects from different parts of their country. Many had been taken from a secular life and "thrown in at the deep end" for total change and needed to learn for a far longer time, as many of our children on Earth need to at the present time. Time was pressing then and it is still urgent today for the false beliefs of the past must give way to the Truth, else Man's progress will be delayed and he will not reap the benefits of the beauty of the Age. This is why we seek to bring together groups who will discuss the Truth portrayed in the words which we share with you. We do not break bread and pour wine, but when we are absent, often there is a communion of food and drink. You do the same thing often - you share with others.

"Those particular words were not spoken, but it does not mean they were not thought. We would not have them erased for many believe and much love and understanding among man have arisen from this simple misunderstanding. However at this last supper the Holy Ghost entered into Jesus. It was to give Him a greater awareness of strength for it was the last direct communication that He had with God the father before going forth to His trial and ultimate crucifixion. Every one of those present, including the Arimathean, received the same spirituality, the same unity with the Christ that He Himself achieved with God."

The Holy Grail.

Questioner: "We have been hearing for so many years of the search for the Holy Grail and I wondered whether this vessel still exists, and if so, where it might be found?"

Master: "It has never existed. The Holy Grail - the search for the Holy Grail - is the search for Truth, the search for the meaning of life. It is indeed entwined with the alchemy and magic of which we have spoken. The Grail, has become a symbol of the Cup of the Last Supper before the crucifixion, where Yeshua and His Disciples and other beloved members of His family gathered together. That particular vessel was but part of the vessels of the inn, where they would all meet over many years in order to be taught and to be in harmony one with another. There was no special Cup from which He drank, any more than there would be in this day and age. Where would a simple man such as he who kept the Upper Room in readiness for the disciples find a jewelled vessel, unless stolen from the palace of Pilate? Even Joseph, who was a wealthy man was modest in his possessions, preferring materials of wood, tin and pewter. At the end of the meal all the plates and drinking vessels were collected together and cleansed until the following meal. These are figments of the imagination which have grown throughout two thousand years because of secret writings, because of misinterpretation, because of mistranslations, all so easy to do, and done more times than anyone can imagine."

The above question was asked by a group that met in London in November 1991.

Chapter 6

The Anointing

Jesus bestows upon those He can trust the power that He has used in His Ministry.

The following question was asked during a meeting in London in February 1992.

Questioner: "We read about Christ and the Disciples healing people who had incurable diseases and even raising people from the dead. Is this an exaggeration, or was it true and if it was true why cannot the healers of today reach the same degree of power?"

Master: "To explain this we need to explain two functions of the reality of the soul and its mission on Earth. Jesus, during His life, was Christed. This means that the direct essence of the spirit of God, the Cosmic Creator, was bestowed upon Him. God has the ability to take life, to give life, to allow the Earth to continue or to allow it to disintegrate and be no more. That particular essence of growth, of beginning, of birth - all these things which comes from the Cosmos - entered into Jesus and Christed Him. When he realised that His life was soon to end and that the things He had been able to do, the power He had used, would go with Him, He knew it must continue at least for a while. Few people had been guided, vast areas of the world had not even heard of what was taking place and being only one man, there was a limit as to where He could travel in the time given to Him. He gathered to Him those He could trust, those with whom He shared facets of the Higher Self, those whom He knew had potential to carry on the work. He had taught them all He felt they would understand in the rather simple and unworldly lives they had led, until it came to the time when not all, but a few - must be an extension of Himself. These he took aside and He called upon The Creator and He asked through incantations and special words of power that this energy be bestowed on them also. Joseph of Arimathea was present and he too was accorded this power. It was a truly dramatic and yet spiritual moment. The Archangels of Light were present in all their magnificence and beauty, the heavens were alight with mystical grandeur, all the colours within creation were there, blending. The Archangels of spirit and all humanity were kneeling, heads bowed, to receive their blessing and this was called The Anointing. Yeshua Himself had within the palm of His hand a small container of certain oils and this was the medium that was used to transfer this energy from the Cosmos, through Himself, to those chosen ones. He made the mark of the equal - armed cross upon the forehead of each one. When they had been anointed, at first nothing was different. When the scene had changed and there was the fast fleeting dusk and the night sky, beautiful in its glory above, they began excitedly to speak of what they had experienced, totally unaware of its majesty and glory and of what they were now capable. That perception came slowly; it came with the inner desire in their hearts to serve. This was intensified by the ritual that had taken place, but each one understood separately, in his own time, the gift that had been bestowed.

"Raising from the dead was undertaken only in very special and very specific times. Very few souls were restored in such a manner and certainly not after they had been received into the spirit sphere. There is a time of waiting; the soul leaves the body and there is a rejoicing with those that have been close and with other aspects of the Higher Self. It is a timeless state and yet it is of great wonder and rejoicing but there is still time for that soul to return. Your physicians, those who do all they can to restore life, do much the same, do they not? Many who have been pronounced dead, open their eyes and live, but if the soul has gone beyond that initial plane then it cannot be drawn back. The cord which joins the soul with the body is severed and once this takes place the soul has no desire to return to the travails of Earth. Then the body is but an empty casket which again becomes part of the Earth.

"The disciples then became Apostles and they commenced their individual journeys and their ministry. It was a wonderful time, but similar things still occur upon the Earth. A different time, a different Age now, but still with infinite possibilities for Love and Truth to be taken into all mankind. Does this answer the question?"

Chapter 7

Jesus the man and Jesus the Christ

Many interesting questions have been asked concerning Jesus both as a man and as the Christ. Some of these questions were of a minor nature while others were profound. This chapter is mainly devoted to a selection of these questions together with the Master's answers.

A question on age.

Questioner: "What age was Jesus when he died?"

Master: "He was nearly forty-two. It is quite an important question, because the Scriptures are inaccurate in that on many occasions it is recorded that he was at least ten years younger. It was not so."

A description of Jesus.

Master: "Jesus was tall and slight. His skin although dark was not sallow but golden. His hair was magnificent in its beauty with glints of chestnut and gold. He had great personality. His eyes were of a deep blue and His great knowledge and immense love penetrated those who gazed into them and felt uplifted by the power which He exuded. His hands were gentle and when He touched those He sought to assist - to bring health and well being - it was like the light touch of a woman giving great love. To Him all mankind was His kin and should share in the wellbeing of total health and life."

Jesus' family name - Yeshua.

Master: "At home and among His friends Jesus was known as Yeshua. He had one cousin who lived in a different country called Joshua and another cousin who was also called Jesus. To avoid confusion when these three were together Jesus from a very early age was called Yeshua and His family continued to speak of Him in this way all through His life."

Note: This may be the reason why some sources have stated that after the crucifixion Jesus lived and died in Egypt.

The free will aspect.

Questioner: "You have described very clearly the influences and the conditions of the people surrounding Jesus' early childhood and how they led Him and encouraged Him in the spiritual way. Was that pathway planned by spirit, by God, prior to Jesus' birth, or was it a result of those childhood influences?"

Master: "All souls that come into an incarnation have a purpose before they are born and His was no different. His soul was aware that it would be a very special life, that all the tuition within spirit would remain in His conscious mind, not only in the sub-conscious as with the great majority of incarnating souls. He also had free will and this was accepted when He was born, as it must be accepted by the rest of humankind. He could have turned away from His purpose, but because He knew that the life of mankind in the future would be directed by His teaching He had a dedication and a discipline seldom seen in humankind. We say "seldom seen", because there are many hundreds who have put this same discipline and desire to help others, above their own quality of life and their own safety. He needed guidance, as all other young children need it. He grew in the same way as others, the main difference was His great enlightenment and knowledge which pervaded all that encircled Him. This meant that if He did not agree with the words of the teachers He would be strong in His condemnation, for He could see so clearly the Truth of an issue and He felt that they were being misguided by dogma, by the written word, even from Abraham himself, for the people of that time and not for those of His generation. What young person of today does not feel the same? Why follow the ancient teaching and laws when life at the present time indicates something so very different? Jesus needed discipline in His early years and this was provided by those who understood His purpose and what might follow later in life. He knew also how his life would end. He could have turned away from it, He need not have returned from India. He could indeed have travelled to Egypt and taken refuge there, or even gone to His uncle's estate in Cyprus or to nearby Greece. He did not. He returned to fulfil the karma that His soul was intensely aware of and which has been such an influence throughout the past Age and will continue to be, as long as life upon the Earth exists."

Jesus as a man.
Questioner: "Would you please tell me more about Jesus and His life as a man and if He made any mistakes?"
    Master: "Jesus the man was an enlightened being from the time of His intended birth. There had been other lives and those lives had opened His awareness to what Truth is, and to the light itself. These

were within His soul and also His conscious mind. He was never as others within that last important incarnation but like an ascended Master. This path, trodden by those that have suffered greatly in their lives in order to assimilate Truth, usually leads forward into the light itself until that soul is combined with light to make a whole. It does not return either to the Earth or to other planes of life but it leads certain beings back to Earth to bring enlightenment to many. Jesus, was there to lead mankind into what was then another new Age, an important Age, that of Pisces, an Age where mankind would be brought from the darkness into the light of knowledge and intelligence and which culminated in many scientific experiments and knowledge of benefit to the world but in some cases to its detriment. Unfortunately, the world is in that state at this time when it may survive or perish, but at the time the Christ was born, mankind had to acknowledge that He was part of the universe and was not on Earth merely to be destroyed.* This part of His ministry He succeeded in accomplishing.

* Until that time Man did not comprehend the part that the planet Earth played in the solar system. Comparatively few studied the stars and the planets and even the most knowledgeable felt profoundly that the Earth was a place apart, that Man entered into life, lived and departed - dust to dust and ashes to ashes, nothing else survived. Survival of the soul was only acknowledged by the deep awareness in some through their reading of great teachings from the past. As they absorbed this knowledge they had a greater understanding of Man's involvement with that which lies beyond. Even so there was no understanding of the etheric self surviving beyond death, but there was a spiritual recognition that something in the self survived. Also a great fear of the God force - of a vengeful god, therefore in many, even priests, there was a great fear of death. In more ancient times the Egyptians were more aware of passing from one state of consciousness to another and the same fear was not so apparent, but we are not speaking of that culture. We are speaking of the time when the ordinary man was aware of life and its purpose as it surrounded him, not with any great sense of the future. He felt that he lived by the sword alone, it was the survival of the fittest. If he did not strike first then it would be he who would be struck down and his life would then be incomplete. If man had any awareness of a God force at all it was with great fear that he would contemplate being called to account for the life that he had led.

Master: "It was the intention, even before Jesus' birth, that He should die in a spectacular way, which would draw the attention of the masses to everlasting life. Even as a small child His knowledge was far beyond the knowledge of mankind surrounding Him. He had a firmness of character which led Him away from the usual disasters that mankind encounter. Emotional problems were not His except at the time when He was taunted by the devil, when He was offered great riches and power beyond all understanding if He gave way to certain temptations of the flesh, but He was steadfast and did not give way.

"There are very few in the world who have this steadfastness of character. There are some and when they return to their spirit sphere they also will find their place among the Ascended Ones, but even they do not have the same richness of character as Jesus, that ability to stretch beyond flesh and be flesh and spirit, united in one purpose. For He was able to do what only alchemists can do - to raise the dead, to heal totally and absolutely by thought as well as by touch, to reverse the damage that nature had done to mortality and He could, if He had so decided, have turned away from the ultimate death upon the cross. But he wished to suffer that Man would see His suffering and also see Him rise glorious beyond the grave.

"He loved, and loved deeply. He had emotions as all flesh do, but He was able to turn away from temptation. He did not marry, nor yet take the flesh as though in marriage, for He knew that he must be abstemious within that life, that He must be an example to others in a similar position of leading and teaching the masses, that they should stand apart and not give way to lust of the flesh, but He had needs, the same as all mankind. He needed comfort, He needed love, He needed understanding, therefore He gathered around Him those who could provide these things, both men and women. Those who looked after His comforts ensured He rested and was fed, and there were many times when His feet were lacerated and sore from walking along the way of life that saddened and hurt Him greatly. The lack of response in man to Truth is disheartening and all those who teach find this. They offer Truth but it is not always taken and assimilated.

"Is there anything else that you wish us to tell you?"

Questioner: "I think that has covered my question. It is really my desire to understand Him as a man - a spirit in Man."

Master: "He was not set apart from others, as some of those in the world today set themselves apart. He did not wear regalia, He did not speak to men as though He had greater light and knowledge than they. He wore a simple garment and often walked barefoot and was at one with the people. Those that did set themselves apart such as those in the temple, those of the hierarchy who ruled including the Romans, belittled

Him as one who had no regard for His own needs, one who did not desire to be worshipped. For it is God the Father that is worshipped, not as Man, but as Spirit, as Truth, as The Way indeed. Jesus suffered greatly many times, not only at the end of His earthly life, when He was scourged beyond all endurance of the flesh. Many would have died with such pain and laceration, but He recovered from that torment and still made His own cross. He was a man who asked for nothing except that God be acknowledged as the Creator of all the universe, that His own path and His Truth should be acknowledged and that Man's spirit and soul within should be recognised and as part of the greater whole. It was only this that He sought to teach."

"May I ask a further question concerning Jesus the man. Was he able to raise Himself above the baser needs of Man? There have been many debates on this."

Master: "He was able, and did so, but many others have been capable of this. A few set themselves such heights but fall from them. The tenacity of purpose within Man is manifold and those that seek light and are absorbed by it are given strength above those who do not seek it to the same degree. He remained celibate all His life, but He was still a man, with anger and passion. Much angered him, especially those things that destroyed the young and crushed their belief in their purpose in life. He spent much time in prayer that He might be strengthened, that He might learn the lessons of life and understand them as lesser men do. Some lessons He failed to understand. You must remember the flesh is weak and if the soul had no need to experience the flesh it could remain in the perfection of the spiritual spheres, but when encased in flesh, the same temptations, the same anger and awareness encompass the body."

"Was the Higher Self of Jesus within the Astral Plane the same as that of ordinary human beings?"

Master: "The Higher Self of the vast majority of mankind dwells over several planes. It begins initially in the plane which is still part of the Earth but of a slightly higher vibration and it moves through to the Causal Plane, the Astral Plane and sometimes beyond. Much depends upon the spirituality and the learning of the soul throughout many lives, so the Higher Self of the Christ did the same. It was more radiant, there was more growth within it, therefore it extended vastly beyond that of average souls."

Jesus - the Son of God?

Two answers to this important question are reproduced; the second one explains the implications of karma.

Questioner: "You must have known Jesus very well and I imagine that you tell everybody that he was the Son of God and there is no other God?"

Master: We do not speak quite in the way that you infer. All men are children of God and we have explained exactly what God is - not the human personality, but the structure of all life - therefore the soul within each one of you is part of that life, that great soul essence of creation, but Christ was one sent with a mission and He was blessed with the Christos, that divine beam of light and understanding - not from birth, as many believe, but when approaching the maturity which was needed to bring forth His understanding of teaching and the spreading of love and purpose among men. Then this light, this power, this Christos entered and raised Him above the level of most of mankind. There have been many teachers that have lived upon your Earth and they have been endowed with great understanding far beyond the normal intelligence of the Higher Self, but the manner of Jesus' life and of His passing is distinct in the memory of mankind and has had great impact, great awareness of how fragile is man, how easily his soul can depart and return to the great spirit realms. Jesus has done this and He has also brought to mankind a great sense of purpose, of peace, as well as of love. And yes, we knew Him well."

The second answer is as follows:

Master: "The man Jesus, born to radiate the Truth as others have been born throughout existence, has been wrongly shown to be the only Son of God. We have throughout our teachings, both to the individual and to groups, been at pains to explain that no one person can die to absolve mankind of sin. The retribution which comes with the soul, comes because of the action of individual Man, as well as collective Man. Those who think and reason must surely realise that not one alone is the Son of God, but all, for God is not of Man but of spirit - the influence of creation, of all that has stemmed from the single cell, the single thought and yet those with great understanding, theologists, theosophists, philosophers, all those that read deeply and find within themselves the Truth, still believe in the principle of the first cause within Man. This is far from the Truth and yet the simple Truth is always the most difficult to accept. The sins that Man commits, he pays for - if not within the present life, in lives to come. But that which the man Jesus did indeed manifest among mankind was Love, total, absolute and without fear or favour of the self, unity with the Higher Self and all that is beyond, the total awareness of the principle of life and the total understanding of the meaning of Love."

Where is Jesus now?
Questioner: "Is Jesus on the planet Earth today?"

Master: "If you refer to the soul of the Christ who came in the Piscean Age to help mankind to understand the purpose of that Age and prepare souls for the present Aquarian Age, this was the soul of a great Master who came but once to the Earth to inhabit a body and bring teaching and love to the Earth while in that body. Upon re-entering the spiritual realms that soul returned to the Higher Self then to the Causal Plane and finally to the Logos itself to enrich the spirit energies and love for Mankind. That soul cannot return for it is fulfilled, but there are souls of many Masters within the bodies of men so as to help and guide and bring peace to a troubled Earth. It is like the Aquarian children who have no need to return for their own progress for they are fulfilled. They come with love to help the world to strengthen the creative principle and understand its own purpose. The essence of the Christ love remains throughout the universe, enriching Man and bringing to him those things that he desires. There are Teachers who come in each Age. They have the light of the Christos within them for that is separate from Jesus the Christ. Jesus came at that time to awaken Man to his individual needs, to understand the Truth, the reality of life and how to absorb that Truth and live with Mankind in harmony and with purpose. Other teachers have a similar mission but they are not of the same. And those who say that they are of the Christ essence speak ill-advisedly for they are not."

The 'Second Coming.'
This is a very popular question and the following excerpts are taken from three separate answers.

Master: "Many have asked 'will there truly be a Second Coming?', and our answer to this is yes, there will, but not in the way anticipated and believed. In fact it is now with you, surrounding you. It is indeed already in the world, for the Christ has no form and need not be within the human frame. The Christ is in that total soul, that at-one-ness which is mankind, the Higher Self and the total reality of existence. It is here, my children. It is with you in your knowledge, gleaned through many, many spiritual lives and it will continue throughout the entire existence of the universe. No one personality alone can accept that burden. There are those, born more recently, who can accept certain responsibilities through their very progress which has taken place throughout aeons of time, but no one personality will again ever accept that mantle of Karma."

A second answer contains the following sentence.
Master: "Those who talk of the 'Second Coming' misinterpret the law. It is a further understanding of Truth that will take place."

To a question whether the Christ could materialise again the Master replied: "The Christ has been assimilated into that wonderful light which is beyond return. Eventually souls no longer desire to be separate individual beings and then the entire Higher Self of each soul merges into the divine light which is the source of life-the creative impulse. It then becomes universal and can be drawn into each individual in the world as a sense of emotion, of faith, belief, love and wonder, but it cannot appear except in a form of great purity to those who have that wonderful faith which surpasses Man's understanding. There are those who, when their vibrations are raised, have from time to time seen visions of Mary, of Jesus and other beings of light. But only those people of very great spiritual acumen and awareness are able to elevate their consciousness to that level and the vision is momentary."

A question about Jesus' temperament.
Master: "Jesus was impatient with those who were not perfectionists, who wandered from the path, who did not have the intelligence or understanding of the different subjects that He himself had. He could not bring himself to study things in which He had no interest because He was impatient with Himself desiring to do the work in hand which He was destined to do and not that which others felt would be right for Him from a hereditary or any other point of view. He was also sympathetic to those who desired things in life and could not have them. He understood lack of opportunity for advancement or

education because He felt very keenly His lack of opportunity to teach in the normal way a rabbi did in the Temple - with the one exception reported in the scriptures. Also He felt that He should have been esteemed more highly by those who did teach in the Temple. His quickness of temper and burning enthusiasm was the desire to allow the self to go forward unimpeded by companionship which would prove a burden and not a solace.

"It was no mean feat to be able to learn as deeply as He did on His travels and not become embroiled in any romantic associations. He had a very great sense of responsibility to the self and to others and He realised in His own self-discipline that He could not accept the responsibility of marriage and a family because He was aware of His future, ultimate end and manner of death. Therefore any children He might have would be without that guiding paternal influence which He felt so keenly that He had lacked because he had an aged father who died after a long and serious illness."

A visit to Glastonbury?
Questioner: "Did Jesus go to Glastonbury with His uncle Joseph of Arimathea when he was a child?"

Master: "Not to Glastonbury. He was taken to Greece, especially to those parts that were of great beauty.

"The flight to Glastonbury was after Jesus' passing. There were those of His followers who came also - His mother Mary was brought for her own safety, for there were many who sought her life."

The nature of the Christos.
Master: "Two thousand years ago, when we ourselves walked the Earth those of you who are here (said to a group in London) were also alive. Not all of you were close to the Christ light, but the world was still a large place and the energy which evolved from the Christ being present upon the Earth, echoed throughout each continent, as indeed it still does. Wonderful light, total power, such as is the Christos', is not limited to one area. It spreads within the spirit - and remember, the spirit is the spark of life which you all share, which all civilisation and all creation shares. You breathe it in, you have it within the inner soul and the silver beam of pure light and energy which links the inner soul with the Higher Self also manifests light and spirit. It cannot be evaded, even by those who profess no truth, no belief, no understanding. They could

not be upon the Earth if they did not share that divine essence of spirit."
At a later date the Master commented as follows:

"You may well ask what part the Christ spirit now plays. It is a very important part. Every supply has a source and if the Christos is to be shared equally among man, there must be an energising source. His soul, now accepted into the great light of infinity, showers this energy and power and infinite love into the hearts and souls of all living men. Because all men do not make use of it, this does not mean it is not there. The air around you is for you to breathe. You may not be aware you are breathing it, but you could not live if you did not. You may not be aware you have the Christ spirit within you, whatever your race and creed, whatever your colour, your belief or lack of belief, but it is as certainly there as the blood that flows through your veins."

A hypothetical question.

Questioner: "If Jesus was living on Earth today what would He be doing?"

Master: "Firstly, we hope you understand that in no way would Yeshua ever return again to the Earth in the same form. The Higher Self, so called, was integrated into the Greater Soul, in other words it became part of Cosmic Reality - the initial sound from which all life stemmed. The personality of Yeshua can still be reached within that great pulsating sound, by those who adhere to His Truth and His Principles, especially those that have released themselves from the dogma of religion and understand Him as a spiritual being who came to teach. Therefore it is very possible to link in thought, to make the requests which many make for healing, for understanding, for His presence in times of trouble, in the same way that all aspects of soul can thus be reached by those who desire it, but no aspect of that soul will ever again return to the Earth. It is therefore very much a hypothetical question. If indeed it were possible, we feel that He might then take up a similar role, two thousand years on, without the same privations, perhaps with more understanding of the intelligence of present day Man, and Man's desire to progress still."

This above answer then led to the following revelation:

A new Christos Teacher.

Master: "Early in the year 2000 an aspect of the Christos will enter a child which will have great bearing on the way forward for mankind. This child will not take the place of Jesus the Christ who spoke for God two thousand years ago, but he will show to the world again the Way, the Truth and the Light. This child will be born in the normal way, will grow, and gather the Children of Light together, teach them and organise them in a very similar way as Christ did with His followers (who numbered many thousands, not just twelve). In many years to come, that child will be acknowledged as bearing the Christos within. All humanity has a thread of that Christos within them, because all humanity has a soul within which carries this Light. The outpouring of Light and Love from The Creator, is the Christos.

"The child will be born in whatever way the soul has chosen for its initial beginnings. We cannot say whereabouts within your world , whether it will be in a crowd of people in a busy Western city, or in a remote place in the quietness of the wilderness. It is for that soul to choose. It may come to a single mother or to an elderly mother who has already borne her children, but come it will.

"The Children of Light have still to grow, and mature. They are very young. At least ten more years must pass (February 1992), and have we not often spoken of the importance of the beginning of the year 2000 and onwards? Around this time you can look for such a birth, but still it will be many years before that child is able to communicate with others and to learn an earthly pattern, in the way Yeshua also needed to learn. It is always good to anticipate and have faith.

"Faith is very important and also, to be positive in all that you do towards fulfilment. Never allow negative aspects to override and take predominance within your life, however grave your situation or however hopeless the immediate future may appear. Look beyond it, time is only in the vision of mankind. The greater vision of that which is taking place in all aspects and spheres of light, has promised there will be beauty arising from what is occurring in the world at this time and all the changes, all the vastness of experience of mankind, will show eventually that spirit, guides, uplifts and helps. If not, why does it exist, why are there spheres of light and Archangels with their supremacy and power? God did not make the universe to go its own way. It is structured, it moves within a rhythm and if anything, however small, should move away from that rhythm, all would perish. Hold on to this and have faith in your future and the future of your children."

Why are we here?
Questioner: "What is our purpose, why are we here?"

Master: "Many ask us this question and collectively we give much the same answer to each one: 'you are here to serve', and that answer is not always clear to those that are listening. The word 'serve' so often gives the feeling of being a servant, of being a lesser person than those that receive the service, but when we look to the beginning of the last age, that of Pisces, and see the Christ Light manifest in flesh, eager to serve, even by washing the feet of others, and bearing food and drink to the table of those that should be serving Him and doing these tasks with love and understanding. That is true service. We do not ask that you should demean yourselves, but that in your service you pass on to others truth and enlightenment that will enable them to have their own sense of reality and purpose in what remains of their lives."

The following past life was given to a Dane in March 1992 and gives a further insight into the life of the Christ.

A servant of Christ.
"Can you tell me if I was present when Christ was on Earth? Did I meet Him?"

Master: "Not only did you meet the Christ but also the one who speaks with you, Joseph of Arimathea. There were many among those to whom we have spoken in the last few years who were present at that time and known not only to the Holy Family but also to those who speak as I do. Some of the Apostles who were the disciples of Christ, and who dwell still in the Causal Plane, share their understanding and memory with us at times when we speak of the past. The accuracy of one train of thought is doubled when it is augmented by other memories in minds that link together. Most people in the World at this time were present also 2000 years ago. Souls congregate at the beginning of an age in order to appreciate the past and improve the future. It was not by chance that Christ came at that particular time, and His influence went far beyond Palestine.

"You were born of the servant class as it was known and much depended upon the intellect and the understanding of their masters for how much comfort and appreciation they had. The Holy Family were born to wealth, although it appears from the writings in the scriptures that they were in essence poor. As we have already explained this was not so. They descended from the line of David and in their own way, although enjoying the simple things of life, they were also very aware of the authority and the influence that they themselves held over many. Joseph of Arimathea was asked to take care of Mary when her husband, Joseph the Carpenter passed to the higher life. They would travel between their homes in Nazareth and in Jerusalem according to need. Jesus knew well both dwellings and also those of His uncle Joseph in Jerusalem, in Arimathea, as well as the estates he inherited from his father in Cyprus and in Greece. And Yeshua would travel with His friends and cousins to these estates. It was considered imperative that He was guarded, for even before His birth there were those who considered that should He live and continue living the State would be under threat. He had a cousin whom He loved greatly and who acted as his guardian when He travelled but with Him also would go a servant. This was the way of those with position and It would be considered ill advised to ignore these simple procedures.

"First your father enjoyed that role and often he would listen to the relatively simple teaching given by Jeshua to those who travelled with Him and those He would speak to by the wayside, for He enjoyed the company of others and conversing with them. And when your father was too crippled to continue and you had reached the age of reason you followed and served and were also a friend, for members of that family looked upon their servants almost as kinsmen and they were given privileges that many others were not. So you travelled between these various homes and you would enjoy the benefits of the estate in Cyprus, especially when there was need for extensive periods of rest. For Jeshua travelling as widely as he did, would often be exhausted and He would need time away from the community, away from those that constantly sought His wisdom and His teaching and relax alone.
Initially, you would sit a little away from Him, being conscious of His need for solitude. And then He would become alert and call you. Together you would sit on the shore and there His way of speaking was often in parables. His knowledge of dialect and language was unsurpassed. And He would speak of that within the Ocean which as yet no man had set eyes upon, the wonders of the coral reefs, of the animal and fish realms that dwelt in the darkness of the bottom of the Ocean. And you would sit listening with wonder and enjoyment to these tales. And always at the completion there would be a parable to help you personally.

"As the time approached when His teaching would come to an end and that which was foreseen within His life would take place, you desired greatly to guard and protect Him and save Him from the rigours of first the lashing and then the cross. But like all others you were powerless. History proceeded each moment along the way, unfolding as it had been ordained. But still you followed behind Him, still you endeavoured to hold Him back from the crisis, from the pain, in whatever way that you could. When it came to the time of the crucifixion, you could not bear it. You ran away, you hid your face and covered your ears from the sounds. And when the great darkness covered the land and the storm came with the lashing of wind and rain you remained in the shadow of a tree, too afraid to emerge to see what had occurred. But then eventually the darkness lifted and there was a deep, deep silence. You came out of your hiding place and went to Golgotha. But all was calm. He had been taken to the resting place in the tomb. And then your heart was full. You tried to go to the tomb knowing His body must be prepared for burial. Here there were the women who loved and followed the Christ. But they were not allowed to go within nor yet were you. You stayed with them for their vigil, until so tired with the sorrow and anxiety of the day you could no longer keep awake and you slept. When you awoke the place was deserted and the tomb was empty. You also saw others within the garden searching for where He could have been placed. You followed Mary Magdalene to the olive grove and at first helped her to pick some olives, as she was very hungry not having eaten for some days because of her sorrow and anxiety over the Man she loved so deeply. But then you were called away and she was left alone to perceive first the stranger and then His transformation into the risen Christ.

"We endeavour to spread the truth to Mankind. Some of the things which occurred at that time are accurately reported in the Scriptures and some have been omitted. And when we speak, we speak of them. But above all it is to the Soul we speak, and the Soul recalls."

Finally two small notes taken partly from a group transcript and two personal tapes.

Master: "We would like to add at this time that the Christ had neither a wife nor children and His life was dedicated totally to the expansion of awareness of eternal Truths. He loved very greatly one of the sisters from Bethany. She was a cousin as also was Lazarus but not a close cousin and the younger sister Mary loved Him greatly, and He loved her. However during His long stay on the continent of India in order to learn and understand the ways of the mystics, who had vows of chastity to enable the soul to express its knowledge profoundly, He also took certain vows of chastity. It was when He was learning how to have continuous life through the etheric body which He needed after the crucifixion, that He took these vows.

"He was aware even before His travels that His life would be very different from the lives of His fellow men and also of His family, to whom he was very close. But quite naturally he had the same instincts as all mankind and he did love Mary deeply and desired her, but they both understood His purpose and she endeavoured to uphold him in His vows. There was no other woman he felt so deeply about.

"There are writings which speak of a relationship with Mary Magdalene, but this was not so. They were very close as brother and sister would be, or as cousins which they were and she had great respect and honour for Him. He, in His gentleness of personality and understanding of the difficulties of the way of life she had been forced into, may have given some who studied that period of history the idea that there was something closer, in the same way that some historians have deduced, incorrectly, that He travelled to India after His supposed death on the cross, taking Mary Magdalene and their children with Him, but this is not so. It is derived from other historic writings which did not correspond to the true life of Jesus, but to that of another sage who came from Egypt and had very similar teachings to the Christ."

A final thought.
Master: "Yeshua had much humour and a great rapport with happiness as well as the suffering of others. He too had strong emotions and could be stirred to anger, as all men. Although endowed with the Christos and with memory and knowledge of what would be within his life He was very human."

Chapter 8

The Disciples

The Master has been asked very few specific question about the disciples and most of those questions were about Peter. This chapter collects together comments and answers directed specifically about the disciples (more information about them is woven into the text in part IV). Some of the information concerning the Disciples is contained in past lives given to individuals. In order not to destroy the beauty of these stories no attempt has been made to extract specific details from these narratives.

Peter versus Paul.
Master: "There is much misunderstanding of the teachings of Simon-Peter and Paul. There was a gentleness within the heart of Peter together with an intense desire for the teachings to spread. Peter learnt the Truth - the teachings, direct from the Master Christ and he kept these teachings simple - as they should be. Paul, educated and a Roman citizen, learnt these teachings from others and without the strong influence of Christ applied to them his own logic - his own personality. The church has been largely founded on the truth Paul bore witness to, but it was Peter who had the direct truth and he has never had the credit due to him."

Taken from a private tape - August 1993.

"And He said to them 'Follow me...' Matthew 4:19.
The following past life was given to an English woman in September 1991.

"I feel that I was alive at the time of the Christ and that I then knew X (a woman). Can you confirm this and possibly tell me who I was at that time?'
    Master: "We are well aware of the part that X played within the drama of the life of Christ and there were those who formed friendships then as in this life - those who were close to one another in everyday being. In that life you were a fisherman and you worked during your youth and young manhood with your father, mending the nets and living your life as tranquilly as possible within that area of Palestine involved with the growth, spiritual development and final passing to spirit of Jesus.

"You knew two brothers who were called to his service, but you were at that time too young, for those that he called were men of knowledge, if not of intellect, men who had lived and had confidence in themselves. You had just begun family life by taking to you your betrothed and having your first child. Yeshua, as we called Him, did not call on those who had such urgent responsibilities. For a while you were envious. You saw the two brothers leave their boats and their nets and follow Him, but to us the word "follow" is not exact. Life and work were not suddenly abandoned, for men were gradually drawn to His teaching and His light and then decided that they would leave their homes, their families and their work and follow Him wherever He travelled. This is not always clearly stated in the gospels.

"For many months and even years that His teachings took place the brothers would, from time to time, return and recommence their work and they would speak to you of what they had learnt, where they had been and of their own knowledge growing within them. There were times when you also would travel, not because you had been called, but because of the sheer desire to travel. Your wife and two children were taken into the loving family of your parents. You accompanied Yeshua and the two disciples to the house of Lazarus. There you were made welcome, and there you would share their repast, their laughter and their prayers and those that waited upon Yeshua and the other male members of the family, would sit and would listen and also would share. The wife of Lazarus and his sisters and other members of the community would come and would listen to the teachings of the great Master and then you would return again to your home and share that teaching. The teachings of the Masters are now being spread throughout the world, the same teachings that we are giving, the same light, the same knowledge, and those that listen are not being asked to give up their livelihoods, give up their families, they are being asked just to listen, to absorb and to remember and in that way they too will share with others and repeat the words of Truth and enlightenment. It is the same then as now.

"You were not present at the time of the crucifixion, but you were aware of it. You were attending your wife at the birth of your third child, sitting quietly outside the door, praying that her travail would soon be finished and the child that you both desired would be born safely. You hoped that your two friends, the two brothers, would return in time for the celebrations of the birth of your first son, and as you sat and contemplated birth and life, you were only too aware that a life was being taken, was ending, and so it is throughout the world, throughout all eternity, that as a soul comes into life, so another soul returns to spirit.

"The brothers returned, albeit briefly. They knew then their task, they knew that they had to travel far and wide and bring about the enlightenment of those that sat in the darkness of spirit. Your friendship continued until circumstances throughout the land made it impossible for such friends of Yeshua to remain without fear of their lives and then they left with the Arimathean, to travel firstly to Britain, and then in some cases to other lands and islands, in order to perpetuate Christ"s teachings, but you remained, you looked after your family and your boats. It was an important job - just as important as those that followed their hearts."

Simon Peter's Son.
The following life was given to an English man in June 1992.

"I wish to know the circumstances of my life at the time of the Christ; what I learnt then and how that can help me understand my role in life today."

Master: "It is seldom realised, because it is not officially recorded in the scriptures that the disciples were married men. They had commitments of their own before they were called to guard, guide and help Christ on His chosen path. Some were businessmen such as the tax collector and there were those, simple in their outlook and yet disciplined because of their mode of life, the fishermen. There were those who within their limited understanding of doctrine would endeavour to help the afflicted of mind and body. They were a mixture of men, but there were also the women, for Jesus loved men and women equally, they had their place in life. He endeavoured to extol them and raise them from the degradation of being the chattels of the men who owned them. Joseph in his own life had believed from an early age in the equality of women and was outspoken in his beliefs, thereby causing outrage among his peers. Jesus also, coming from the same stock as His uncle, believed absolutely that love should be shared and not demanded, that it was not given as a right, but as a reward. As we have already stated Jesus had taken the vow of chastity because of the training He had received, mainly in India from those who had themselves restricted their lives in order to be able to guide and teach and show others a way of living. And because He himself had great awareness of His purpose, to leave a wife and family behind at the mercy of vultures was no part of the rhythm he had accepted. He still loved and the love of humanity can be greater than the love of a father for his children, or a husband for his wife. Such love demands sacrifice but it is still part of the rhythm of life and thereby important. We have spoken of laughter but love is even more important.

"There was one named Simon Peter, a man of great depth and yet a man initially of great ignorance. A member of a large family with a wife and children of his own, hard working, industrious and freely spoken. In this day and age he might be called coarse, without refinement, a rock that had not been polished in any way, but he was strong in upholding others and giving them strength.

"Simon Peter loved one son more than the others, that son had been born crippled, mentally and physically. The mother had sustained a great fall and normally this would have led to a miscarriage, but because of the love of her kinswomen, who insisted that she rested and looked after herself and the child within, that child was born. Almost immediately it was realised that he was not perfect. He did not react to life or love and had little sense of reality. There was great grieving. Simon Peter hoped that the child's life might ebb for he was aware of the difficulties surrounding men and how they were discarded unless strong and fit. At first he did not wish to see his son, but when he realised his wife's great sadness for she loved this one as much as her other children he realised that withholding his love was an act of cruelty. Now whatever Simon Peter was he was not cruel. He forced himself to look upon his son. The child opened his eyes and smiled at him and immediately there was love between them. He helped the child slowly as he grew to have certain accomplishments within the limited framework of his life. He would take him into the small boat and talk to him as he fished for his livelihood. He fought other men when they mocked him for being less than a man to father such a child. This child was weak in frame as well as mentality and yet he showed much love even to the fish as they were loaded into the boat for those that still lived he begged his father to return to the water. And laughing with his great laugh, for Simon Peter was a huge man and to please his son he threw back much of his catch. And when he returned to the shore and his catch was less than that of others, he said "But these fish are of quality, they have been chosen by my son." Years passed and the time of Christ was nigh. He passed that way and He sought Simon Peter and his brother John. He knew they were very close and He desired to have as His disciples those who respected and loved each other. Therefore he chose the two brothers and as is known in the fullness of time He referred to Peter as the rock. (The Master confirmed that this was indeed Simon Peter's brother John who, unlike Andrew, did not actually become a disciple). The name of Simon was no longer heard, but many who loved him referred to him as Paul. The name Paul meant "righteous one" and Peter above all others was able to retain the truth, the teaching and share it with others. He had great powers within him, not only of strength of body but also strength of purpose and mind. When it was found that Jesus had the ability to heal where others did not, he requested that his son be made as strong, both in mind and body, as his other children and the children of his kinsmen. As was His way Jesus bade him to sit and listen and He said to him " Would you have your son as he is, gentle with the ability to love and care even though he is small in frame and in mind not as strong as others, or would you have him lose this quality and be as strong as you, as full of purpose and strength and ability, and yet without the gentle quality which you do not have as yet?" And He bade Peter to think about His words. At first he was angry, he felt he had been abused, restrained from natural love towards his son, by the one man he respected most greatly, not for his great physical strength for Jesus was not strong physically. He was tall and slim and had strength of character but not of body, and Simon Peter in his own weakness found this difficult to accept. Being so great in size and strength himself, almost as Atlas, he could not totally respect those who were weaker. And it was this quality in Jesus which Simon Peter felt was lacking. He discussed this problem with others, and one said to him, "Why do you not discuss it with your son, ask him what it is he desires from life and what he cannot do because of his weakness." This was a new idea to Peter. He sought out his son once more in the darkness of the night when they were seeking their catch and he asked him this question. The son said "You have been speaking with our Lord.", Peter agreed that he had, and there were certain possibilities that he could be healed, but that he might indeed lose his gentleness of spirit, which came with his weaker frame. The son laughed and said to his father "That is my personality, it is within me whether I shared your frame or that of a weakling. I do not think my personality would change if I had stronger purpose in life." So Peter returned to Jesus and told him that he had made his decision. Jesus asked him how and Peter replied "It is the decision of my son only and I have told him to seek you out and speak with you." And this the boy did. Many days passed, Jesus and Peter's son who was called Eli were together on an island much loved by Jesus for its solitude and peace. And when they returned at low-tide, when they could walk across the sands to the mainland, Peter eagerly ran forward expecting to see a transformation within his son and he saw it was not so. He still walked irregularly, he was still of slight frame, he still spoke hesitantly, but there was a light of purpose that shone from his eyes that had not been there before. Peter said to Jesus "Have you healed my son?" and Jesus said "Healing comes with words of teaching and direction as well as the laying on of hands and the imbibing of spirit. In a certain way yes I have healed your son, but only as much as he himself desires." And Peter had to be content with that.

"This was the early days of the ministry of Christ before He bade His friends to leave all that was theirs and follow Him. Then the one who was left to care for both the younger children and his mother was Eli, for Eli had great love for humanity, he understood his purpose, he desired nothing more than to be able to show compassion and love to those close to him, to thank them for the years they had spent in devotion to him.

'Peter saw few of his family again and never his son, but always Eli's youthful radiance shone within his heart and he remembered him as his own gentler side, that he found so difficult to reveal because of his great size. We are sure that by now you realise you were this son Eli and that much of the gentleness that reflected within that other aspect of your soul reflects within you now. Do you ever feel that you lack in any way strength or determination? You do not, you show them with compassion and love."

A midwife in the Holy Land
The following life was given to an American in January 1992.
"I have been reading a book about the times of Jesus Christ and about the Essenes, this touched me very strongly. I felt as if everything I was reading I already knew and it was just re-affirming it, as if I had been

there. I would like to know if Saul of Tarsus was actually married to Mary Magdalene?"

Master: "No, he was not; in fact they never even met."

"Because this book touched me so much I wonder if there is a reason; did I live in those times?"

Master: "Indeed you did have a life at that time and we will explain this to you.

It was a very traumatic time and you were very young when the actual crucifixion took place. The greater part of your life was after this, but your real drive and determination for living arose from it. You were born as the result of an accident to your mother during her pregnancy. Bearing in mind that at that time the mortality rate was exceptionally high, very few infants would survive a pregnancy virtually terminated by accident. There were no life support machines and little knowledge. Also, children were so easily begotten that the mortality rate was welcomed, rather than grieved over, especially in the Eastern countries, but your mother had longed for a child throughout her life. She was already approaching middle age. At first she did not realise that she was with child and continued her arduous daily life. She was married to a man younger than herself, whom she treated very much as an elder child, giving much to him, pampering and waiting upon him. He did nothing to help her. While some husbands would fetch the water and would help their wives with the difficult tasks, he did nothing except sit in the sun - a visionary thinking of the future and wishing that he had saved himself for a much younger woman with whom he could roam about and enjoy himself, without any kind of domesticity or difficulty. He was fond of your mother but he looked upon her more as a mother to himself. It was at a time when she was fetching a particularly heavy vessel of water from the well that she slipped, she caught her foot and she went down very heavily. The water spilled and when she tried to arise from the ground, she slipped again on the wet earth. She fell over the bucket and injured herself quite severely on the abdomen. Although in pain she managed to return to the dwelling. At first she thought it was the pain of the injury and then she realised that it was more severe. When the contractions had gained momentum she realised with astonishment she was giving birth. Neighbours came and helped her, but you were born prematurely and very small. It was only the intense love of this woman and her desire, once the child was laid in her arms, to nurture and sustain you that allowed you to survive.

"Within hours of the birth, one of the neighbours, who was aware of the ministry of Yeshua and of the Disciples who followed Him, sought Him. One of the Disciples who was nearby hastened with her to the dwelling. You were very near death and yet still only a few hours old. Your mother was weeping, holding you close and trying to encourage you to take her milk, that you might gain strength. When Peter entered the dwelling his radiance filled it. He placed his hands over the infant's head and said an incantation that he had been taught by Yeshua. It was as though the young child was flooded with life. Immediately its eyes opened and it began to take nourishment. From that time on you gained in strength.

"The crucifixion of Yeshua sadly took place when you were but two years old. Your mother endeavoured to keep you away from the scene, but other children of the neighbours who were older than you and who were consumed by curiosity went there and took you with them. Kept well back by soldiers and other people who felt it was no place for young children, you watched unnoticed from afar. To you it was a profound experience. The scene at the cross was so different from others executed in a similar way, no weeping, no screaming in pain or outrage, just quiet stillness, resignation, determined dignity, and then darkness. It was as though the sun had become eclipsed, a dark cloud covered the sky at the height of the bright sun of the afternoon. All went still and quiet, there was no sound from the great crowd and even others who hung upon their crosses were stilled in awe, and from that great darkness the wind began. Within an hour the soul had left His body, and then the darkness lifted and the wind was stilled. Those who loved and cared for Him, eventually were allowed to take His body from the cross and he was taken from your sight.

"You had been told many times by your mother of Peter's healing. Being so very young you had little understanding, but you remembered these things and as you grew older they were recalled more often and in your sleep you occasionally felt that there was a touch, a communication to which you could not give words, as though the renewal of energy and life was repeatedly taking place. When you reached adolescence you learned more about the tragedy of the crucifixion and what had led to it. You made a vow to yourself that you would endeavour to help others at their time of need, especially regarding women in the pain of labour and that if your ministrations could help keep alive an innocent child they would do so. You found you had a gift for this. You became a midwife, as it is known, and you attended many births, especially those that came too soon or were difficult, for there were those who, through hardship and poverty, had no help and therefore the children when they were born, came with great anguish. You found that when a child was born, you had only to place your hands over its head and life would surge within it.

"It was not until you were a fully mature woman that Peter returned again to the Holy Land very briefly, before being recalled to Rome, where he was tried and also crucified. You met him and spoke with him and recalled to his mind his healing at your birth. Then he had been in middle years and now he was old, white - bearded with long white hair, bald, large and slightly misshapen beneath his flowing robe, a man who had suffered a great deal with imprisonment and floggings, but in his great heart and vibrant voice there was a determination to teach and bring others to the way of Truth and Light. You spoke with him for a long while and he agreed that you had that touch to impart life and that it came from the mantra, the incantation that he had spoken, given to Him by the Christ.

"It was not long after that, that his soul departed from the world, but you felt you had been rightly drawn to your own life of service. You did not accept a husband, nor were you taken in an act of love, but dedicated service to the infants of that time fully made up for any other lack within your life. You did not bear your own child, but you had loved many children."

The beginning of Peter's Ministry without his Lord.
The following life was given to a Jewish English woman in September 1990.

"May I be told if I was on Earth at the time of Christ and if so, what I was doing? 'X' (a woman) and I feel a great rapport and we would like to know if this is related to past lives?"

Master: "It is indeed. Throughout the spectrum of living your souls have been together many times, in different guises, in different parts of the world. This is no different from many others who feel a similar friendship and partnership, and many of those who listen to our teachings were indeed present upon the Earth at the time of the Christ life. They took part in various ways in spreading the teaching and endeavouring to eliminate the evil which was spread then, as it is now, by ignorance.

"You were indeed present in Jerusalem at the time of the crucifixion. Many indeed who had not met before were united at that time in their purpose of endeavouring to delay or postpone indefinitely the atrocities which indeed took place because it was so destined. But men were not aware of this destiny, therefore they endeavoured to release the Christ and prevent His assassination. Those who had come from many parts, Israel, Egypt, Jordan and other places had experience of the teachings not only of Jesus, but also of the disciples who travelled far more extensively than is revealed within the Gospels - in fact the Gospels are totally inadequate at expressing the true wealth of knowledge and teachings which were in the world at that time.

"Before you journeyed to Jerusalem, to join the multitudinous gathering which endeavoured to prevent the crucifixion, your own soul had many times arisen to the Truth and the Gospel of the Way without even being aware of the specific teachings that were taking place. The spirituality of the soul will often arise and give voice because it is united with the spirit realms from whence all Truth descends, and the outpouring of Truth can come to mankind in the most remote areas of the world. As adults, certain hermits or those who have taken a vow of silence may possibly never meet or speak to another but still have the Truth of the Holy Spirit within them.

"In that life as a woman you had taken yourself away from the world. You had a disease which was considered to be one which many could acquire should you touch them, or if intercourse took place with you. Voluntarily you went away from your village. You inhabited a cave with others who had a similar disease. There is nothing at this time which is comparable, but it was a wasting disease. The blood did not reach the extremities and therefore the digits upon the hands and feet would slowly disintegrate and fall away. It was not leprosy but similar and in that part of the East leprosy was not prevalent at that time. This disease was caused by minute mites which entered the body through feet walking in tainted water. They moved through the bloodstream, firstly destroying vital organs within and then in the later stages attacking the flesh. It was an extremely painful, debilitating and noxious illness.

"Several of you lived together in this cave. You then heard that there were those who were healing, who were transforming the most hideous of diseases into perfection, that the blind were able to see and the deaf to hear, the lame to walk and even the dead to rise from the grave. The little band of women who lived together travelled, with you as leader, many, many miles to find those who were performing these miracles. As you approached the place where you knew these healers to be you heard of the sacrilege which was taking place. This Man who had such love for others was to be executed; He was being charged untruly with things He had not uttered because of the fear of those who ruled the city that His love and compassion would prevent their tyranny. Thus you were present at the crucifixion, but you realised that you could not mingle with the people. You found one of the disciples, one who loved Christ greatly and yet he had denied knowing Him or being with Him. He was in tears, distraught, preparing to destroy His life because of what he had done. You approached him - there were six in number - and standing at a distance you asked that he might heal in the name of his Master, and looking upon you and seeing the travesty of youth destroyed by disease, he then realised the importance of living, of going forward and continuing that which his Master had begun. But as he gazed upon the woman with such profound and advanced disease he felt that such healing was far beyond his healing abilities and he said: "I cannot heal you but I give you my love and the love of all of us who speak in His name", and then he turned and left.

You watched this act of sacrilege from afar, but you felt within yourself that indeed a healing was taking place. You led the little band of women to the great lake. There you immersed yourselves and when you arose and came again to the shore, it was to find already those blisters upon the skin were beginning to heal.

"You returned to your home. For many months you remained within the cave, until those parts of the body which were ulcerated had become healed. It was not instantaneous, but it was progressive and when healed you then covered your faces, because many of you had lost a nose and some the lips. You covered the lower part of your faces and down to the bosom, then you went forth and you taught of the wonders of healing. Does this put at rest some of the doubts and thoughts which had been within your mind?"

"Well it makes sense of the fact that I have this need to work with people who are HIV positive or have AIDS. It may not have a spiritual link, but for me I have a feeling for people who are often regarded as no longer acceptable in society. Thank you so much Master."

Master: "And this is, of course, your link with Peter, as you have probably understood and Peter is indeed part of the group who speak with you, and whose knowledge is absorbed among you."

More about Peter.

Master: "He was indeed a rock that many depended upon, a strong man within a group that often would have liked to turn and run when faced with adversity. He could block their way physically filling an aperture within the wall through which they would flee, turning them back to face the truth within themselves and to realise that their purpose had been specifically chosen and they must accept this, but he also had great depth of character within his spiritual knowledge having spent many years of his life in contemplation in a boat upon the open sea as he fished with others for his livelihood. He was used to loneliness, he was used to the stars above and the elements, making decisions and asking for the help of the divine in his path in life. He was also a kinsman of Yeshua and His family and was the first to be chosen to join Him as a follower and companion.

"Many things occurred to the disciples, especially to Peter. The agony of mind that was his throughout the time of purgatory, throughout the trial, the agony which was his Lord's was his also. All those that were with Him recognised the divinity, the Christ light. They knew that that incarnation was the first and the last* and many of the majestic things that occurred were known to them only - the tears, in the private places of the heart, the searching for the godhead, the desire that the flesh should not be hurt. However conscious man may be of life within light, of how unimportant the body can be, it still feels pain and there is still the fear of pain. The Christ was no different from His fellow man for this and when He had passed, those that carried the word forward lived in constant fear also. Prayers and services were held by Peter within subterranean passages and deep caves, as those that had pledged themselves and their hearts to continue preaching the word would meet quietly in secret. Children also came, for it was as important then as now that the young ones should understand truth and acknowledge a Master and yet some might cry and otherwise create noise that would attract attention and often they did. Seldom did all that meet escape the attention of the guards and many were whipped and scourged, to make them relinquish their belief. This happened far more often than is recorded within the gospels, Peter was scourged, his flesh was whipped from his back and he would cry in agony that the pain might be relieved. Those among the apostles with the healing touch could alleviate the pain of the body, but seldom of the mind. Each knew that as the years passed, they would stand witness to what had been and what would be in the future time.

"Peter was a man of great stature and when he himself was put to death, the agony that had been his Master's became his own. He had endured many lives before that, but as we have said many times the truly spiritual life is often one of pain and sacrifice and those that are to join the Higher self and move to the causal spheres must understand truly all there is to learn."

The above is taken from a group meeting held in London in April 1988.

* Jesus' incarnation was different from that of other souls because His soul had not entered into life before that particular incarnation. It was therefore His Higher Self which entered into the body of Jesus and absorbed the Christos before His true work began. There are those who feel that the soul of Jesus encompassed the souls of Elijah and other great prophets. Certainly the awareness of the Christos was within those prophets as God spoke through their Higher Selves and allowed the great teaching to emerge from very simple men. It was not so with Yeshua. His was a complete life - the first and the last - and those who repeatedly insist that other aspects of Jesus have been reborn and is indeed living now are misguided and misled.

General information about the Disciples.

Master: "It is never by chance that people meet in life and look at one another and sense the past, perhaps not understanding totally when or how they have met, but deep within themselves the reality is clear and the soul recognises and cannot turn away. If that is true now, why should it not be so in the past? And as Yeshua sought those who were to accompany Him as he travelled and taught and lived and loved, He realised that they had been born and had arrived in that place, that He might choose them. Here we have the first error of truth in the Gospels, where it is implied that within a short while those He chose were made His Disciples. In fact it took more than twelve years to find them and choose them and there were far more than twelve. Do you have only twelve friends? Do you have only twelve people whom you can trust, can speak with and share? With many it may be only one. With another it can be more than a hundred and can it be conceived that a man whose heart was full of knowledge, would share this with only twelve? And as He progressed through His life many of the things revealed were changed later by those who wrote of Him. The most ignorant and humble of His followers revealed their innermost hearts to scribes, and these scribes faithfully wrote exactly what was revealed to them. But many of these words have been withheld from Man that he may be subservient to those who seek to suppress the truth, that essence of Love which is universal and which should be shared by all beliefs, all peoples, and not just those who have received the label of 'Christian'. There is no label. You cannot call yourself by that which you feel, by that which stems from deep within your hearts and overflows as would a chalice of great worth and great understanding and Truth.

"Gradually, as we meet in this way, as we extend our hands towards you in this life, as we have in the past, as you walk with us through the valleys of understanding, as you remember within yourself events from the past which remain in the consciousness, for they cannot be obliterated, we will share memories and in that sharing the Truth will again be withheld from none. It will be reborn, for each one of you present has known either Yeshua or His mother and father, his step-brothers, his cousins and uncles, the Disciples and all others who lived and walked and made Jerusalem a city of light. At this time we will leave you to contemplate these thoughts. We ask only that you hold on, not to the irrelevancies of the past, but to that which will be revealed in the future - not only by him with whom you speak, but by others who give voice to the one Truth, the one Light."

The above was given to a group which met in London in June 1991.

More about the Disciples - given in November 1991.
"Some time ago Master you spoke about the Disciples and you said there was very little in the Bible about what their real work had been and how much they had travelled. Would you enlarge on this?"

Master: "Again it seems that the Bible concentrates upon but a few - those who had perhaps a little more intellect than the others, those with greater powers of oratory and also did not fear mutilation and death as much. There were some who followed their ministry in a quieter way - rather in a way that we suggest to those to whom we speak at this time - by innuendo, by gentle encouragement to those who fear to believe, to follow the light, to be positive in their ideas and their way of looking at life. There were those who returned to their homes, who did not travel far, but their very demeanour had changed because of the enlightenment that they had been given. There were many more than twelve, as we have said, but those that were beloved of the Christ, to whom he spoke most often, who tended and cared for Him and protected Him along His travels - to these He imparted His secrets.

"There was much more to the teaching than just the word of God. Teaching the uninitiated how to heal, how to raise from the dead when it is warranted, and many other magical effects which did indeed take place. It is not easy to share these things, and those who were chosen to be close to Him were those to whom He felt would not share with others. Those who could not be told these special things should be available as a shoulder upon which to lean in times of trouble. There were some who died as a result of punishment and torture when the Romans found them and imprisoned them. There is nothing as far as we are aware within the Gospels which speaks of their trial and their ultimate death, other than that of Peter, and there were those who did indeed flee the country, that they might retain their freedom to spread these truths in other lands, but those who left the country did so at His request; Those who remained within the land to shed what light they could before they themselves were killed, did so upon instruction and there were, as we have said, those whose lives would draw to a natural close very soon.

"Some had special powers. There were those who could heal, not just through mental attainment, but through the means of their livelihood like the physician Luke. They were not all ignorant men, although those most loved were men taken from the Lake of Galilee and given the task of being protectors."

Judas Iscariot - his real motive in the betrayal.
A question taken from a group which met in London in April 1988.

"Is it possible to reveal the truth of the betrayal of Jesus? Was it in fact Judas Iscariot who betrayed Him and if so what was his real motive?"
Master: Judas was the vehicle. You are aware of the laws of karma and there were those within the community of Christ that longed to love and revere and understand and yet because of their past, as well as the

lives that they led within that time, put upon themselves the cloak of envy and greed. It was destined that what transpired should be and therefore there must be a vehicle that would set in motion those acts that culminated in His death. It was indeed Judas Iscariot, not from greed, for money, but for power. He truly thought that he would be revered and understood in the same light, and he had light, but it was dimmed by the action. There are many now and always have been that shine brightly and yet their lustre is dimmed by the thoughts and actions of the body."

Chapter 9

The Crucifixion and
The Resurrection

From a Christian perspective this has to be the most important chapter of this book and much of it is devoted to understanding the nature of the death on the cross and how the resurrection was effected. After a reminder that all His life Jesus knew how He would die (and what horror it would be if we all knew our destiny) there follows a statement as to why a cross was the chosen method of execution at that time. This is followed by a detailed picture of the site of Golgotha. Then, through a past life, details emerge of attempts to fashion a suitable cross for the infamous act and how this was thwarted by the Roman crucifixion ritual. There is an important revelation regarding the position of the cross followed by reasons why Jesus needed to be crucified. A detailed picture of the resurrection and the nature of the etheric completes this chapter.

Knowledge of the future.
Master: "If tomorrow you were told that in a few months time you would die a horrific death what would your reaction be? Your fear would be intense, no way of evading death, no miracle of medicine, no euthanasia, and whatever you did to help others and uplift them, heal them, raise them from the dead, your destiny would be as assured as sleeping at night and waking in the morning. The darkness that shrouds you during the night hours and the day with its light are constantly repeated, never vary and never cease. You are born into life, and at a given moment you enter the portals of death and are resurrected into the true life of the soul; but that is the peaceful passing. What if you had to die as He did, before many thousands, for a sin He had not committed enduring the pain of the cross?"

The above was taken from a text given to a group which met in Gloucestershire in December 1991

The Cross.

Why a cross was the method of execution.

Master: "A cross was used because it was a general form of death at that time. Those who ruled the land did not recognise Jesus as anything other than a troublemaker, a person assumed to be descended from the royal house of David and therefore trying to be king to the Jewish people. It was through fear that they desired that He should leave the world, should not be present. None truly understood His mission. This is the case with many. Fear holds back reasoning, it holds back logic. Jesus was indeed heir to the throne of David. If He had desired to take His rightful place, none could have stopped Him, but that was not His purpose.

"Crucifixion was given mainly to criminals. We hope now to put paid to many rumours and many hypotheses that have been written for it was Jesus Himself upon the cross, upon Golgotha and He was not released through poison. We know that many speak of these things and many who endeavour to disprove the rising from the dead will put forth many plausible stories."

The above was taken from an answer given to a group which met in London in November 1991.

The site of Golgotha.

Questioner: "Would you please tell us the actual location of Golgotha?"

Master: "Joseph (of Arimathea) had built a house on the outskirts of Jerusalem, in what was then a very beautiful area containing many gardens. There were gardens of rare beauty and gardens in which the olives grew. It has changed very greatly throughout the Age, despite the fact that this part of the world has changed less than other places. This house was built on the side of a rocky face. Beneath it was hewn the tomb which was subsequently used for the burial of Yeshua - at least His body was laid in it. Already the physical body was no more. The etheric body was alive and already had been seen in other places, well away from Palestine. The front (so called) of the dwelling looked out on green hills - very bare. They were windswept, very little grew upon them. At one time it had been known as the burial place, the place of the skulls and was felt to be an eerie place. No-one desired to build there, to walk there or even to attempt to grow trees on that very barren and windy place. It was quite steep. Golgotha could be seen from all aspects of the town, even from outside the walls of the city. No more public place could have been created. The back of the dwelling - of Joseph's dwelling - was built on rock, and as we have said, beneath it was a tomb which took much time to hew and to form into a place where a body could be laid. This had only been completed a matter of weeks before the crucifixion. There were several chambers, one for the immediate family and one where the mourners could gather and light their tallow candles and say prayers for the elevation of the soul.

"There was also a small secluded garden - a matter only of a few feet square - around the entrance to the tomb, sufficient for mourners to sit and communicate with the soul of the deceased. Beyond that perimeter was a large delightful garden planned by Joseph's family and used extensively. There was a small natural wall which prevented those in the garden from interrupting anyone meditating or praying within the small area which was tree-lined and very quiet. The general noises from the road outside would not be heard within that area. It was especially built and chosen for prayer and meditation.

"Joseph valued this house more than any other, except perhaps his home in Arimathea, the ancestral home, where all members of the family from wherever they were living would come and speak together on Holy Days and days of family rejoicings - or commiserations. This house was quite different.

The windows at the front which had looked out upon this hill, when it began to be used for that purpose were filled in. Further windows were placed looking over the garden, therefore none could witness from the house anything taking place on the hill. It was quite near, the outline of those upon the cross, hung there sometimes for weeks, until only the skeleton was left by the carrion birds. Often it was not until the bones fell from the cross that they were taken away. At other times those crucified would be taken down and buried in a mass grave at the back of the hill, a deserted, woody area where no one ever set foot. It was said to be 'haunted', by the souls of the departed. To go there at night would mean that the following day one would be insane. Whatever took place, none knew, for none would return and be able to communicate what had taken place. There is indeed evil and it manifests where injustices have been done to innocent humanity. Who would wish for windows to overlook such a place? But that home had stood there for many, many years, long before the hill began to be used for those purposes, for it was indeed the occupying Romans who invented these indecencies for those who dwelt within that beautiful walled city."

The above was taken from answers given to a group which met in London in November 1991.

Cyprus and a cross.

The following life was given to a woman from the Caribbean in April 1991 and has been included because it shows how Joseph of Arimathea, the disciples and others, came to terms with the inevitable fact that Jesus would be crucified and attempted to try to ameliorate His sufferings in any way possible.

"Master, I understand from our meetings here that all who are here were present at the time of Christ and I would like to know what my life was at that time."

Master: "We sometimes wonder whether all those who were present would really desire to know the role they played. It is a vast subject, for there were many there, not only those members of groups which we direct and teach, but the host of people, some of whom were instrumental in the death of the man Jesus, many of whom led Him towards His fate. There were many also who were open in their cries against the Jewish people. All these are still included in those who now dwell again on the Earth, who have deep within their consciousness the awareness of the past and its karma and of whom many are drawn to listen to the words which you also hear and absorb. That life, so full of karma and potential, so great was a guiding ray for many into what would become an experience so profound, so deep within themselves, that however long they lived upon the Earth it could never be erased.

"In that life you were born a man. You lived not within that part of the country initially, but in the island of Cyprus. He who speaks with you, Joseph, travelled greatly in other parts of the world, for as well as being an Elder of the Sanhedrin and a Rabbi he had also inherited his father's business concerned with the tin mine industry and as a young man he travelled widely, that the business might do well and the family have the abundance to which it had become used. Gradually this side of the business waned as Joseph himself became more and more the counsellor and friend of those who sought the interpretation of the law.

Also his family commitments became more arduous and when the father of the Christ passed to spirit then Joseph became the guardian of Jesus' mother, for she was still young and she had great responsibilities towards her son Jesus - Yeshua, as he was known within the family. One of the countries visited many times was Cyprus, a place of great beauty, a place of refuge for many who were sought by the Romans for misdeeds which they had no awareness of having committed. At that time Cyprus was well wooded, there were many areas of great beauty and trees of some rarity. There was a house there which was inhabited during these visits by members of Joseph's family, especially the elder son, who continued the tin mining industry as the father became more involved in the courts. This industry did not take place in Cyprus which was a place of refuge and solitude. Your family lived there, not a large family but one united in purpose and strength and it was upon Joseph's estate there that yourself and your father worked, keeping the wooded lands clear, propagating new trees and generally looking after the wildlife in the woods.

"As you grew strong and purposeful you were placed in charge of the felling of trees, many of which were shipped to different countries to be used in the building of dwellings and other purposes. Joseph requested that you accompany him first to Arimathea and then to Jerusalem. Here, within the garden where Christ was to be entombed, was his house built upon the face of the rock, with as we have said the tomb beneath it. A large consignment of trees came to that place and was used to complete the building of the dwelling, as well as the natural rock and stone face. Most of the houses in that area were built of stone, for the inhabitants had no way of finding the right wood that would endure the heat and the climate. Here you accompanied him and you looked after the different consignments of very strong and special wood.

"To keep the story short for it is an emotional one, after the trial and the proposed death sentence, the wood for the cross had to be found. Mostly the wood used for these executions was of the roughest timber. This was the usual way of executing criminals. It mattered not how gnarled the lengths of wood might be - it was a purpose to an end. When those who loved the Christ and understood His teachings, realised that the death sentence would be carried out, come what may, it was then arranged that He should be as comfortable as was possible in the circumstances. You were in charge of the cutting, the moulding and the sanding of the wood, which you did well. When this was complete, after a period of repose, you returned to Cyprus. However this wood was never actually made up into a cross for it was discovered that part of the ritual for the person to be crucified was to prepare his own cross by hewing down the fairly rough wood adjacent to the site of the crucifixion. Some time later, when the disciples were being sent to different parts of the world that the teaching might continue, it was to your home that some came and remained for a short while before continuing their journey and you and your family made them comfortable, gave them refreshment and a place to sleep. Lazarus, who had been raised from the dead, was also there within your domain with his sisters - the Bethany sisters, as they became known - before they travelled towards Britain where they continued their lives. One of the sisters went on to France after a time, but another sister, Mary the Mother, Mary Magdalene and others who tended and looked after them dwelt in the place called Glastonbury, where the teachings began in the land.

"These things you know, but we reiterate them for your interest. Lazarus remained in Cyprus for a long while. But as was the way with all these countries and all the disciples and the teachings, they did not remain in one area for the remainder of their lives. It was their duty to teach, to spread the Truth and this they did, but in many areas of the world they had sanctuary, they had safe places of refuge when there were those who sought to maim or kill them. Simon Peter found refuge there when he was being sought after.

"It was a time of great wonder as well as a time of anxiety, but each person whether they hear our words or read them, all were involved in some way with the activities of life at that time.

"It is a talent, you know, to be able to mould and smooth wood. It is a most beautiful medium. Largely it has been lost, except by those in the Eastern countries who still take pride in their work and fashion things to be worn or to be ornaments within the home of others."

The position of The Cross.

The following question was asked by an English man.

"Are you able to tell me if the greatest Master that ever lived died upon the cross?"

The Master replied: "No, He did not. This particular episode in life was not fact but the stories coming down through time. It was established at the time of the Romans of that era that certain people would die upon the cross with their heads down and their feet up, not in the way depicted in the pictures that you have seen. The blood drained from the feet to the head and stopped the heart beating and so people died. The cross was common punishment for those who broke the law of Rome which was the predominant law of the land at the time.

"The Master Christ was the essence of love born in man. He was a great teacher, healer and spiritual adviser and therefore those in authority sought means of preventing His freedom of speech, for men in their ignorance had accepted the poverty and restrictions of that age. Christ, the enlightened One sought to bring understanding that there was a life beyond that of the material, a spiritual life in which men could join together and receive abundance. This is one of the laws of the universe and provoked anger and dissension among those who ruled the country. Punishments and the full rigour of the courts of that time therefore were brought into play. Remember we are speaking of a man with high spiritual understanding and knowledge. The Christ aspect was within this man but he Had a body and as such that body must die, and so the punishment was carried out.

"After the scourging which took place in the forecourt after the trial Yeshua was left in such a weakened state that He was unable to walk. He was laid upon a structure which to all intents and purposes was a cross and He was taken from the court to a place where he was able to rest for a while before the ceremony of the crucifixion took place. It was deemed necessary that he should be able to walk to the place of execution in order to fulfil the full word of the Law, otherwise the crowd could well cry out and say He was already slaughtered. Simon Zelotes, the faithful servant of Joseph of Arimathea, was sent to the court house to do all that he could to revive Yeshua for the rest of His ordeal and he was permitted to travel with Him the short distance to Golgotha. There he helped Him to cut the wood and tie it together to form His own cross, for this was part of the Roman crucifixion procedure, and then to help Him carry it to the highest point of the hill where it would then be driven into the ground. Yeshua was tied to the cross while it was still laid flat on the ground and then it was raised with His head towards the ground and His feet uppermost virtually three feet or so above the level of the ground. Within a short time the blood had run to His head and He no longer existed within the body. But the etheric self was immediately released and so strong was His spiritual power that that etheric took form and later He could be seen as clearly as the physical body and as such He walked among the people and He continued his teaching. He left the place where He had done the greater part of His Ministry and he went to other continents that the word and the light might be shining in as great an area as possible. And when His ministry upon the earth was complete He then rose spiritually from the etheric into the soul body. The etheric fell away as would any discarded thing and he moved rapidly throughout the spheres of light teaching the souls in their elements as He progressed. Time we cannot measure, but eventually he was observed within the greater Logos which is the creative element existing for all time. Man must endure the law of the land at the time He lives and if such is the punishment, then man has it inflicted upon him. But man is everlasting, it is the body which perishes and the mind and the soul continues and if he is elevated in intelligence and understanding that soul can instantly form an etheric self.

"Those pictures which show the man Jesus upon a cross with his head to the sky - no - it was not so."

Note: It was revealed in another personal tape (November 1991) that the cross was actually in a slanting position. '...the crucifixion took place the reverse way to the normal crucifixion of criminals. The head was where the feet would normally be. The cross was not totally upright, it was at an angle. The downward flow of blood to the brain allowed the senses to be withdrawn very fast, so He did not suffer too greatly. The true suffering was when the nails were driven into the feet and the palms of the hands. He was also tied to the cross to keep Him in position...'

A discussion with the Master on the advisability of including the above in this book or in any other publication. (Brussels, March 1990).

Questioner: "The sacredness of the Bible is a deep and ancient belief and the idea of being crucified upside down, or slanting, goes against the deep reverent feeling that millions of people had, and have, for the cross and the words of the dying Christ. Is it worth it?"

Master: "It is vitally important. The truth cannot be masked because of tradition. All who read the Holy Book understand that the cross was upright only because in none of the Gospels did it actually stipulate how the cross was placed. Traditionally at that time criminals were crucified in an upright position so that their death would be as slow and as agonising as possible. It did not as far as we are aware state that those of more noble birth, those with ancestry which was undisputed, who because of the law of the Land still received that form of death were allowed greater mercy. There are those who have been allowed to regress and have seen that particular position of the cross. Those who were present in that past life have the memory within and we know of four who have had visions of the Christ upon the cross in the position that we have stated. Now even if this is considered to be against the tradition of the Scriptures, it is still the truth. Also it is important to remember, it is not only older people who will be reading this book. Young people, and soon the Children of Light and those a little older than they, will read these words as well as those with open minds who have great spirituality, a great longing for truth and something within them from the far past will say : "At last we hear words of truth, and not words of tradition". Gradually older people steeped in dogma and creed will be leaving the face of the Earth. They will be travelling to a place of Light where all will then be made clear to them. We cannot write the book only for these older people. Allow them to enjoy their Scriptures but allow those that are growing into the Light to be made aware of the absolute truth from all sources. As every man does not read every book that has been written, so there will be countless millions who will not be drawn to this manuscript, but there well may be countless thousands who will be and who will appreciate that certain details omitted from the Gospels are now put with great clarity and certainty within its pages.

"Speaking of the words, who remembered them? Who at that time was capable or even desired to record them or read them? Remember the ignorance at that time. Most could not read or write and those in authority were not present. Those who were present were the ones dearly loved by Him and even they were not allowed to approach the cross itself, except by permission of the Centurion who guarded Him. There was Mary His mother, Mary the younger of the Bethany sisters who loved Him so dearly and there was Mary Magdalene who recognised Him as both master and teacher and she also loved Him very dearly. There were therefore three Mary's grouped around the cross and they have since become known as the Holy Mary's, although in some Gospels and documents it has been assumed that one of them was the mother of one of the disciples (e.g. Mark 15:40. "... and Mary the mother of James the younger...") but this was not so for it was indeed Mary the sister of Lazarus.

"His Mother was allowed to come and wipe the blood and the sweat from His brow. Another, known as the Beloved disciple, John, was also allowed to stand beside Him, to hear His last wishes for the family He loved and the Mother whom He loved above all others. None of these people would write down the words whispered to them by a dying man - dying in body though not in Spirit - whose Soul was about to manifest in the etheric body, to live again for a while before departing to Spirit. Think of the facts and think of life at that time, of its ignorance, its cruelty, its barbarism, with a powerful nation ruling Judea endeavouring to destroy its tradition. And then believe that certain things written in the Holy Book would be the words people would desire to hear and not necessarily those which in the agony of the last moments of life were whispered to those He loved."

In answer to a similar question asked in October 1992 the Master gave those present around the cross as His mother, a brother, a kinsman and one of the Disciples. At a later date the Master was asked about this apparent discrepancy and his answer is included because it gives an interesting insight to that horrific event.

Master: "There is no discrepancy when you realise that Yeshua laid upon the cross between 7 and 8 hours and during that time there were several who asked permission to come and speak with Him to see whether life was still present and if there were any wishes that could be attended to. Two changes of guard took place throughout those long hours and some guards permitted visits others did not. The disciple's as a whole were not permitted to come close in case they performed some miraculous act which would result in panic from the crowd. So it is all in essence true."

What happened to The Cross.

"The cross was taken away by the Arimathean and he received word from the Archangel Gabriel that it was to be ritually burnt and the ashes were to be used in a second ritual which we cannot explain to you because of its deep significance."

Given to a group meeting in London in April 1988 and to a questioner in June 1993.

Why Jesus needed to be crucified.

"I believe that Jesus knew that He was going to die on a cross and He shared that knowledge with Joseph of Arimathea - yourself - also, perhaps through His own siddha powers He was able to avoid death and therefore it seems to me a question as to whether it would not have been better for Jesus to have lived longer and been able to teach more, and more widely, than to die so soon?"

Master: "His purpose at that time was two fold. Firstly it was to show, through His own example, that the body is resurrected after death. Secondly to continue with his teachings. What better way to show that death releases the etheric body containing the soul into life, than by enabling many to be aware of Him, to speak with Him, and walk and listen to teaching for some considerable time after the crucifixion. There were times that he appeared to others than His disciples, to groups of interested people who had accepted His teaching. He would appear and speak with them, allow His body to be touched. If you remember, initially He discouraged this until the etheric was well established within the form He wished to take, but after a while it was easy for Him to return in that way, to bridge the difference between the earthly world and spirit and to show himself almost as humankind. He would speak, He could be touched and those who within the work wished to establish it in both Palestine and Britain were then indeed able to reveal that they had seen Him and touched Him in that manner. It was more important then than it is in your sphere of life to be aware of the tangibility of a person who had, to all intents and purposes died. It is more generally accepted at this time.

"There was much conjecture at that time as to what occurred after death, as there is still today. So many people do not believe in the afterlife or they fantasise regarding it, but the etheric body which cloaks the soul is as real within its own sphere as your human body is real upon your Earth. Eventually, the etheric is no longer needed. When the soul realises totally that it can go forward to a higher plane where there is more light and teaching and understanding, it loses that facsimile of the physical personality, or it returns again into life, in order to learn further. Because of Jesus' abilities, He was able to transmute (see page 120) His etheric self so realistically that Man could see Him in person. Normally the vibration is much higher than that of the physical presence, and therefore man through his normal sight cannot be aware of it, but He was able to reduce that vibration, to slow it down so it harmonised with the rhythm of the world and within the spectrum of sight which mankind uses to see. In that way he was visible to all who desired to see Him. He could use His etheric body in the same way as all souls within their realms of light, to appear where He desired to be, to disappear from that place and appear elsewhere, or even to be in more than one place at the same time. He could do that and people could still see because of the change of vibration, the lower speed of the etheric. Others too are able to do this. There are many who are called magicians who are able to disappear from sight and reappear elsewhere, because they have mastered the alchemy of this change. We say many - they are in fact but few considering the millions upon the Earth, but there is certainly more than one. In the same way that you can be aware upon waking of a presence in the room where you sleep and recognise that presence as someone you have met in life. Because they can travel in their etheric body, their soul body, during sleep, they may not be aware except in a vague dreamlike state, of having been with you and normally you may not be aware of their presence, but something awakens you and alerts you and you see them. It is all the same principle and when you are asleep your vibrations are very much faster than they are when awake, and when you first awake, you are still part of that accelerated vibration."

The above answer was given to a group in London in November 1991.

The Resurrection.

Master: "Throughout our teachings we have been at great pains to speak to you of Universal Law so that you might understand its presence within your spiritual self and also surrounding you within your world. That law of love is so profound, and yet all other laws within the universe are part of it. But Love is not an illusion, it is a fact. There are illusionists in your world, but the way they perform is only to show others who look upon them that they have sleight of hand and their magical gifts do not truly exist. The Christ in His body was of flesh. He was as unable to transmute that flesh as you, but once he released that body in death, then the Etheric Self was not only transmuted, but also became a spirit entity, changing its vibration and therefore its concept of earthly transgression. (Transgression, because human beings transgress in their understanding and their concept of life.) Before the act of crucifixion the Christ had to rely on the prayer and loyalty of His followers, in the same way as all other human beings. He was mortal, He had an intensity of love for mankind and total understanding and awareness of spirit and its procedures, both in the Realms of Light and upon the Earth, but change the course of events He could not.

"When you are faced with possible disaster the alternative to running away, full of fear or attempting to hide, is to face what is there before you and pray for strength to cope with the situation, to hold your head high and to be sure that once the earthly life is extinguished there can no longer be pain. Therefore any infliction of pain must be transient. Of course He suffered pain through His execution, but it was speedy. We have explained before that the method of crucifixion for those who have achieved either notoriety or respect, was speedier than those executed for civil wrongs. By placing the cross with the head towards the ground, the rush of blood rendered the person unconscious and when the body is unconscious there is little awareness of pain. It also meant the act of death itself took place many hours earlier than it did with others surrounding Him. Life was soon extinct. Those of us close to Him who had already pleaded with the authorities for clemency and failed were given permission to remove Him from the cross and prepare His body for entombment.

"As you know the next day was the sabbath and also the Passover. It was not permitted by law either to exhume or to lay to rest within a tomb a recently deceased body upon that day. The laws at that time were very strict, far more than in the present age. There were other reasons than law - there was no way of preserving bodies such as you have now. Jesus was laid to rest, His body was anointed with oils and covered with a shroud, as was usual. The shroud had been lovingly prepared before by those who were aware of His imminent passing. Like the robe he wore in life it was seamless - and that life-giving robe was never soiled, it never showed any form of dirt, it never needed to be washed, always it was fresh and beautiful, enhancing His form and blending with the colours in His aura. This robe had been removed from His body before the crucifixion by Joseph (of Arimathea). It was put in a place of safety so that it would not be rent by many who sorrowed, who followed the party to the Mount, clamouring, endeavouring to save the man they had grown to love from being executed. This new robe, the shroud, was also made in one piece, woven by those women within His entourage who loved and cared for Him throughout His ministry and this was wrapped round Him.

"There was a general air of great peace. Within the atmosphere there was no feeling of death as though all was ended. There was a feeling of expectancy, since even those whom He had taught the truths of life and death expected Him to rise immediately and again go forth. There came after an air of disappointment that this was not so. Jesus was at peace, but life was extinct. There were those who went forth intending to pray, but they found the words would not come, for without their master, their leader, there seemed no point in prayer. The tears flowed and there were those who emulated Him by hanging themselves from trees, desiring to be with Him in that spirit land of which He spoke with such love and there were also those who watched. All waited in the darkness which was dense for there was no moon nor stars to light the way of the traveller. Those who waited in the garden, ensuring that none might come and take away the body of their Lord, could barely see each other in that deep darkness.

"Eventually sleep overcame all but one. That one was vigilant, still hoping for a miracle, desiring beyond all thought that a figure might emerge from the tomb, human, loving, full of the essence of life. All had to learn one lesson that had not been absorbed, the lesson that although all lives are one, there are different vehicles in which the soul lives. Upon the Earth it is a mortal body of flesh that harmonises with the beat and rhythm of Earth, but the spiritual body is lighter; few can see it, for the speed with which its molecules move cannot be traced by the human eye, only by the inner eye of those experienced in alchemy, but none present were experienced in that way and none saw Him approach or felt Him touch them upon the shoulder and bless them in their sleep and sorrow. It was not the first time that those whom He loved had slept while on guard, but He knew the vagaries of man and how the heart desired and yet the flesh was weak.

"When the dawn came and the tomb was found to be empty those who entered were very frightened. They feared that those in command of their city had come in the night and taken Him and destroyed what was left of His mortal flesh. Within the tomb there was a great light which blinded them. For a long while they could not see the bench upon which the body had been laid, but when they did, they found that there was no form upon it. Most returned to the garden, desperate to know where they could go, who in authority could help them without knowing who they were and perhaps punishing them.

"It was much later in the day that the other disciples came, having arranged for the burial to take place the next day and they also sorrowed greatly that their beloved Master had been taken from them. One among them had a great sense of the psychic, as well as the spiritual. Many times he had seen auras surrounding fellow man, he had heard voices within his mind and also had been told that he was mad, insane. Twice he had escaped the punishment of death because of his hallucinations, for none would kill a madman, and he insisted that he could see an outline upon that bench. "He is there", he assured them, "transmuted and changed, but he is there". No-one else could see this form and they still searched.

"Again the darkness fell, but not as deep as before. Most had gone to their dwellings, exhausted by what had taken place, but again those He loved the most kept vigil, in case whoever had taken the body returned, perhaps having re-anointed it, or found a more suitable place for burial. It was at this time the stranger approached and asked why they waited, why they were not already speaking of the wonders of rebirth, of life continuous in all its beauty and majesty. No-one recognised Him and most were angry that He should interrupt their grief. They thought that He was one of the soldiers who had come to mock them. Eventually they left that place in fear of their own lives, for such a body still remains property of the law of the land and the governing parties that rule.

"That which is accurately portrayed within the Holy book also shows to man who reads and understands, that even those close to one who has all knowledge cannot always absorb the truth, because they themselves do not have souls which have ascended. It is only those who have returned countless times to Earth throughout the Ages, who can absorb these truths, so that they are indeed part of the knowledge of all life. We have spoken of alchemy and this allows man to strip from his eyes the blindness of ignorance, to truly hear with the inner self that which God the Creator of the Universe desires man to hear. Intelligence will often hinder. Mankind has been given freewill to reason, but uses this unwisely. True beliefs can only come when the body is stripped away and the etheric sees truly that which is real and cannot be denied. The man Jesus was as all others, except it was His last incarnation and all knowledge from the past remained within his conscious mind, from the time of His birth to the moment of His death. There have been others similarly blessed, who have tried to teach the world the great truths and enlighten mankind. You know yourselves how difficult it is to concentrate on words which are not familiar. If another language is spoken, of which you have no knowledge, you cannot think, interpret, nor yet absorb, and the language of spirit is such as this, it must be learnt. Slowly mankind must accept, accept the Higher Intelligence that knows and not attempt to reason, any more than you reason with a magician, who appears to disappear and reappear before your eyes. The Christ did not disappear, He underwent transformation. It took time for the Etheric Self to manifest. The physical body had gone through great trauma, not just at the time of execution, but for many weeks before this. He knew He could not turn away from death, He knew the mode and method of His passing, He could relive time and time again the cruelty of the bindings that held Him to the cross. The lacerated flesh was part of His conscious mind from the moment of the trial. You cannot emulate those who die because of their beliefs, but you can uphold them and watch with them, giving them strength, letting them know that you love them and will be loyal to them, whatever may occur because of it. And yet how many do? How many turn away with fear that they themselves might suffer?

"You have a great task ahead of you. Throughout this coming decade many prophecies that have been part of your world for countless hundreds of years are gradually manifesting themselves. Events cannot change because mankind wish them to. Karma takes its course in man and in the world. Much of the fear encircling man is of death, because he does not know how he will die. Do not fear death, it is painless. It is the fear that brings the pain. Whatever you may be asked to do to help mankind as time continues, be strong, communicate with spirit in your minds, do not be afraid to ask for help and strength and the means to tolerate whatever may be, for it will be, as the morning follows the night and the moon rises in the darkness of the sky, but you will be uplifted, as other chosen ones have been. Some were part of the throng that cried for blood, and others sobbed, that the flesh might be saved and some present wept at the graveside and others did not recognised their Lord. At some time we will speak further of this. The time is not yet ready for you to know all that will befall, but life is sweet and has much fruit for you to grasp. Eat your fill and do not worry about tomorrow."

The above extract was taken from a group meeting held in London in April 1990.

Transmutation.

In the answer just given the word 'transmute' appears several times and therein lies the great truth which is the foundation of the Christian religion - the nature of the resurrection. It is therefore considered essential to include part of the text given in answer to a similar question (March 1993). This explains in greater detail exactly what happened in the tomb and what is meant here by 'transmute'. Although part of the answer repeats itself, no attempt has been made to rewrite it because of its importance.

Master: "It is assumed by many in their thoughts that the actual body of Christ was resurrected from the tomb. It is amazing that so many people, although aware that when the body dies it disintegrates and eventually becomes as dust, still believe that Christ tried to prove the resurrection of the actual body with His own death. This was not the case. The etheric body is that which enters the spirit world, it is the etheric which has continuous life. As we have already stated It was His etheric body which appeared before the disciples and Mary Magdalene within a matter of hours after the crucifixion and before the disciples on one or two occasions. It was the etheric body that continued to travel in other areas of the world continuing the teaching although He was not recognised as being Jesus the Christ, but just a humble traveller who had great knowledge, great humility and great healing ability. As we have stated on more than one occasion that etheric body looked and felt exactly like a physical body. There are others who have existed in their etheric body. The great sage Babajee, who is well known in circles in India by those who follow His teaching and his faith, that body went through many centuries in the etheric but not in the actual bodily form and there have been others that have descended to the Earth for great teaching but they have not needed sustenance, they have not needed rest because they are of spirit and not of flesh. Is this clearer now?"

Questioner: "Yes, but maybe you would explain the transmutation from the physical body to the etheric body. You have said that there was a transmutation but did the physical body completely transmute so that nothing was left physically?"

Master: "That is so, it took place in the tomb as soon as death took place, although not death as it is known in the world at this time. The Christ had entered into a state of unconsciousness, very deep unconsciousness, and death had been wrongly pronounced. After He was removed from the cross He was immediately placed within the tomb. During the next few hours He was with angelic forces, those from the planes of light, sent particularly to help this transformation into the etheric so that it would appear to be a body of flesh. It was the Christ totally transformed, each cell, each organ was transmuted into the etheric counterpart in-situ where the body lay upon the slab. When it arose, it arose in its transmuted form. Therefore there was no physical body to dispose of, because each cell had been changed, in fact the four Archangels of Light attended Christ at the time of transformation and He then became the true Christ, the essence in total of absolute truth, absolute knowledge that He had been prior to His birth upon the Earth."

Questioner: "So physically he did not look the same because the etheric had different features."

Master: "It was not different features. In the explanation that we have given to many in our teachings regarding the auric manifestation which is around all mankind, which holds all qualities, all being, it is this that Man is in tune with when becoming acquainted with fellow man. When you look at a person you meet for the first time you do not immediately see the physical appearance for the third eye - the etheric eye which is in the forehead, looks into the surrounding aura, which is the soul-self, the soul-personality. This is why there is either an instant rapport or revulsion. It is not from the sight of the physical body which may be very beautiful and yet repulsive or even excessively ugly and yet instantly attractive; it is based upon the soul essence and its progress through the ages. In the kind of transformation that took place with Jesus the total soul body reflected within the aura is also part of that etheric self. It is not separate, it is not surrounding the body, it is of the body and this can confuse those that look upon it. They are used to seeing the etheric self projected, surrounding the flesh and when it is not there, there is instant fear because the recognition is not from man to man because the etheric to etheric cannot take place. Is this clear?"

The above answers were given to the questioner in London in March 1993.

Further details about the nature of the Etheric Body.

Questioner: "Would you please explain the law behind the etheric manifestation, also in The Gospels it is reported that the risen Christ was at first not recognised by Mary Magdalene (John 20:16) and again He was not recognised by two others when travelling on the road from Jerusalem to Emmaus (Luke 24:13). Why was this?"

Master: "The etheric body, although in many ways a duplicate of the flesh, contains the knowledge of the past. It is formed, as is the aura, from this composite knowledge. We mentioned the Higher Self and how it absorbs all aspects of all the lives that the soul enjoys. It becomes full of wisdom, it is a living energy of great beauty. It surrounds Man throughout his life on Earth and is seen as the glowing colours which are called the aura. Between the aura and Man's fleshly body is a dark line which is visible when seen through the third eye in meditation, or in any form of spiritual awareness. This is the outline of the etheric, that which unites earthly Man with his spirit. Immediately after death of the body comes its transformation into the etheric. This 'body' is recognised in spirit, as it goes to the sphere of light which it has earned throughout the earthly existence as the soul desires to progress. It is a 'carbon copy', a duplicate of the body of flesh and of the personality it has chosen and used for the years on Earth, but at the same time it also reflects the superior wisdom of its Higher self - though this is not easy to understand initially. Dwell upon this in your thoughts and meditation, but the reason why Jesus' loved ones did not instantly recognise him was twofold;

"First, for many weeks he had suffered greatly. His physical body had been greatly abused. Under these conditions the body changes physically. Those who surround that person become used to the changed state. They are inclined to forget the strong, the healthy, the radiant and become aware only of the depleted personality. This is one aspect of the question. The second is that the radiance of the Higher self is far beyond normal Man. Jesus was radiant and that is difficult to appreciate with human eyes. It is blinding. Any features are behind the radiance and not easily perceived. If you wish to prove this, stand with bright sunshine slanting across you, and ask a friend to look into your face. That friend will probably turn aside, blinded by the reflection for It is as a mirrored image, greatly emphasised. So these people saw Him - and remember - they thought Him to be dead, ravaged by His torture and the last hours upon the cross and did not recognise the perfected soul. The etheric, manifested from the life now completed and the greater radiance of the Christos, which was then in its totality within the etheric combined with the radiance which shone from Him prevented instant recognition, but nothing can change the love within, expressed in the voice. A voice does not change, the vibration remains the same and even one word, softly spoken, brings recognition."

The above question was asked by a group which met in London in April 1991.

The extent of Christ's Freewill.

Master: "Often a past life entails the remembering of that which is hurtful, that which is painful, either to the senses or to the memory. There is much within the Christ life which to many brings back fear, brings back a haunting feeling of failure, of having permitted such things to be endured by One whose path was of Love and yet it must always be remembered that His destiny was written within the scrolls of life and it could not be changed. Although aspects of freewill were woven into His life they were limited as in the case of all those who have a true spiritual depth of understanding and a path to tread. The more profound the guidance of the Higher Self the more elevated the understanding and therefore less freewill is operative. Those with total free-will are those who do not listen to conscience, which is the Higher Self. Therefore although many were present at the Trial and Crucifixion very few could have changed by word or deed what ultimately took place."

Chapter 10

The Ascension

The detailed explanation given in the last chapter as to the nature of the etheric body makes it possible to understand that there was no actual Ascension as depicted in the Gospels. In this chapter the Master adds a further explanation as to what actually happened after the resurrection.

Master: "It appears in the written gospels that the Ascension took place quite quickly after the Resurrection. There were in fact many, many months between them, and when the Ascension did occur it was not in the manner recorded, which is very dramatic and far-fetched, because there is in fact no place within the sky where the etheric body travels. The spirit worlds are all around you. They occupy exactly the same area as you do, but because their vibration is faster you are not aware of them and after all when you do see them, they are not hanging from the roof, are they? All these things will gradually be made clearer to you."

The above was given to a group which met in London in November 1991.

In April 1992, the Master said: "Now many thought that Christ ascended into the Heavens for that is what they saw. However, in actual fact His etheric self gradually faded before their eyes, so that He was totally of spirit and merged again into a spiritual existence. To many this appears as though there is an ascension taking place for a body dematerialising seems to those watching to be lifted into space."

In answer to a similar question about the Ascension (March 1993) the following more detailed reply was given.

Master: "There was a time when, on more than one occasion - only one is actually reported in the scriptures (Luke 24:32)- where Yeshua, or the Christ as He had become, would simply melt before their eyes - would simply cease to be. If you recall in another part of the scriptures there is word of a man called Enoch* - "Enoch walked with God; and he was not,..." (Genesis 5:24). Now many of the ways in which these things have been written are ambiguous, but in this case, as also with the Christ, at one moment the etheric is visible, there is speech, there is understanding, there is awareness, and then the etheric ceases to vibrate in a manner that can be perceived upon the Earth. The vibrations are raised and no longer can the body be seen for it is then part of the spheres of light and this happens in a split second. The words "...He was lifted up, and a cloud took Him out of their sight." (Acts 1:10) have been misinterpreted. He did not rise as though toward the heavens but He was taken from their sight. The vibrations increased so that they were no longer aware of His presence among them and of course He appeared at different times in a similar way. He could be present with them whenever He desired. He could travel wherever He wished, completely invisible to the naked eye - to the human eye - and then He would appear. You could call it a grounding, but it is difficult to find words that can completely explain the phenomena. He would be there and their awareness of Him would be complete - not necessarily as Yeshua, their friend and teacher, but as a man who was among them."

* Enoch was the son of Jared and father of Methuselah, an outstanding man of God of whom it was said he was received into God's presence without dying.

Interval of time between the crucifixion and the 'ascension'.
Questioner (June 1993) "Was the interval between the Crucifixion and the ascension years or just several months?"

Master: "We feel that the confusion arises from the conception of the Ascension. This is synonymous in the minds of some Christians with the transformation that actually took place when Yeshua simply ceased to exist in His etheric body on the earth and returned in spirit form. There was of course no actual Ascension as depicted: as we have explained He simply faded from the sight of His followers. Possibly one to two years of travelling occasionally alongside His companions took place. It is difficult to be precise but they were aware of Him, especially where two or three were gathered together discussing their work. Then He would appear and converse with them and this period of time is inconsistent with the records. Certain scrolls which have been found are at this time being read and a decision made as to whether to make them available to the public. But the actual ceremony of the Ascension which was the fading of view from those that were travelling with Him took place a few months after the crucifixion. We need to explain this a little more clearly. Yeshua felt that His death had been precipitated before He had a chance to allow His disciples to truly understand their role. Therefore He needed to return and to continue to counsel and teach them. This occurred in private places where they would meet together, on the beach for example, in caves and in the homes of one or another where they could be silently aware of Him. We suppose that in this day it might be called a seance, for they would call upon Him and He would appear. He would then speak with them, counsel and teach them and this gradually became less and less as they became more aware of their task and their mission.

"It is very similar to the way that we at this time are counselling many. There will come a time when they will understand the purpose of the work and at that time we will come less. We will establish a different rhythm of teaching from the present way and if you look upon it thus it will be with greater understanding of what took place when Christ's physical body had been destroyed. We cannot be accurate regarding months or years."

A note on reincarnation.
Questioner: "We understand what we had to learn from the death of Jesus and yet it seems as if the idea of reincarnation has been totally removed from present Christianity. How can we know and somehow prove it? We understand it, but others do not."

Master: "The idea of reincarnation did not commence at the time of the death of Jesus for it had been part of many religions for countless thousands of years. The Egyptians were extremely aware that the soul passed from the body into another life, which is why some of their rather macabre ways of burial took place. They also thought that they might return at a later time and need their body, hence resuscitation and also companionship of others. Perhaps they did not reason in quite the same way as people now, but certainly they believed in reincarnation. Reincarnation has always been a matter of controversy among many different peoples, according to their spiritual understanding and also the factual and scientific arguments they use. The process is certainly not as simple as we ourselves endeavour to portray it. At some time we will go into greater detail as to the actual process involved in the decision to reincarnate, how this is connected to the process of family life throughout the ages, the genes within the family and other relevant factors, for it is all linked.

"We are aware that some of those to whom we have spoken regarding a past life have awareness that perhaps part of their soul has been manifest in a relation less than one hundred years before. They recognise that personality through photography, or even through having met that person. This is indeed a vast subject and many would be frightened by it, so we have spoken very little of it, but we do feel that as time passes and as the Children of Light, with their greater capacity for memory of the past, grow to maturity, they will change some of the archaic ideas and the ignorant beliefs of mankind into a more logical way of Truth."

The above question was asked in a group which met in London in November 1991.

Part II

Under the Roman yoke

Chapter 11

An insight into the life and times of Jesus

The following past lives, most of which were at the time Christ was alive, have been selected primarily because they paint vivid word pictures, often including intimate personal details, of how life was under Roman occupation. Some of these lives contain very emotional situations which reveal dramatically the working of the Universal laws of reincarnation and karma.

Fourteen past lives have been arranged under the following headings:

Life in the Roman Army.
- *A soldier.*
- *The life of a Centurion.*
- *A Centurion who deserted.*
A raising of the dead.
Healing.
- *The blind young man who chose to remain blind.*
- *A life among lepers.*
- *The miraculous water.*
Lives associated with Paul.
- *His father.*
- *One of Paul's disciples.*
- *Another of Paul's disciples.*
The Sanhedrin.
- *An Elder - a friend and ally of Joseph of Arimathea.*
- *An Elder on the side of Caiaphas.*

A handmaiden to Mary the Mother.
A stonemason employed by Joseph of Arimathea.

Life in the Roman Army.

A soldier.
The following past life was given to an English woman in June 1992.

Master: "Your life was initially spent in Rome where you were born. In young manhood, for in that life you were a male, you were enlisted in the Roman army in which all young men, of sound mind and limb, had to do a period of duty. If they enjoyed army life they would often remain there, rising through the ranks and travelling to different areas of the world as Rome extended its empire. Most were loyal to their officers and in time became legionnaires and others achieved high ranks within that great army. During the occupation in Palestine there were many legions who would come and go after a period of time and they became part of the life of Palestine. In the same way that many occupying forces in the world now become part of the countries that they rule, many became interested in the culture and had a certain sympathy for the people. Not all were tyrannical and many indeed grew to love the people and some were allowed to intermarry.

"There had been no formal betrothal in Rome when you joined the legion that was to be sent to Palestine. You were still very young and aware that upon your return there might be a marriage that had been arranged by the family, but that was far from your thoughts as you made the arduous journey feeling like many others ill and distressed by the sea voyage. But many were kind and considerate and looked after you when you arrived. The journey from Phoenicia to Jerusalem, where you would be stationed seemed to be just as arduous for now you were on foot. You passed those on the roadside who were chained, many prisoners of the State Army who had done things against the law and the leader's demands. These men worked on the roads to make them as strong and even as possible. Many camels and donkeys travelled on these roads, and rich people and those that ruled the land, passed by in carriages. Though you were tired and footsore as you walked the many miles there was also much to see and wonder at, including the desert area.

"He who speaks to you was influential in the Sanhedrin and he would sometimes be attacked by those who felt an injustice had been done. It was not always possible for one of his own kin to guard him but there were many he trusted within the Roman forces and this was his opportunity to teach and to show them the way of light. And when you were settled in your quarters and had begun to understand the rhythm of your life, you were often one of those chosen to accompany Joseph into the desert or even to other areas where he had dwellings. The house in Arimathea was always well guarded for many who lived in that region had little reason to love influential people whether of Jewish blood or not and there were times when his servants, who were like family to him, and his own kin would be attacked.

"You became almost one of the family and you were particularly fond of being with the eldest son. There was a time when you were asked to guard the younger son on a journey that he had to make to Syria. There he was buying and selling silks for his Father, although the main business was with the metal tin in Britain. You enjoyed the visit to Syria, but could not stay there because there was duty in Jerusalem to which you had to return. Therefore the younger son had to return alone at the end of his business commitment, but before leaving Syria he fell ill, and suffered extreme exhaustion. Eventually he returned to his family and you were sorry you had not been there to help him on his journey.

"You were present at the time of The Crucifixion. The Centurion there had to hold back the crowd, for there were many who wished to see the end of one who they believed would tyrannise Palestine if he were allowed to live, and who wished to perform that act of sacrilege themselves, while an equal number wished to rescue Him. So many within that Legion were on duty to control the crowd and to keep what peace was possible. The Centurion is well known to us in this life and often we speak to him, to that element of soul now active within him which desires to heal and counsel and make use of the knowledge he attained in that life. And it is the same with you. The qualities that were yours in that life remain within your Higher Self, within the soul's structure. Although the soul within you in this life is a separate facet it still has knowledge and deep memory. You are capable of doing and receiving many things and we feel that you have friends now who may have shared the atmosphere of the Christ Life even if they had not known Him or heard Him speak, for His influence spread throughout the world. Boundaries and barriers do not prevent this nor yet oceans for that which enters the atmosphere of life is shared on a deep level of understanding."

The life of the Centurion referred to above.
The following past life was given to a Scotsman in London in April 1990.

Master: "Many were involved at that time for the vast resources of the Roman Empire had spread to many parts of the world. Many areas were occupied by Rome and those who ruled in Palestine sometimes did so wisely and sometimes not, for as in all forces there were good and bad. There were those who tried to show wisdom and clemency whereas others followed the law to the n th degree. So there were those that harmonised with the new spirit dawning and those that did not, but all soldiers had to follow their commanding officers and obey them. The penalty for disobedience was death though within their hearts they might have decided that an action was right or wrong. Many would listen to the teachings of the Nazarene and were touched by them. A realisation of the total Truth was gradually born as a seed within and its result would show in their treatment of those soldiers in the ranks who looked to them for help and advice. These officers would temper discretion with mercy. Where some might have died they would be allowed to live and there would be a different punishment.

"You were in command of what would now be known as a battalion of men. At that time you were strong and fearless, but you would also strike with your sword those who had committed trivial offences. You were often present when the Nazarene would speak and His words reached your soul, as words of initiates always do. And you would be present upon the hillside, waiting with others under your command, should there be rioting or anger among the people (and there never was) and in the stillness when all who listened, learned, yourself and those in your command would learn also. You were present at the crucifixion and you and others that were there had to keep control, though unwillingly, of those that fought to save their Lord from the gallows.'

"I thank you Master. It has been quite a dramatic experience to hear this because I remember some aspects of it."
Master: "That is the awakening of your soul to that which has given it purpose."

More about the Centurion.

In June 1991 this man asked the Master various personal questions about his present life and his past life as a Centurion. The following extract gives a deep insight into life at that time seen through his experience.

Master: "In your past life there was a companion to whom you were betrothed who was not of your race, but she had been brought to Rome from Britain, first as a slave then released under the orders of a governor who had understanding and compassion. That governor lost his life in the service of truth to mankind as others stronger in character and more aware of the need to subjugate others in order to obtain obedience took over many areas of Rome under the Emperor. These were harsh times; human life was held in scant respect and many who came from Britain were considered to be wild arrogant people with little understanding of compassion to one another. Many of those who had been bound and taken from their homeland were women, and they served men, especially those that were in the armed forces of the state, many because of their nature were quite willingly enslaved, for they were used to subjugation. Women at that time in all areas of the world did as they were bid. Celts were no different from other races in demanding obedience and ensuring that their women remained in the background and served themselves and their family well. In some places it was considered right that they should also serve their friends and honoured travellers. Times have changed greatly and women are now taking their rightful place in society, side by side with their partners in life and their understanding is accepted and respected. It has taken many centuries for this to be acceptable and understood.

Referring again to the life that we are revealing to you, your enslaved wife, once released from bondage, took her proper place within your home and you had children with her. When you were sent to Palestine to serve for a while you had been content with her presence in your house. You valued her loyalty and love of the children you shared and for the home which she kept ready for you and also her love and respect for you. There were many who would have treated her very badly while she was still a slave, but you had not, for you had a gentle nature, but there came a time within your service, especially when you were with a battalion in Jerusalem, where there were other women who attracted your attention. Many of those with whom you served were strong men of ardent natures and desires, with little respect for the inhabitants of other countries, especially subjugated places under their command. There was a time when women were stoned and beaten for prostitution and yet they had been driven to this through the state, through privation and starvation, through the men who had been betrothed to them being taken away, imprisoned and often killed for their beliefs and attitudes towards life and desire for freedom. There was no way at that time that women could preserve their own identities and their beliefs and still remain alive without starving and being homeless. It was a very difficult time for many women, even those who were highly born, for they were not permitted to be betrothed to another man once their initial partner had died or been taken permanently away. If the family could not support them then they were forced to support themselves. The whole region was rife with these women and many would use them for their own purposes, for as little money as possible. They also stood to be punished for it was forbidden within the armed force to consort with such women and yet many did and there were those that would take one and harbour her and keep her away from other men so they might not need to share and therefore would escape the punishment that would be meted out to them for being outside the law. Yet when these soldiers returned again to their own country these women were once more alone with no means of support and very often with children. Some of the soldiers would take the children with them especially if they had a son and many of the women once left would submit themselves to stoning or being thrashed to death as preferable to living and starving.

"You witnessed many such scenes. Often you would turn away, your gentle nature full of horror and disgust at those rabble seekers who were herded together and given stones to throw and bags of coins were scattered before them. Many were beggars, many had diseases which soon would take their lives. Many men also were in great pain and agony of mind which left them demented. At the sight of coins, and bidden to throw the stones as sport, no longer would they reason or turn away with natural horror as they would have done in their youth. They would do as they were bid in order to live. It was one of the duties of those who served Rome to scatter the coins and provide the weapons for the torture and the stoning. It was not only the women who were berated and stoned, this happened also to men who spoke against authority and the state.

"You were present at the stoning of the young man Stephen. He was strong and had great beauty of countenance. His father had authority within the Sanhedrin, but that did not save him. There were many who hated him for he believed also in the great Truths and expounded them. It was not only Yeshua who spoke and preached and was enlightened. There were others stirred by the Holy Spirit within them who endeavoured to enlighten Man and give him understanding of the wholeness of life, the continuity through the gates of death into a life where there was peace and knowledge. It was witnessing such scenes that turned you totally against the regime of the state and yet you were also afraid knowing how easy it was to be executed if you turned from your masters. Always there were those who could not be trusted, who would lurk quietly in a hidden place and then return to others who would give their orders and a quiet execution would be carried out. Many were burdened with fear and you were not different from them. Authority you had over those below you, but those above you had equal authority and it was those that you feared. You helped to bind the wounds as the blood flowed but you were unable, like the others who also helped, to staunch the tide and allow life to remain.

"Because of this act of compassion you were taken, imprisoned for a while and flogged. You understood well the feel of those who were lashed but you were not lashed beyond reason, for still you were valued, you were respected and this still meant much in an army that had become delinquent with power and so you were released again for your duties before being returned once more to the unit and then again to Rome.

"You desired greatly to take with you the woman who had been your solace during your stay in Jerusalem, but you realised this would not be tolerated and when you left it was with the full knowledge of her probable fate. You tried to leave her with one who you trusted, who you felt would respect her and enable her to live quietly and unobtrusively without the need to beg nor yet to sell herself, but there was too much fear, the whole area was rife with fear. So many were leaving and joining together in small groups. Those who had become known as the Zealots were not the rabble-rousers of youth, but dedicated to Truth, to change, to the desire that once more their country should be free, that the religion of their ancestors could again be followed and not subjugated to those who had no true belief or understanding except the pagan gods. They worshipped an older man who desired to travel to

Rome to establish there a Church and when he arrived he too was bound and lashed. He was a big man, a strong powerful man, but already past the first flush of youth and he would draw many to his place of hiding whence those such as yourself had begged him to travel that his wounds might heal and that the power which he had within him to teach might be released. There were many caverns and places to hide in the areas of Rome and beyond and you would bring those who desired to hear the true teachings. They interested you also for they were the same teachings as had emanated from The Christ before His crucifixion.

"You would guard the entry into the caves. Many would be there. The cool atmosphere of a cave would be turned to the hot humidity emanating from human bodies, many of whom were in fear, trembling that they might be found and accused and yet drawn to this man with his powerful voice and vivid personality which shone forth. Yet he spoke with gentleness and humility and when one area became suspect and his life was again in danger there were those under the cloak of darkness who would help him to move. You travelled widely in your own capacity, shielded him in guises of many kinds and often there was your own fear as openly he would preach and when he spoke to the governors of different areas you would hide so that you would not be recognised and punished. He would chide you and call you one of little faith but you loved him and he you - the love of respect and understanding of a teacher.

"Eventually you left the service for you had become an invalid. You desired now to return to the woman who had made her life with you, who had remained faithful, who had indeed endured much to protect you when you were absent without leave, but you had one last task, and that was to be present when your master himself was crucified as His Master before him, to tend him, to speak with him and eventually to help his soul to pass. That teacher was Simon Peter, as he is known in the gospels, but among his friends he took the name Paul - this is not Paul who had been blinded. The Truth that Simon Peter shared and came to believe was always part of himself. Paul did not have the same clarity of vision as Simon Peter and those who called him Paul did so to shield him so that his name could stand pure and clear in the annals of the teachers. This is not stated in the Holy Book and yet it is revealed in the scripts which as yet have not been released. One day they will be and all Truth will stand clear and Man will no longer be in doubt. The name Paul has a clear meaning - a leader, a teacher of men, one with Light, also a Christed one. Simon Peter had the same kin as The Christ and great was their union and their love and when he taught the light shone from his eyes and the words he spoke were not chosen they were inspired and he was magnificent to see."

A Centurion who deserted.

The following past life was given to an English woman in June 1990.
Master: "Christianity came through the ideas of Man, not those of the Christ. Christ taught the way of life, the universal law of love and directed His disciples and all others who followed Him towards love, compassion, healing and understanding. The disciples also endeavoured together and separately to teach that vibration of pure love. It embodies all mankind whatever their creed or faith - whether they be Gentile or Jew it matters not - it is the creed of love. And all those who surrounded our Master Jesus at that time had their own individual tasks and each one needed to fulfil them before returning to a spirit sphere earned throughout that life. As well as the disciples and the close attendants and followers of Christ, there were legions of men and women with whom He came in contact during various times within the passage of His life. Some were more important than others and many followed Him after healing. Many also turned away from their way of life in order to protect Him and you were one of these.

"In that life you were born a man and not a woman. In that life you proceeded through your early childhood and into puberty in a normal uneventful way, following the traditions of your family and the rulers of your land. For you were within the legions of the army that had settled in Palestine, but who originated in Rome. Many of these were cruel in the extreme, they had been specially chosen to subjugate those in that land.

"The Jews were greatly hated - they were powerful - they had almost total jurisdiction throughout the country. Where law and religion were concerned they were a force to be reckoned with and those who were Gentile often feared greatly the interpretation of the law made by the Jewish Sanhedrin. It was this body of men the Roman Empire desired to subjugate, to destroy. But few of those who ruled beneath the cloak of Rome had the strength and direction that was needed to overcome their power.

"More and more legions of soldiers would be sent to ensure that the occupants of the great cities should obey totally those that had overcome their land and desired to subjugate them. You rose through the ranks. At the time of the uprising within the city some were for the protection of the Christ and others demanded his defeat and death. By then you had command, but you had listened faithfully to many of the teachings. You and those underneath you had been sent to watch over and control the great crowds that would go to the hills and the sea-shores and listen to teaching and report back to those in greater command whether there was any desire to take over the city, to dominate. But you soon realised that the teachings were of love and health. You were present in the temple when the Christ's anger arose within Him and he desired to destroy that which was Caesar's and preserve that which was God's. It was you who restrained Him. At that time He was bound and taken from the temple. He was interrogated for a long while by officers senior to yourself, but then allowed to go His way. You were present at the scourging and you were present at the crucifixion. This made a profound impression upon you. You wished also to follow the guidance and accept the teachings of the way of love and you deserted your regiment. The clothes that you wore you destroyed and stole from another, while he was sleeping, the simple robe of one who was a beggar. At a discreet distance you followed the disciples and learnt more from them and their teachings.

"Despite your high position you became humble - you waited upon them at table and you helped to guard the life of Peter when it was threatened, because there were times when with his great love of the Word he allowed himself to be endangered but you saved his life which allowed him to continue his ministry.

"You played an important role and from time to time after you returned to spirit many of your future lifetimes were humble so that you might regenerate your spirit in lives which did not demand sacrifice or dedication to duty. For this is the reward that is given to a dedicated soul.

"The lives that we have given to you were important at the time of their telling so that your Soul might be energised and reminded of its purpose within this life. There is an optimum time when the Soul should learn and be taught and it is but recently that we have divulged to certain people their role before and now. If Man is told of his obligation too soon fear might arise and prevent him from moving forward to attainment and if it is told too late the opportunity may pass."

A raising of the dead.
The following past life was given to an English woman in 1990.

Master: "You were one of those who sought the help of the Master Christ. You came from your dwelling and walked many miles knowing that He was speaking in an adjacent village to your own. The path was rough and wild and there were those that lurked in the darkness who would take the purse you carried beneath your skirt. Within that purse there was the last of the money that you would receive for a long while. Your partner in life was very ill, close to death. You knew that once he passed it would be difficult to gain sustenance from any avenue of life other than humble begging. You loved him dearly and wished for his life to continue and yet your soul was aware that you also feared poverty. If his spirit left his body and you were destitute what then of your child? But this conflict within your mind was not conscious. It is often the subconscious thought which is the reality that mankind seeks, but cannot see. Many times you fell by the way as tiredness overcame you and fear of the shadows that lurked behind the trees on the path and even this was symbolic of your life - the fear of the veiled - but you did see the strength of the dawn as it rose behind the hill. And then you saw those that hurried to learn and to hear. You joined these and far away in the middle of the crowd you saw Him speaking. Your eyes burned in their intensity to draw His attention. He had that faculty of knowing if a mind was drawn to Him and needed His help, and He stopped in his speech. A path was made in the crowd as He walked towards you. Before you were able to speak he said: "Lead me to your Husband."

"The journey back seemed so different from that hazardous journey there. You had travelled two days and yet it seemed barely an hour before you entered again your home. Your daughter and a servant met you in tears. Your husband had died and they had laid him within his tomb. The Master Christ demanded to be led to the tomb. He stood outside the door and bade the soul of your husband to arise and join him in the open. You all waited with bated breath, then He turned to you and said: "Child do you believe?", and you said: "Rabboni, I believe." The veil parted at the door of the tomb and your husband came towards you. The illness that had wrought such ill effect over the months which had left him so weak that any effort had made him faint had vanished and he was strong again, but he had knowledge that his spirit had indeed left his body and knowledge that it had returned. His spirit had indeed been with you on your journey, helping and sustaining you. If you had been aware of this your fear would not have been so great. You all rejoiced and the servant prepared a feast that all could share.

"Your husband was Lazarus. From that time he joined those that loved The Lord and followed Him and you being content to be at his side travelled also and you were among those who accompanied Joseph of Arimathea to the golden isle of Glastonbury in order to begin the church that would show mankind the Way. Your memories, that you have seen so many times both in dreams and meditation, now make sense do they not?"

"They do Master and I understand why the cross affects me so much."

Healing

The blind young man who chose to remain blind.

This past life was given to an English man in November 1990.

Master: "You were born a Palestinian son of a Roman soldier. Your mother was one of the women of the streets in Bethlehem and then moving from area to area. She went to Jerusalem and there she met and loved your father. During the time that he was in that great town, before he returned to Rome, they lived together and loved each other very deeply and you were born. But you were born without sight and as you grew into boyhood, it did not seem as though your lack of sight inhibited you, for you had a great sense of touch and your hearing was sharp, but you had difficulty with speech at first. Mankind does not realise how much is learnt through reading the lips of others, and when the faculty of sight is withdrawn the hearing also becomes limited. But you grew and as you reached puberty these other defects meant nothing to you, for within your imagination you pictured those things you touched. When you touched your mother's face, you knew her to be beautiful and when you touched the face of others, you drew your conclusions as to whether they had beauty of countenance, or whether they had ugliness of nature, for the two are never combined. There is no radiance with those that cannot bring beauty into life. There is dullness and anger is represented within the contours of the face. The time came when your father had to return to his country and he was forbidden to take with him the woman who had lived as his wife, especially as her past had not been salubrious. There was great crying and great sadness as he said goodbye and you desired then to be the man of the family, to care for and support your mother, for she again went back to her old way of life in order to live. This saddened her and when you realised what was taking place, you could not bear it within your heart. You came to the Temple Courts and it was indeed Joseph himself to whom you spoke. You released the anguish that was in your heart and asked for help, for you feared your blindness and your inability to work. Joseph told you to go to the Disciples and ask for an audience with the Christ that He might restore your sight. You explained that you had been born without sight and that which gave sight to Man was not within your eyes. Joseph laughed and said that that it was not beyond the man Jesus to rectify and so you sought the Disciple who lived near you. He took you to the Christ, where He was speaking with many and when He had finished you were taken to Him, He looked upon you and touched your eyes gently with his fingers. He said "you may open your lids, my child, but when you do, the world will not be as you have pictured it. You may desire to continue to live within your illusion, for your illusion brings peace. The reality of seeing things as they are might even be destructive."

Then you explained about your mother and the Christ said to you: "She has freewill; if that is the path she chooses to tread, it is her choice and only she can turn from it. You can have your sight if you so desire it, but it will not change your mother and her way of life." You chose to remain blind, but you did go back to your mother and tell her what had occurred and that you had chosen blindness that you would not see and be aware of the changes within her and her life, but that you would indeed help. It was your words, and your words alone which turned her away from her path and she relied upon you. In that life you drew - you drew beautiful pictures in the sand around your home. You also used rocks which had a blue tint and you would use these upon surfaces where that which you drew had purpose to those who looked upon them, thus you were able to show people the true way of overcoming disability, and in that way you supported your mother and then later in your life, your wife and family. Your mother did not return again to that path and you never desired to be able to see clearly that which you felt within yourself.

"You see you learnt a great deal from that life. You learnt to trust your inner feelings, your inner needs and it is this, which is important. If you do not trust your inner needs, you cannot go forward and share and grow.

"We know that the emotion of understanding that which is past can be overwhelming, but it is good that it is so, for from now onwards you will accept more willingly the path before you. You will embrace it with joy and with gratitude.

"Our peace surround you and bring you comfort."

A life among the lepers.

The following past life was given to an English woman in 1991.

Master: "You were not in any way implicated in what took place with Christ at that time but you did live in that area, you were in Palestine and you were aware of what was taking place. You attended more than one meeting where the teachings were shared. You were even at one time within the dwelling where a meeting took place, where food was prepared and laid before those who came to hear the Master speak, but you came as a traveller, one who sought healing and received it, not from touch, not from implication, but from the words that were spoken.

"You were a man and you had been working with lepers, endeavouring to help them particularly to ease their pain, for it is a very painful condition, and you had contracted the disease. A kind of doctor, you were dedicated with your hands and could mix the different potions well. Some were ointments to relieve pain and there was also a preparation which could be taken internally, but would often burn in its passage down the gullet and cause vomiting. You sought to find a way that was more gentle and soothing. But all this meant that you were exposed to the disease and one day when you looked at your skin you saw that whiteness which showed the death of cells and within your heart was great fear. For a moment you stood still unable to recall the past or visualise the future. As you saw your reflection in a pool in which you washed you felt fear. Because of the nature of your work you looked for the Christ. It was a long while before He was able to communicate with you and His time was short. He knew at what point He would return to the etheric and that His ministry upon Earth would not be for long. You did not realise that only the command of His voice could help you, you demanded His touch and had faith in it. As you were known to have leprosy, you were not allowed to come into the presence of others nor yet were food was prepared. So you bound yourself and covered your flesh with cloth that your disease would not be apparent. But there were those present who recognised your voice and they denounced you. But before you were taken from that place with great anger of those present the Christ bid them be still and He said to you- "Go back to your colony for you are healed." And gradually as time passed the white cells turned again to their normal shade.

Those areas where parts were missing began to grow again and you realised that indeed your faith had made you whole. But it could have made you whole without His presence and His command and that is what you have learned today. He is not present in body but He is present in thought. And that which emanated from Him at that time continues, and man is able to regenerate himself and to be whole through faith and acceptance of the true rules of life. It has taken a long time to learn that lesson and in this life you have had cancer and you have had to accept Him mentally - is this not so?'

"Yes Master."

"So hold fast to the knowledge of the Christ within, for He is present in all the children of Earth in that flame of light which emanates from the source and within each soul that flame burns and that knowledge exists."

The miraculous water.

The following life was given to a Belgian woman in March 1992.

"I would like to know if I lived in Palestine at the time of Christ and who I was? Was my friend Y, (a woman) who is Jewish in this life, there also?"

Master: "Firstly the fact that your friend is Jewish in this life bears no relationship to her race in any other incarnation. It is true, to a certain extent, that where contentment and happiness is found within a race the soul may decide to use that form of belief or understanding in subsequent lives in order to achieve the true purpose of the path of life as it passes through generations and ages, but there is no certainty that one life is followed by another where one would be of the same race or colour. So the fact that your friend is Jewish within this life would not necessarily make her so in a life 2000 years ago. In fact, as we spoke with this woman, we felt that there was confusion in her regarding links with her race which indicated to us that there was not a Jewish link in the past as strong as that within her present life.

"We would perhaps have spoken to her regarding a life at the time of the Christ if it had been relevant. It is extremely difficult to link once that aura is removed, but you did live at that time as did your friend also; the great majority of people in the world at this time were alive 2000 years ago. It was the beginning of an age and there are souls that desire greatly to be reborn when an age is beginning. There is a form of excitement in the changes that take place as one age recedes and another emerges. Also that particular time was one of great moment within the earth's movement and cycle but there were, of course, lives other than those in Palestine. The world existed as it does today. There were fewer people upon the earth but most certainly there were those all over the world those who felt the Christ expression even if they were not aware that He was alive and this is why a soul will return to be aware universally of the light of different teachers that are to be born, or have been born, whose teaching and love may spread to them wherever they may live. There was less freedom of movement at that time, travel was restricted to that which could take place on foot upon an animal or by boat. There was no other method of transport, whereas in the present age if certain events are taking place and men have the means they can travel there and feel the vibration more closely.

"You were not born in Palestine, nor were you Jewish; you were born in Egypt. Your beliefs, your way of life were totally against that small minority of Jewish people who had taken up residence in the region where you were born and lived. There were great difficulties between races then as now. Such difficulties have existed for many thousands of years.

"The desire to propagate understanding is a very strong motive in mankind. It stems from the desire of the soul to learn by the means chosen at birth. It will never truly cease unless all mankind become as one and this is not likely to happen in this Age whatever may evolve at a later time.

"Your father loved to travel. You were the elder male child and therefore were being taught his business. There were times when he needed to travel to Phoenicia and beyond by means of the many fleets of vessels which followed the shore line to other countries close at hand. Your father's particular business was with fabric. It was unusual at that time for such an interest to concern a single member of the family and not the greater family as a whole. He loved the touch of fabrics, their richness and silkiness. He would travel to India and be gone not just for many months but for more than a year at a time while he negotiated with those there who were able to buy his products and sell their own often primitive products and yet when he returned triumphant with a new colour or a new texture the whole family would rejoice and forgive him for his absence.

"The family greatly increased and then tragedy struck. There was an epidemic, a very serious illness which was carried from one person to another at an alarming speed. The death toll was horrendous. At least half the population within the metropolis died within a matter of months. Those who ruled the country spiritually as well as the leaders of that country were in a state of tension and near panic. If this dreaded disease continued their safety would be at risk for there were always other countries which would endeavour to conquer. There was a great fear that the powerful Romans might do so and that the liberty of the Egyptians would then be removed. It did not enter their consciousness that with such an epidemic another country would fear to invade Egypt.

"All available forms of medicine were used and then it was discovered that there were certain waters in another part of the world which appeared to contain a healing balm and these were in the northern reaches of the Indian continent. They had been discovered by your father on his extensive travels for having a malady and feeling ill he had drunk from these waters and immediately slept. He had awoken refreshed and full of energy with the illness gone. Filling his water skin from this small source he then went on his way. Some of his companions also were unwell and also found relief from drinking this water. He had brought some back with him having kept it for this purposes. He then asked for audience with the Pharaoh. He was received and his gift was accepted.

"An army of men was sent forth. They chartered a boat from Phoenicia and were absent a long time. The illness was still rife in Egypt and the mortality rate was high. These men went with as much speed as they could. They returned with many skins full of water and this was distributed first amongst those first that ruled and then other members of the population who were considered essential to the life of Egypt. It was indeed a miraculous cure.

"You were growing during this time and had a great interest in what was taking place. You had heard of the influence of the Christ and that He had spent a great deal of time in India and being intelligent you wondered if there could be a link with this spring of water and with the workings of miracles by the Christ which had been reported. There was no way of being certain of this. You desired to travel to Palestine and seek audience with Him. But when the news was circulated of His trial and death you realised that your opportunity had gone. Being of high intelligence you desired to examine minutely some of this water. Although by now your father had little personal influence, the influence of his name was still quite great and you made use of it. As was the way at that time within the Age, things which appeared to be miraculous, or outside the conception of normality were kept in a place where they could not be violated and lost. The most common hiding place was in the tombs of the Pharaohs and at the time of a passing these were opened and many would be admitted. You obtained permission to take this small phial of this water and to place it within one of the tombs. It remains there my child. As with other events in the history of mankind, particularly in Egypt with its vibrations, the children of light when they grow older will hold the key to many of the answers to the known hieroglyphics which defy translation as well as those that will eventually be found. Eventually these children will find this phial. This water was indeed used to immerse the Christ at a time on his journey when exhausted, dehydrated and starving, He found this pool and laid himself to rest in it and asked that the waters might be for ever blessed.

"We regret that the evidence one always so greatly desires will not be available until the century to come as these children grow and become interested in Egyptology. But it will be so and it will be interesting to know at that time how many realise the importance of these miracles performed by Christ because of His nature and because of his descent from God."

Lives associated with Paul.

His father.

The following life was given to a Belgian in October 1991.

Master: "You were already elderly when Yeshua returned from His studies in India and began His ministry in Palestine. You were well born and had risen through society. You had your place in the Sanhedrin as a respected Elder and Teacher. There were many who sought your wisdom, as well as those who by reason of their rank or their birth were entitled to learn the great languages, to interpret the Truth through that understanding, and to be the future inspirers and teachers in the Temple. You were well known to all who served including him to whom you speak, Joseph of Arimathea, but there were two camps of ideology and light within that place. There were those who were inclined to follow the teachings of the Torah alone and there were those who enjoyed interpreting Greek mythology and also were able to visualise the future and had many out of the body experiences. You were one of these. So also was Joseph, but to a limited extent, and you would speak to him for many hours. You would visit his home in Jerusalem and share wine and eat together, but he was not a man easily led and he found it difficult to accept new ideas, new teachings, being steeped himself in his hereditary Jewishness and longing for liberty and light within his land. You were older than he. You met his family and delighted in them. There were those members there whom you felt with your mysticism would perish and as time passed you were shown to be right. His elder son distraught at the death of his cousin Christ, ultimately took his own life, while his younger son fired with enthusiasm and zeal for his tribe and race to become free became a Zealot and perished at Masada. You shared these visions with Joseph who became distraught and begged you to stop.

"You had a son and that son was called Paul but he had been named Saul at the time of his birth. He was a boy of inward thinking and great fears. He longed to make something of his life and be strong, though his strength was poor and his stature puny . He idealised you and he longed to be as you, with the same influence, with the same love of humanity and desire to learn, but he was more like his mother, frail and lacking in wisdom in many ways. However you as his father delighted in him and gave him all you were able both in riches and in whatever wisdom he wished to share. Joseph would endeavour to help you in this manner, but Joseph without his later foresight could not possibly anticipate what would happen to Saul at Antioch. Indeed he felt that the lad was spoilt and that as he grew would be a trial to his family as indeed he was, but the friendship between the two men remained constant until that aspect of your soul that dwelt within the father passed to spirit.

"You desired greatly that Joseph would oversee your son and make him a stronger man, which he endeavoured to do. He failed, but that is the way of the soul, it will go its own path and if it desires greatly to mature because of certain circumstances, nothing will deter it. However your life was exemplary. Many things were written regarding you that were derogatory to the real man, but Joseph knew your strength and weakness, but he knew also that you would never speak ill of those who had the spark of divinity within them and that you were knowledgeable and a learned man.

"Since that time an aspect of your soul has returned more than once into the world and has taken on the cloak of Judah. They have been known as "The Chosen People" and they have been so. History, looking back even beyond the reign of David sees the descent so clearly and yet Mankind fears and much of their fear is well founded for the knowledge that is deep within the soul of that people cannot be eradicated by any action of Mankind."

In March 1992 further questions were put to the Master on the above by those involved in the compilation of this book.

First Questioner: "You referred ,Master, in this particular tape to an event that took place at Antioch, perhaps you would tell us something about that event because when I first heard it I thought of the one on the road to Damascus -of the vision where Paul was blinded - obviously it is not that one that you are referring to."

Master: "We were in fact referring to that point. It was not on the road to Damascus. If the book is to have any credibility as to its meaning which is to state the truth many things that we say will need to be accepted. If everything was exactly as it is in the Scriptures, there would be no need for it to be re-written. If your book omitted that detail, there would be less credibility and not more'."

Second Questioner: "Another point -as a child -St.Paul was my hero and I loved to study his life. According to the New Testament Paul was born in Tarsus,was a Jew and a Pharisee, also a Roman citizen and he studied in Jerusalem at the feet of Gamaliel. However I would like to know if it is possible that his father was in the Sanhedrin in Jerusalem and a friend of Joseph of Arimathea"

Master: "Most definitely yes to both questions. Paul's father had great power. He was an Elder. And the friendship with Joseph of

Arimathea lasted from early manhood and continued until he passed to Spirit, at the time when his son was beginning his own inspired ministry. There are, as we said initially, certain facts which have been omitted from the scriptures, either because they were not considered relevant or the details were not there at the time to be included in the various writings. Some things in life at the present time are not noted historically because they are simply not considered worthy of this. So it is those details that we give to the individuals. We take great care to include all relevant details to make a clarification of that person's life. However we agree that certain things we have said will indeed be questioned, and we are prepared to clarify them or to say whether they should or should not be included if you feel strongly regarding them. But that which we have said is true."

"Yes, it is just that when St Paul's talks about himself he says that he came from Tarsus which is in Cilicia and that he was born there so I was just wondering how his father and he came to be in Jerusalem?"

Master: "As with many others they travelled there and they had their residence there. In the present world, people do not always stay in the place where they are born and as Paul's father initially was a merchant who travelled greatly in different areas of the World, before taking his place as a revered teacher and counsellor in the Sanhedrin, his two sons were both born in different places of residence which were quite temporary. The younger son was actually born in Jerusalem. The family remained there for many years before obtaining another property which was further away from the activity and the business of Jerusalem and eventually they lived there even after the father had passed to Spirit."

One of Paul's disciples.
The following past life was given to an Englishman in May 1992.

This man had just had a holiday on the Greek island of Naxos and asked the Master if he could tell him why it was that he had such very strong feelings when he was there. Was it an echo of a past life and if so why was it necessary for him to experience it and what had he learnt from it.

Master: "You were born and brought up on the Island of Naxos and you listened to those such as Paul when he accepted his role in the Ministry and travelled often with friends who sought to guard and protect him as his life was often in danger. You were already in young manhood when first you listened to the Teaching. For a long while it was even abhorrent to you, but you were drawn more and more to listen. Paul himself did not present a very strong picture of Christhood. Avid as he was in his belief and desire to teach, he was short, extremely thin and bony, a person who many would turn from, feeling that if he truly had such a wealth of knowledge he should have used it for his own personal adornment, but like John the Baptist he scorned fine clothes. Coming from an affluent family, a father who was in the Sanhedrin in Jerusalem, a palatial house in which he lived, he had cast aside all these things in order to travel lightly and to be able to share his conversion with others.

"You found him physically abhorrent: a Greek yourself, you longed to enjoy such teaching from those who had a greater sense of presence and beauty. You sought the teaching of Peter also, feeling that he had a sense of majesty and presence. A towering man who had within himself great magnetism, one easy to follow because of his directness. And yet in many ways, you found his teaching not as satisfying as that of Paul. And soon you began to realise that this was because in Paul there was the initiate, there was the convert. As for Peter he had for years absorbed the only form of teaching that he had known. To him there had never been another Truth. And gradually you began to merge your knowledge with that of Paul's.

Eventually, you left your own home which had great splendour and you followed Paul to other lands. You became his admirer in the true sense of the word realising that despite his deficiencies, despite his awkward manner and lack of eloquence, the real Truth lay within him and this he tirelessly and endlessly shared with others. You were present at the time of his death and you helped to lay his remains in a place of safety. You wept with many others at his passing and the manner of it and not until then did you return to your own land and tried there to bring Truth to the unbeliever.

"Never in that life did you truly succeed in casting away all the signs of splendour and glamour. Proud of yourself and the personality that you portrayed you saw it as part of the Teaching and not separate from it. You learned a great lesson in that life, one of many that have been learnt as the years have come and gone and your lives have revolved around growth. You have learned that it is what is spoken and taught and not so much the manner of the teaching that is important. And you have learned to lay aside personality and accept the knowledge which the Soul contains, rather than the person expressing it.

"We are in no way surprised at your reaction to those places where so many things had occurred in your life. Your childhood and young manhood, the reflection of your beliefs - shared with those who could not accept them, the sadness, the tears and the brotherhood with those who travelled, shared and talked together are all there. We are sure that you will return and when you stand and gaze across the ocean and allow your mind to open to other times - other voyages in the past, and you see coming towards you across the deep seas the kind of vessel in which you also sailed you will know that all lives are indeed one, separated only by the Eyes of the Soul."

Another of Paul's disciples.
The following past life was given to an Englishman in 1991.

Master: "You were born at the time of the Christ's life but when it was approaching its end. You were the son of one of the members of the Sanhedrin in the Courts of Law in Jerusalem. There were many at that time endeavouring to overthrow a rule which had become increasingly arduous. The civilian population was subjected to great hardship. Many had lost their sense of identity, wondering why it was that they were alive and what life could hold for them except harsh punishment for the most minor offences. Those of us who served with that body of learned men endeavoured to explain the law to those of our own religion. He whom you know as Joseph of Arimathea would help those of the Jewish order and he who was your father would help those who were not of the Jews but Gentiles. Your father had had more than one wife and was quite old. His latest partner was youthful and had two sons, who shared the womb at the same time. One of them was yourself, the other died upon birth. This has a profound effect upon life of the surviving twin and so it did with your life. The influence of the soul of that twin in spirit was considerable. You would have hallucinations, or as they were known - visions. You would see another child in your home, sharing your meals, your growth, with learning and times of play which others could not see and it was the soul of your twin brother growing with you. This is quite common. It is not common for another child to be so acutely aware as though it were indeed a human form. Your father was concerned by this and he approached the other brethren within the Sanhedrin to ask their advice. It was suggested that perhaps your mind was not completely clear, even madness might be approaching, and so that you might do no harm to yourself and others you should be placed under restraint.

"Your father was a man of great kindness and normally of great vision, but it was clouded upon this issue and you were taken from your home and your grieving mother and you were placed in an establishment and those that dwelt within there were diverse. Many were deformed in limb, many could not see or hear or speak and were therefore considered imperfect in their intellect. Time then was quite different from now both in tolerance and in knowledge. For many years you lived within that place losing all memory of your father or yet of your mother and then you became adult.

"By this time the Christ had passed to spirit by way of His crucifixion, but there were many who walked the earth in His name, preaching and healing and teaching. One of these was St. Paul who had, as you know, been miraculously brought to the faith when he had endeavoured within his life to bring punishment to believers. He found that his way of life had changed greatly and the spirit of God stirred within him and he could not bear to see so many caged in the way that they were who he felt with a little understanding and teaching could lead a full life. Some of those that he saw within your establishment were released by his intervention. You had long since grown out of acknowledging the spirit form of your brother, but your intellect had been impaired by being only with those who had little or none and were not allowed to express it. However Paul recognised your qualities and he insisted that you personally assist him along his way, not as a servant, but as a friend. Therefore you travelled with him to many places and soon any cloud that might have shadowed your intellect was dispersed and you became of great knowledge of that which he spoke from the heart. Then you returned to Jerusalem.

"There was great sorrow as one of the leaders of the Sanhedrin lay dying in great pain and anguish from bodily afflictions. Paul and yourself went to see him summoned by his manservant. Laying on of hands and prayers for health were said, you assisting Paul in this task. The spirit of the man eventually left his body, but that body had been released from pain, the mind had cleared and the old man's failing sight returned with clarity as he looked upon you, saw himself in you and recognised you as the son long since banished from his house. When you knew that this man was your father you were overwhelmed with emotion, but at that time you could not forgive him despite the teaching imparted to you by Paul regarding the importance to the soul to forgive. However you were gentle and kind and understanding to this man and helped his passing. You never truly forgave him for his desertion of you, but in other lives you and he have come together in many different relationships. However in this life there is or will be one whom you will need to forgive. It will indeed be a facet of the soul of your father and there will be a wrenching within you as the deep feelings arise. But it is important to forgive totally, absolutely and without recrimination and you are preparing yourself for this, you are becoming more enlightened. We feel that when the moment comes you will not be found wanting."

The Sanhedrin.

An Elder - a friend and ally of Joseph of Arimathea.
This past life was given to an English woman in May 1991.

Master: "You were born a boy in a noble family of Jewish heritage and as a result of this when a man you automatically became an Elder in the Sanhedrin . It was a part of the Jewish heritage that those who followed the path of Truth and enlightenment would have the power of teaching Truth to others. From an early age as a male child you were taken to the feet of the Elders. You were taught Sanskrit while Hebrew was your native tongue. You also learned Greek both written and spoken. Your father, a merchant and a good friend of the father of Joseph of Arimathea, would take you upon journeys. From Phoenicia you and the young Joseph were taken to places within the world where your fathers had business to do. Joseph's father was a tin merchant and your father dealt in magnificent materials with colours seldom used in your native land. There was the influence of India, your father brought back from India an Indian woman of noble blood with whom he had a child. This child, your half-sister, entwined herself within your heart and you desired her. As she grew older your desire became greater and you confided this to your friend Joseph. Although of high principles he was a man who understood the ways of flesh, having himself had a friendship - a love affair with a woman by whom he had a child. He understood well your desire and your need, but he did not encourage it knowing that these relationships were incestuous and thereby outside the law, both of the Jews and of the Romans who ruled the country, but this sister shared the desire and it was fulfilled.

"There were those in the Sanhedrin who were loyal to the High Priest and those who were loyal to the more liberal faction led by Joseph and also by Nicodemus, another good friend and they betrayed the confidence that had been given them. There was great debate and argument within the Sanhedrin and it was decided that the death penalty should be given to the woman. Immediately your friends encircled you and it was decided that the woman should be sent to a far place where her child would be born. India was not possible for there too principles would have resulted in her isolation or even her death. She was taken by boat to Greece and there had her child and brought it up. From time to time you would visit her as a patron as it was not to be understood that you were indeed the father of her child. You were allowed your life unimpeded, but deep within yourself was a sense of loss and also of fear and at times you would look within yourself and wish that life could end, but your great friend Joseph would speak with you and discuss the teachings and would not allow foreboding and melancholy to drive you to extinction.

"All this time the drama of the Christ and his teachings were progressing. Often you would be present with your friends to listen to the teachings, even disguised so that you would not be recognised by those who might report your activities to the High Priest and thereby to the Roman Governor. You became deeply touched by that which was being preached. It reached a chord within you which constantly vibrated and could not be stilled. You realised that your actions had been wrong, but you also believed in forgiveness - self-forgiveness, not that of an unseen force which has no power over the soul. It is in the soul's power to forgive or not forgive the actions of the self.

"You were present at the trial of Christ and your voice was raised with those who desired that He should be pardoned - those who felt that He was not one who wished to usurp Roman authority. Your action comforted you. You could not bear to be present at the crucifixion, having witnessed the flogging and seen the anguish which was inflicted upon His body, but you were there soon after the awakening when He walked again among men."

An Elder on the side of Caiaphas.

The following life was given to a Scottish woman in April 1991.

"Would it be appropriate, Master, for me to know if I had a life on this earth at the time of the Lord Jesus Christ?'

Master: "It would be appropriate for us to speak to you of your life at that time and awaken your memory. But before we tell you of these things it would be wise to understand the context in which they are given. All souls in their pattern of life through eternity are drawn to each other because of the karma which has been attained throughout that passage. This means that aspects of the total soul return time after time into life to learn one from the other and to have a similar growth pattern of spirituality.

"Having said this, you were indeed born in that part of Palestine where Jesus himself was born and raised. You were not part of His extended family, but you were part of the friends, the servant and disciple energies which surrounded him to a far greater extent than many visualise. The words written in the Book of Life, the Holy book, do not adequately describe the depth and vision of that life. Many things have been omitted which were known to those scribes who wrote of Him, words which could have depicted the wider aspects of His life and teachings. It is that teaching that we, in a limited way, are endeavouring to bring back into the world so that man may grow inwardly in spirit and cast aside the mantle of religion which has grown throughout the centuries limiting him in his concept of the greater energies of the universe, bringing fear instead of the beauty of total understanding and growth. This it was that Christ endeavoured to do, to bring truth to man. Some who were drawn to Him were simple men, others were scribes and had great intellect, others were powerful and sometimes misused their power.

"The Elders of the Temple in Jerusalem were known as the Sanhedrin. They were the spiritual rulers of the Jewish people and interpreted the law to those who could not read or write. Only those who were of ancient lineage received education. Jesus, who was of the line of David, learned from the Scribes and the priests in the temple and since you came of an ancient line you were also able to study there. You could speak Sanskrit and Hebrew and understood Greek. You studied the law and in that life you were male so all things were open to you.

You were wise but did not always use your wisdom well. Unfortunately in the Middle East even at this time women are still prohibited from learning and opportunities are only given to certain classes.

"This was the time when Jesus desired to bring the truth to men in simple words that they might learn. It was also the time in which the Elders of the Sanhedrin were afraid that their authority might be usurped and that the Roman rulers would destroy this authority if others spoke out This great body of men who made up the Sanhedrin was split with controversy. Those led by the High Priest Caiaphas were against civil liberties, spiritual growth and knowledge; they obeyed the Roman rulers and trembled in their shadow. The other faction, among them Joseph of Arimathea, were more open to spiritual truths and desired that those who could learn might be given the opportunity.

"When you became an Elder amongst this throng of clever men, it was to Caiaphas that you turned for your guidance and your teaching. You came also to others such as Joseph the Arimathean who taught you the beauty of the Hebrew language, so that you might read and speak in such a way as to bring purpose to your life and to the lives of those who sought your wisdom. But at the time we speak of you were solidly behind Caiaphas. You also desired the death of a man who was in fact innocent of any plotting and scheming to become King of the Jews.

"After the crucifixion and Christ's spirit had arisen and left the Earth and Joseph had taken his group of followers and Mary the mother, (who feared death at the hands of those frightened of truth), to continue the teachings, you looked within yourself. You did not like what you saw and what you had been. You followed in another boat in the wake of those who sought freedom and liberty and eventually arrived on the shores of Britain. You were met and welcomed as though all that had passed had never happened . You were absorbed into the society of the wicket church in Glastonbury and all the beauty of that environment became your life. There were those who travelled extensively throughout Britain that they might spread the teachings among the primitive men who lived there. They were not barbaric but primitive, there is all the difference in the world. You also followed Joseph and those close to him to Scotland and there you met the Celts and learned and taught. It was there that you gave your life for one whose life was in peril. There is no greater deed that man can do to achieve progress for his soul than to give some part of himself to save another and you might ask, but why return, would not that deed have allowed my soul to continue through spiritual paths away from the Earth? And we say to you it is that which brings the return of the soul that it may share and spread and give understanding on a higher level to those that seek.

"Go forth, as many of your friends are going forth, share with them that which is deep within you, give words to truth. That is your mission and how you do it, in what guise, in what manner, is your choice. If it is by giving healing, either of the body or of the mind, then so be it; mankind has choice, freewill. Healing is to be used, but used with care, love, involvement, and however humbly to spread truth. So learn well, listen well and share."

A handmaiden to Mary the Mother.
The following past life was given to a woman in 1992.

Master: "The part that you played was handmaiden to Mary the Mother. At first the position was supposed to be temporary, but as these things are wont to occur you wove your way into her heart and she into yours, you became so much a part of the family and her confidante that although there was another who looked after the young child (for he was inclined to be wilful and to follow his own path) you remained with her throughout her entire life span until she was laid to rest on the Isle of Glastonbury. Your name was Martha and as we have said you were constant in your love and devotion to her. You assisted her in the birth of Yeshua's two brothers and you also helped to rear the youngest child who was sickly in health and who did not survive beyond her fifth year. After the events of those times in Jerusalem, culminating in first the crucifixion, then the resurrection and ultimately the ascension to the spheres of light, there was the fear of persecution of those involved in the life of Yeshua. You were taken with Mary and others first to the isle of Cyprus, to the estate of Joseph the Arimathean, and you stayed there until it was safe to undertake the journey across the ocean to Britain.

"Your devotion to Mary was great and knowing how fragile and how near death she was from the privations that occurred you were always close to her. Your own health was not always good yet you felt for her not duty or compassion but love and you remained with her until she passed to spirit and was laid in her simple grave under the Wattle Church. Eventually the remains were removed from there to the mainland where another and larger church was planned where more people could come and worship. Eventually it was this sanctified spot that housed the first of the two abbeys built there. In that ground there are several of those living at that time, Mary Magdalene being one and Joseph of Arimathea another. The bones were removed at the time of the Reformation and we have already spoken of how they were placed for safety in another area. To those who listen to our teaching and follow the Light of Christ in its Truth and not in its fiction, we shall give - when the time is right - information as to where the remains are and what should be done with them, if they are allowed to be lifted; but this in the future.

"In that life you had a Jewish father and a Nubian mother. Your mother had travelled from Egypt. She was herself a princess from a powerful dynasty, but she was taken as a slave,chained and brought into Palestine to serve. Very soon after her arrival she was bought by another who had great power in Palestine and was taken to Jerusalem to serve within a harem in that area. She was freed by a Jew who admired her great beauty, her pride and aloofness in the degradation that she had been brought to. He respected her greatly for this and felt that she deserved peace of mind and respect.

Therefore he released her from bondage and she became free. Ultimately he loved her greatly and became betrothed to her. The child that was born first was an element of your soul, of your Higher Self. Unfortunately this man incurred the wrath of the Roman Empire and he was assassinated, leaving his family at the mercy of those who ruled. Joseph of Arimathea, who had been a great friend of this man, took the family under his wing, gave them refuge and found work for them that they might be independent; thus you found work in the home of Mary and Joseph the parents of Christ.

"You were very like your mother of that life in both stature and your beautiful ebony skin, but you also had pride in your Jewish heritage and the two facets in your life were not confused but blended and gave you a sense of purpose and your own sense of majesty. After your mistress had died it was not long before you followed her.

"You may feel that after such a life of service, none of those present at that time needed again ever to return to the Earth, but this is ignorance of karma, shared by many. There were very few who did not return again. Those that did not were the Apostles and also Joseph of

Arimathea but only because their life then was the culmination of other lives of that which the soul sought. Mary the Mother of Christ and her husband Joseph did not return, but many others did. Those known as the Bethany sisters, cousins of Christ, returned two or three times and the wife of Lazarus also. Another aspect of the soul of Mary Magdalene returned and her mother also. Many, too numerous to mention, are upon the Earth at this time ready once again to spread the Light and the Truth so that their part in the teaching should be continued although you must be aware it is a different facet of that soul, of the Higher Self. The same facet does not return except in special circumstances where perhaps the help of that facet is needed to bring some strength to the one now living."

A stonemason employed by Joseph of Arimathea.
Finally, the past life of a Belgian woman given in May 1989 is told here because it shows another activity being undertaken in readiness for the inevitable crucifixion. In fact this project was finished only a few weeks before the event took place.

"When I was younger I had a strong feeling that if Jesus had returned to earth it would have been so wonderful to be with Him. The feeling is so strong that I think that I might have been in His presence or in His country or knowing about Him when He was there. Is this so?'

Master: "All those who are very active in those things that we seek to express were with us at that time in some capacity, though not necessarily in Palestine or in Jerusalem. There were many who were in Britain when we were there and also in the Greek and Spanish islands and Gibraltar.

"An aspect of your soul was however in Jerusalem and you were present when the Christ was tried and crucified. You were one of the crowd. You had not what we would call a special place in the life of those who lived and worked with Him. But one of your tasks, as a man, was to help to hew from the natural rock the grave in which the Christ was placed after His crucifixion. This particular grave was part of the land of Joseph of Arimathea. But it had to be made right so that those who would be laid in it at the time of their passing would find a quiet resting place for the remains of their earthly body. It had to be a place where their memory would be revered and love would remain. This was an ideal place wherein to lay the body of Christ and only those who showed spiritual virtues were chosen as workmen. They were rewarded well in kind and in blessings for what they did.

"You were watching from a nearby hill the desecration which took place of one who had so much love and understanding for mankind. And you were among those who cried in a loud voice that He should be released while others cried that the criminals each side of Him should be released. You also were scourged for having expressed love for the Saviour, but you survived this and bore your wounds well for the love of mankind. There comes but one life of such deep purpose."

Part III

Joseph of Arimathea

Chapter 12

Joseph - some unanswered questions

What do we know about the Arimathean? Very little, if we had to rely on the Holy Book, even though he is mentioned in all four Gospels. He is described as a good man, but would Joseph stand up to todays investigative journalists? From the revelations in part I we know -using modern jargon - that he was born into the privileged class of the day. His father was a wealthy man, the owner of a successful family business which was a small conglomerate. The core business was in metal - the selling of tin - but there was also a thriving business in timber and smaller interests, including acting as a middleman for silks from India and China.

Joseph was not only very well educated in the Jewish faith but had at least a working knowledge of several other religions and had been to India in his youth. He was also versed in several languages (he could write and speak Greek, Aramaic and Hebrew).

His father wanted him as the elder son to take over the family business and he trained his son for this position taking him on his long journeys to teach him the practical side of the business. As a youth Joseph had already made long and hazardous journeys to Britain to visit tin mines on the south west coast. However he had other ideas - he wanted to be a rabbi and teach in the Temple.

On the death of his father he inherited not only the business but the magnificent family house in Arimathea, a holiday home on the beautiful island of Cyprus (where he was a big landowner), and a property in Greece. Later, using, among other materials, special magnificent hard woods imported from his Cyprus Estate he built a pied à terre next to Golgotha in Jerusalem. This was mainly used by Joseph himself while working in the Temple, for it was too far to commute from Arimathea. While still young he fulfilled his boyhood ambition by becoming a rabbi, an elder in the Sanhedrin (the ruling body of the Jewish faith in Jerusalem) and a teacher and counsellor in the temple. He enjoyed fine clothes and particularly bright colours and dressed opulently, especially compared to other rabbis.

Alas, this comfortable life style was not to last. He received a revelation from the Archangel Gabriel that his nephew Yeshua - Jesus, had special powers. He was descended from the cosmic God and the light that shone within Him was pure. Then Joseph was told how Jesus would die and although he could not change this he had to help Him as much as possible. Joseph then had to keep this secret for the next forty years!

This involved great responsibilities for Yeshua's father was old and Joseph had to assume the role of parent to his nephew. This started after the death of Herod when he helped bring the young Yeshua back from exile in Egypt and under cover of darkness took him to the safety of the Essenes. Joseph supplemented His education with special lessons, took Him to Egypt and masterminded His long stay in India - probably the most important part of Yeshua's educational programme. Then on the death of Joseph the Carpenter the Arimathean became the paranymphos (guardian) of Yeshua's mother Mary.

However life had its rewards, for Joseph was always present where action was taking place. He was present at Yeshua's baptism and at the wonderful anointing where he too received the very special powers. He was present at the Last Supper and later removed Jesus' special robe so it could not be rent. He obtained the body of Jesus after the crucifixion, wrapped it in a shroud and put it in his own tomb and under special guidance ritually destroyed the cross.

The negative side.

All this sounds splendid, but if today a journalist from a tabloid newspaper was reviewing this he might well start to ask probing questions, such as why did Joseph not fulfil his ambition to become High Priest? As a respected elder of the Sanhedrin he had everything going for him, well educated, wealthy, a successful counsellor and a magnificently imposing figure. So what went wrong? Was his Jewish faith suspect? Did he commit some indiscretion? Important questions, for if he had been High Priest instead of Caiaphas he would hardly have condemned his nephew to death! And there is the question of why did he not use his considerable influence as a respected elder of the Sanhedrin to get his nephew off the charge? Anyway where was he when the crucifixion was taking place?

These questions are answered later; but first are revealed through past lives intimate details of Joseph's family. These gives great insight into life at that time and more details of what life was like with Yeshua. Also that Joseph's life was a difficult one and fraught with many disappointments.

Chapter 13

Joshua and Abram - Joseph's brothers

The following past life given to an Anglo-Indian presents further insight into Joseph's early life.

Joshua - a brother of Joseph.
Master: "We also wish to tell you that the feeling of recognition that you have within you has the basis of the Truth. At the time of Christ, two thousand years ago, you did indeed have awareness of him who speaks with you, for you were his brother Joshua in the flesh. Joseph came from a family where there were two brothers close in age and younger sisters ,who died in childhood, and a much younger brother. There was often sparring between the two older brothers because the elder Joseph would inherit the considerable wealth which their father had both acquired throughout his life and inherited from his father. The two brothers were very similar in height and stature and in their ability to assess life. Their feelings of awareness of spirituality however differed. Joseph, the elder, received through enlightenment and revelation a great awareness of the role he would play in the life of his nephew Jesus as He was born and grew and Joseph dedicated his life to the mission given to him by the Archangel Gabriel, knowing that God - the All Powerful - is aware of every facet of life and its need for spiritual nurturing. He gave his life in order to establish that this truth would be recognised and spread about the globe, but his brother Joshua felt that he wished to partake of the joys of the flesh. Joshua believed that Joseph would not use the riches wisely and that much would be given to those who did not deserve it, he felt that if only he inherited the wealth that money could be used for himself and his family.

"Joseph loved his brother Joshua deeply and sought to allow the spiritual to arise and be recognised, to bring within his brother's immediate family the knowledge that could become love instead of desire and lack of respect. Duty to the family and to the heritage was strong within Joseph, but not within Joshua, and yet the division became less as the brothers obtained knowledge and wisdom through age. It was with great sadness that Joseph buried his brother upon his death. Joshua was indeed fighting for his honour, aware that the very name of the family was in jeopardy because Joseph had chosen a different way of life. The loyalty between the brothers was such that they would gladly lay down their lives in order to protect the other and Joshua did so, thus earning Joseph's love and respect for the remainder of his life which was indeed long and lasted into great old age.

"Joseph accepted the responsibility of his brother's family and looked after them as he accepted the responsibility of many as they entered his life and needed his love and upliftment. It was to Joseph's shame that he had not made his brother aware of his great love for him before he was slain.

"Although that facet of soul that is within you now is not the same as that which lived at that time it is part of the same Higher Self and as we have said, the Higher Self has awareness of the purpose of every life, so certain feelings that have arisen within you at times of contemplation and meditation are correct and now you can rest quietly in that knowledge, know that your act at that time was appreciated and accepted and because of it your brother lived and continued his purpose. This life is less arduous and contains less responsibility. You may not totally accept this, but it is so, and when this facet within you has achieved the spirituality you seek in this life there will be no need to return to Earth to learn more."

Abram - Joseph's youngest brother.

"Joseph knew little of his much younger brother who had inherited a family illness which in his short life kept him away from other children and members of the family."

In December 1994 a Belgian was told he had been that brother.

Master: "You were born at that time into the household of the senior Arimathean, Joseph's father. There were six in that family, one of the twin girls was still born and the other two girls died in childhood, which was quite common at that time.

There was a lack of correct nutrition; plagues and many disease were rife and also a lack of general cleanliness. Although it was a wealthy household, many viruses and diseases are airborne so some of the children did not survive. Of the three who did there was the eldest son

Joseph himself, his brother Joshua and then a long gap before the girls were born and died quite quickly. Then you were born as a male child. Delicate in health, you were greatly loved by both father and mother as being part of their closeness together, the life they had achieved and the warmth of their relationship despite the arranged marriage, a custom prevalent at that time.

"Joseph the elder brother, was often away with his father learning the trade which he would inherit. Joshua did not have the same awareness and feeling as Joseph. He was indeed jealous of his older brother but he loved greatly this young child who had survived a famine in the land which had given their mother great ill health during her pregnancy. Also she was much older at that time and not expected to survive the birth - though she did in fact survive but not for many years. You yourself lived until puberty when another great disease spread throughout the land. It was with sadness that both Joseph and his brother laid you to rest in the family home at Arimathea.

"Your great pleasure was to be taken to the coast where the family had a fleet of ships. There a family servant would often take you out in a small boat where you would learn to fish. When you were brought back, because your limbs were not strong, you were often carried for quite a long distance in the arms of a servant whom you cared for greatly and he loved you as a son. You loved and were loved greatly during your short life.

"Although subsequently you have had several other lives you learnt then the lesson of utter love, the acceptance and the giving of love within that life. May it serve you well in this life, and may all the possibilities that were denied you at that time reach fulfilment now, for within our heart you are both son and brother."

Chapter 14

Miriam - Joseph's wife

In 1991 an English woman was given a past life as the wife of Joseph of Arimathea. As some lives of the past can help us to understand and guide the present life she set out to learn as much as possible about Miriam. Between November 1991 and August 1993 she had seven tapes with the Master, asking many details about her life and their life together at that time. This chapter contains extracts from those tapes.

Miriam's family and the alliance with Joseph's family.
Master: "You were born in Phoenicia where those who dwelt along its coast were seafarers. Your father was a a wealthy man. He owned a fleet of ships and those who worked for him would travel to many areas of the world carrying merchandise from one country to another. They would travel to India or China and there great bales of silk and other fine yarns would be placed within the hold of the vessel and would be taken to other areas such as Europe. Many months were spent upon the seas and many vessels would be shipwrecked.

"Your father was old when you were born; you were his only daughter and he loved you greatly. His sons inherited his wealth and also his fleet of ships but you inherited from him the priceless gift of total love and admiration that only a father who has longed for many years for a girl could possibly surround his child with. But you were not spoilt. You were a well adjusted child who respected your parents and elder brothers but within that life, as all who dwelt in that part of the world experienced, there was the arranging of marriage and this was done very soon after birth. This betrothal to Joseph was quite normal. The parents in large houses, the merchants and similar people who had vast riches desired to keep these riches within certain family units and channel the money into the areas which would best benefit the families concerned. Therefore they would often arrange with friends and neighbours to bring their children together in a marriage contract which would enable the flow of money to continue.

"Joseph's father was a tin merchant by trade although he also had silk interests in the Asian continent. These were beautiful fabrics, wonderful designs and colours but his overriding business acumen had to do with tin within the world and he had a friend who was similarly employed. They were both extremely rich and wished to unite their families in order to use their experience and extend their merchandise in other areas of the world. It was therefore quite natural that Joseph's father should marry his elder son to the daughter of his friend and this was accepted from their earliest days.

"A betrothal which would establish the rights between the man and the woman would take place approximately at the age of five or six years and then throughout the time from then to puberty both that boy and girl would not see each other, would not meet again, to ensure that there should be no prejudice. They were discouraged from forming other alliances and they knew that at the age of 15 or 16 the betrothal would become a reality and that they would marry in the eyes of God. And this occurred in your life as it did in the lives of your elder brothers. Throughout your period of childhood, you anticipated meeting again the young boy to whom you had been betrothed. Your parents would speak of him, of his wealth and the position that he would inherit from his own father who also was the possessor of a fleet of vessels similarly employed to those of your father."

Joseph has other ideas.

"Within his own experience Joseph was beginning to feel that the ancient custom of betrothal in such extreme youth was against the physical and mental well being of those concerned. He was very aware of attraction to others but he was also aware that within these great ancient families tradition meant far more than the actual happiness of their children. Joseph's own family of course, came from the House of David which was influential, extremely powerful and rich. The affluence of Joseph's father extended to estates in other lands where the family could live together when he travelled. As we have mentioned before there was such a place in Cyprus which was very beautiful and covered many acres of that island, which was at that time larger than today. The actual domain and most of the forest has now been eroded but this of course has happened in vast areas of the world with the progress of time."

The Marriage.

"The time came for the ceremony and also the meeting once more with your betrothed. Like all young women you were full of anticipation and yet of fear as to how he had grown and whether you would find the personality as attractive as the idea. Because both families had amassed great fortunes, no expense was spared for the festivities and these would take many days. There would be feasting and two ceremonies and between them the marriage would be consummated.

"For the first ceremony you remained veiled and Joseph was not present. It was a renewal of the vows which had been made before the parents and the rabbi who, because of the importance of the families, was the High Priest. This was followed by the ceremony of the exchange between the man and woman, after which the families considered themselves united within their children's marriage. On this occasion you met your betrothed, now grown to a young man of eighteen. You were no more than fourteen summers and very beautiful, but the young man although aware of his responsibilities and that he must take part in the ceremonies as his parents desired had seen great unhappiness within his own family. He had seen his father loving other women because he had little in common with his wife and his mother experiencing deep unhappiness through these infidelities.

"You went to live with Joseph and during that time together you became extremely close. There was never the form of love which comes from a chosen marriage where there is passionate love, but there was harmony between you. You were the traditional wife of a Jewish merchant, obedient and carrying out that which your husband desired; bringing the children up in the right attitude of mind for the background which was theirs and also following implicitly the customs of the Jews."

Miriam - a personal profile.

"One of your gifts was sculpting in marble and plaster and fashioning ornaments of great beauty for the home. You would often model the head of Yeshua and sometimes his entire body. As he got older he would become restive not wishing to sit for long periods of time for he lacked the necessary patience. You found at one time a companion who taught you to draw. You may remember that your husband delighted in colour and was looked upon as being flamboyant in his dress for others wore robes of single colours. mainly white in bleached cloth or black cloaks. The beautiful silks that Joseph brought back from his travels were used to adorn himself, his home and his family. You had beautiful gowns which were made from many of these fabrics. And Joseph would delight in his raiment, especially that of deep purple, and he preferred to wear silken fabrics to cotton. Of course for practical reasons many of these cotton fabrics were used for their coolness.

"Joseph enjoyed your creativity and often visitors would be pleasantly surprised at how professional were the things that you had created for the home. You also enjoyed covering certain furniture with some of the fabrics brought back from such places as China and India. They showed an awareness and an aptitude which many in their wildest dreams have never attained.

"The average home was so simple; it contained no furniture. Woven mats covered the floor and people would lie on these in repose and sit on them to eat. There would be at most a low table on which the food was prepared and yet in the home of the Arimathean there would be seats on which to lie and to eat and drapery on the walls. There were open archways into different areas and a beautiful pool in a shaded part of the house open to the garden. The floors, ceilings and pillars were of marble and there were coloured rugs and low divans upon which to sleep.

"Your life was one of elegance and riches. You were respected, nourished, nurtured and taken care of. You were never abused and your husband never flaunted his feelings for another before you."

Family life in Joseph's home.

"It was quite different from life today. There was not, as in today's small home, the sharing of work and meals. For a great deal of time the wife would remain with the children and other members of the female side of the family - be they honoured servants and friends or friends from outside. Meals were not shared as in modern times. But on the Sabbath the entire family would be together at eventide. As the sun set the candles would be lit. The menorah (seven branched candlestick) would stand in the centre of the table where the meal had been laid by the servants. There would be a simple ceremony. The male members of the family would enter led by the father - Joseph - who would stand at the head of the table. Upon it would be a simple meal of fruit. No flesh of any kind would pass the lips on the Sabbath. There was unleavened bread and there were on occasion cheeses made from the milk of goats but mainly there were fruits of all kinds. The male members of the household would stand in respect of the seniority of their father and he would read from the Torah and there would be certain statutory prayers spoken either in Hebrew or Greek - according to the occasion. If it was a particular religious event the ceremony would be longer. Then the female members of the household would enter. The wife would enter with her daughter and would sit at the opposite end of the table from her husband while the daughter would sit at her father's right hand. When all were seated the eldest son would light the candles in the menorah and there would be further prayers and further reading of the Torah - that part which the female members of the Jews were allowed to hear and to relate to. For there are parts of those great words that only the men could hear and this is so even to the present day. All this was strictly adhered to in the home of the Arimathean. There would be blessing upon the food. First the bread would be broken and wine would be passed around the table very much as in the Baptism or in the blessing of the bread and wine that takes place in many churches at this time. And as the wine was passed round and the blessing was given the meal would be enjoyed by all present. There would be no discussion on that day but the solemn statement of belief in the truth of God's hierarchy. There could however be a discussion on an important aspect of the teachings of the greatest of the Jewish prophets such as Moses or Abraham or even David himself.

"Then the men would stand and the women would leave. And shortly after the men would also leave and go to an antechamber where they would undress and wash. So at the closing of the Sabbath the scriptures were fulfilled that before the working day began each one would be washed and dressed in clean clothes. The women would follow a similar ritual, so all were cleansed for the beginning of the week."

Miriam's relationship with Joseph.

"There was a great deal of happiness and also times of pain and sadness when you could not agree though these difference were solved by goodwill. You were never treated as a chattel by your husband as so many women were. You had among your friends those whose husbands spoke to them only when they desired the sexual act, whereas usually they were abandoned to their own society or that of other women. Even among Jewish women there were those who remained veiled outside their homes. So throughout the ages it has not been just the Moslem women who have been subject to that degree of restriction. You however were allowed your friendships and your ideals.

"There was a very deep and sincere regard and love between the husband and wife but not that passion which many feel is prevalent today. This love was beyond passion, it was a total trust. There was a belief that neither would harm either each other or the children born to them. So in that respect there was a difference between the feelings of a husband and a wife then, to that which exists today. And that respect lasted throughout the life of both Joseph and Miriam. There was never that passion which at the present time seems so important between men and women This is known as desire, in which love plays little or no part. True love, true understanding of each other, is born of respect and this there was in abundance.

"There were times when Joseph would chide his wife when he felt that she had spoken unwisely on intimate matters to others - the ladies of her household perhaps, or to her daughter regarding her future nuptials. For it was considered that comparisons should never be used in order to impart knowledge.

"And when you entered into the home of the Arimathean the servants were as free as the members of the household as they had been released from bondage and given independence. They lived there because they loved to live there, because they honoured their Master and subsequently their Mistress. But you had to learn self-confidence. So in many ways you were shy until you were encouraged to come forward - to allow the timidity to fall from you - to express yourself - to realise that you could be as knowledgeable as any man and perhaps more so than most. The difference between yourself and Mary of Magdala whom Joseph loved was that she had accepted from the beginning of her relationship the importance of manhood and had disguised herself as a man in order to win praise and respect. And then when she became known as a woman she had already won respect.

"It took you a long while before you felt you had earned respect. And yet you had indeed done so by your devotion to your duties and by making them not just a duty but a need and a desire. There was always tenderness, always the understanding of the needs of the wife as a woman.

"Again you must appreciate that men at that time could and did have any woman they desired and would often do so to relieve the wife of commitments which were sometimes arduous for them. But this was not so with Joseph. He was not one who sought relief in that manner. He felt that if a woman deserved love she deserved honour. Therefore you were not called upon to play that role beyond your desire or your strength. And you also realised that neither would he seek that in areas of Jerusalem where such women could be found and bought cheaply for this was not his way. It must be understood that prostitution was quite commonplace for it was the only way that women without means could live; it was more a way of life than has been assumed."

Miriam's relationship with Joseph's household.
"A wife's expectations today are very different. She expects to be a partner to her husband, to understand his hopes and fears and to go forward with him hand in hand, facing all obstacles and sharing all burdens. In the past this was not so common. A woman was normally kept quite separate from the working arrangements of the household. There would be servants, there would be children, there would be other women for companionship and as we have already said the only time that a husband would relate to his wife would be in the marital chamber. This however was not the case in your marriage for Joseph had been brought up with enlightenment and he and you were aware of the teachings of the Essenes. Moreover the whole of the Holy Family in all its branches were with the Essenes in their knowledge, their teaching and their education. The Essenes believed totally in the equality of women. Therefore the Arimathean desired that the female members of his household also should be heard, seen and their viewpoint shared. And he extended this not only to his wife but to his daughter who was encouraged to share her ideas and beliefs with her brothers and also with her father. There were other close associates of the family who were Essene members and within that Brotherhood and within their own home they would unite in a different way from the average Jewish household. There would be times of meeting, discussing and sharing and opportunities for you to express your views and many times sway the opinions of your husband before he took decisions. You would balance the true Jewish female outlook with that of the more open life of the Essenes. However you were always conscious that in certain aspects and friendships you must be the more remote Jewish wife and not allow your friends to be aware of the closeness that you

could attain - how you could direct matters and how you had a life of your own that was not purely the life of a harem. You were very gentle, very quiet, but there is a saying that still waters run deep and we would say that this applied to you, for you would think very deeply on certain issues and have marked feelings towards them. And these were not always the beliefs or feelings of your husband nor yet of your sons.

"Sons in a typical Jewish household would mean far more than the wife or the daughter. But the Arimathean home was not a typical Jewish household. It was rather a typical Essene household. You were not brought up as a child to be an Essene and you married into an Essene household having been very briefly introduced to the community during the time of your adolescence and growing into womanhood. It was there that you were first aware of the man that you would be plighted to. And it was there also that you were first aware of the Holy Family - of Mary and Joseph.

"It was not a lifetime's knowledge. You had to learn through experience."

The Children.
"Joseph had desired to choose his own partner and had largely distanced himself from Jewish customs having even in his youth visions of the future and knowledge of that which would take place as he matured. In his mind he did not see the young child to whom he was betrothed but had a vision of another whom he had not yet met. But he was obedient and the ceremony was performed. At first you lived in Arimathea - the family home - and soon you were with child. The first was a girl and you loved her greatly. You felt that no other child would be like her. So like you in looks, thoughts and attitude to life was she and yet as you were not, fiercely independent and almost outside parental guidance.

"Aware of your husband's feeling of independence you had agreed that any children that you bore would be allowed free choice which he himself valued above all things. He desired that his children should reflect the freedom of their souls. You had no reservations, being at that time totally secure and happy with him. When his own father passed over as yours had soon after the betrothal, he then became heir to the fortune which he did not wish for. He wished only to serve God. He wanted to be a rabbi and he craved also to be eventually the chief priest within Israel and he worked hard toward this aim.

"Another child was born, a son, and after several years yet another. The two sons were very different. The elder was strong desiring to manifest his strength in all things, in words, in actions, in thoughts. The younger son was a visionary with great hopes for the future and like his father he desired to serve God rather than Mammon.

"At this time both Joseph and yourself were extremely orthodox but Joseph had an awakening. The inspiration that was portrayed to him through the Angel Gabriel has already been mentioned, but this revelation went further and covered Joseph's life after the crucifixion. This was indeed a time of true awakening and his whole attitude to life, belief, relationships, began to change. He realised that this total obedience, this ownership and belonging were wrong. There should be more freedom of choice, more free expression of love.

"At first you could not agree with this but gradually you became more attuned to your husband's desires in allowing the children more choice in their betrothals, but at that time it was very difficult. If a child was not betrothed in youth that child would often be passed by in marriage upon maturity. This happened initially with the daughter and the elder son.

"Joseph had great sorrow within his life but Miriam was always a consolation. He admired and respected her and depended on her strength. There was never at any time a rift between them not healed by their equality of understanding and faith. Miriam understood totally her husband's desire for the woman who bore his daughter; the fruit of a very brief liaison. You never met either the daughter or the mother. Joseph's respect for his family was such that he endeavoured to keep this apart from them and it was again in anguish that he realised that his dearly beloved younger son had formed a liaison with this daughter. Karma is a very harsh master. The karmic values in life are not always easily understood, but is true - so true that the sins of the father are inherited by the sons to the third and fourth generation. It is that which can never be disputed, but as in all karma it must be accepted and transmuted and in that manner it is then assuaged. That is as true in the present time as it was then.

"Love was growing between Joseph and Mary of Magdala and he felt very conscious of her need for protection. As he observed the child - Mary - growing he became aware of her great beauty. Joseph also realised that at some time he could be recognised - visiting her mother for the young child - was becoming observant. Joseph was essentially extremely aware of propriety and loyal to his home and his family. This was a time of division. There were other elements to do with the work in the temple and the Sanhedrin - the disloyalty among the elders and the hatred that was rising as the young Yeshua grew, for many felt threatened by His presence. And one of the reasons why He was sent to India was in order to create within himself more knowledge - more ability for He was very outspoken. He had great inner knowledge that He wished to share with others of His own age and older. Therefore it was considered expedient that he should leave the locality and should complete His education elsewhere. Again Joseph was split between loyalty to his family and his work and his desire to accompany his nephew to India. Eventually he did not, but remained in Palestine. However when there is a deepening awareness of prophecy, of its fulfilment and the inability to change it - to stem the tide from moving forward to its completion - it affects the ability of the personality to continue with life unimpeded. Many of the difficulties arose from this. At that time men were supposed to rise above such difficulties and not to share them with those dependent on them and although much was shared between you, you always felt protective towards him.

"So there was not just one reason for the difficulties between you, but many. Your own health at that time was also giving alarm. In order to remain harmonious within yourself it was important that you should not again conceive. At that time there was no form of birth control; It was forbidden within Judaic law that there should be the emittance of seed that was not to be used. There was a punishment if it occurred and was known to be so. It was a law of perpetuity and as Joseph himself was one of the interpreters of Judaic law it was important that he should not be found wanting."

The affair with Mary of Magdala.

"By that time you were aware that your husband's love had moved from you to another, that he had met the woman of whom he had dreamed incessantly throughout his childhood and whom he had desired to marry before he was even aware of her existence. And they had met, they had consummated their love and they had had a child. As we have already said this child you were aware of, although you had never met her, nor yet had you met your husband's mistress. At first there was intense disbelief within you but then you realised that loyalty is more than of heart, it is also of mind and that he served you well with his wealth. He would speak with you and share his life with you, also you had the love of your children and you realised that many women did not have such honesty from their spouses. Gradually you accepted that he loved this woman whom he had put from him and she had returned to her place of birth which was called Magdala.

"This liaison cost him the priesthood that he had desired. Caiaphas became the High Priest and Caiaphas greatly loved the Roman rule, admired those who governed the country and had reduced many of its people to rabble. Your husband knew that he stood little chance against such collusion and yet he worked hard for those who desired to be free.

"The circumstances that surrounded the life that Joseph led with his wife and the affair which occurred fairly briefly and resulted in the birth of a daughter had quite profound repercussions throughout the years and disturbed Joseph much because he had a great sense of family obligation and love for his family and he realised that in showing his humanity and vulnerability he had jeopardised the family life.

"He made Mary of Magdala as comfortable as he possibly could and took great care of her. Although the initial feelings that had motivated his actions had subsided he realised the importance of having brought a life into being. This child should be protected and he had the influence and the ability to protect her and for the remainder of the mother's life the daughter was cared for. She was aware of his affection but she did not have his presence and at no time were you asked to release your legal husband so as to permit him to be with the mother. He would not have done this realising his responsibilities and having spiritual principles which guided his life. All men are open to temptation especially in a marriage arranged without initial love. But love grows and respect grows, the joining together and producing children brings about respect and admiration in Eastern people unknown in the west. It is understood by the men that they must take charge of their families who are not subservient to them, but respect them and their ideals and their direction and that they are responsible for all the children born to them. This you would understand totally being the wife of an elder who took full responsibilities to his family, it would not have been considered necessary to ask that this position was relinquished."

Miriam and Mary the Mother of Jesus.

"You and Mary were very close being both mothers with young children. Your son Josephes and Yeshua were as brothers and loved each other deeply. They thought as one person; the anguish which was Yeshua's was also the anguish which was Josephes and Josephes ended his life very soon after his cousin's death.

"As a child and a young man Yeshua was very close to the entire Arimathean family. He would visit often - the only time that He was at a distance from them was when He was in India. It was Josephes great regret that he was withheld from travelling with Yeshua and being His companion. However, as we said earlier, another close friend who had been accepted into the family accompanied Him in his place, as Josephes was busy with the estate and the family and as the senior son could not be spared.

"You often would speak to Yeshua and his thoughts were again often yours and you would discuss these thing with Mary His mother. She was very young, very innocent and you would counsel her and help her to understand that which lay ahead for her first born. There were other children that followed Him but never were they as close nor meant so much to her as her first born special son. It was the same with you, for although you loved your other children, to you Josephes was very special. His younger brother was completely different in his nature and needed much love and gentleness, which you gave to him, but Josephes to you was almost his father. He looked like him, spoke like him, had the same commitment and often the same arrogance, but he could give to you all the love that you desired and though unfortunately for a period of time this love was withheld, he was of your womb and of your heart."

Chapter 15

Joseph's family

In July 1990 an Englishman was given a past life in which he was Josephes - the elder son of Joseph of Arimathea. Over the next four years as he recalled more and more details of that life he returned to the Master for guidance and for confirmation or otherwise of what he had remembered. The Master supplied him with more and more information and the following are extracts from twelve tapes.

Josephes - the elder son.
Master: "Two thousand years ago there were many who sought to serve - those who became the Disciples, the Apostles and those who waited upon the Christ and His family. There were those also who could not understand Christ's teachings largely because of the difficulties of living under Roman occupation. It was a time of great cruelty. Only the elders of the Temple were given any freedom and even they were limited in the teachings that they could give to those that sought counselling and help from them. The soul of he who speaks to you was one of those in the Temple. There were many who sought help from the elders that their lives might be uplifted and not depressed by the laws of the land and the indecencies that were forced upon the labourers and other human beings. We sought to comfort and give love to those who sought our wisdom for it was a time of little liberty and great hatred.

"Christ's family was numerous. The man Jesus had brothers, sisters and cousins. There was one who was very close indeed to Yeshua, his mother's uncle, Joseph of Arimathea. The soul of that man was within you for you were his elder son. In many ways you were able to listen as Yeshua expressed His fears about that which was to be placed upon His shoulders. He did not feel that it was possible to go through life being so totally aware, as He was, of His ultimate fate, experiencing many times the death pangs that would be, and many times He entreated his Higher Consciousness for the burden to be taken from him. When His fear was greatest He would turn to those he loved. The Disciples looked upon Him as a Rabboni - a Master - and He had to be strong for them and to teach them. For His own strength and upliftment He had to turn to those who knew Him as a man and not as a God. It was then that Yeshua would turn to his family and beyond the immediate family to the greater family. You were of the same age and brought up together to play as young children. Who else could He turn to for comfort and acceptance of Himself as a man and not a God? When you learnt that Yeshua had died upon the cross you wept as others wept but you were as helpless as all of us. He could not avoid the ultimate fate for it was His karma*, and all have karma, and all must accept it and use it for their advancement and not seek to evade it.

"Yours was not a long life, for having been wrenched apart from one whom you loved as a brother you walked into the Sea of Galilee. The waters closed over your head and you joined many others in the spirit world who had rejoiced in Yeshua's company, companionship and teaching. It was a long time before you returned again to the Earth, but there must be many material lives as well as spiritual lives for the soul to learn greatly and distinguish the true value of what is to be learned from one life to another. Always remember it is often as important to be a cog in the wheel as to be the wheel itself. Without that cog the wheel cannot turn."

* Karma can also be expressed as 'destiny'. It seems difficult for man to think of karma without immediately thinking of something he has 'earned' through misdeeds. Karma may be good or bad, but also the destiny which the soul seeks out in order to learn or, as in the case of the Christ, simply to help man to progress.

Josephes' education and boyhood.
Master: "It was a prosperous home and those that lived there wanted for nothing. Like their father the children were versed in Hebrew and Greek and as they grew older they were instructed as to how the languages came into existence - their roots and the loom on which they were woven. Also they were taught to appreciate the beauty of Aramaic which Yeshua spoke at home more than Hebrew.

"Your grandfather was a man of great warmth and it was from him that Joseph learned to relate to his family and children in a much more personal way than most fathers of that time. There was no segregation in the family between the girls and the boys as was usually the case in Jewish homes. Both the girls of your grandfather's family and your sister - the first born - were given the same love and understanding as the boys. Very often in Jewish families the girls were kept separate and had very little honour bestowed upon them but this was not the case with Joseph's daughter. The family would meet in the house in Arimathea which was very large with many rooms. It was fairly close to the coast and the children would learn to enjoy sailing small boats and under supervision would be allowed to go and fish. They also liked to watch the merchant vessels entering the port and putting to sea laden with different goods collected through the land. They particularly enjoyed seeing the merchant vessels return with a cargo of beautiful silks from India and China. Joseph clothed his family and himself in these wonderful materials.

"The holidays on Cyprus were also happy family occasions. Children from neighbouring estates were encouraged to come and play as otherwise the children would be thrown upon their own resources and might have become narrow and selfish. So other children, whether poor or rich, would come and bring variation into their lives. It was in this way that many long lasting friendships were made. The house was large and very airy, there was a roof upon which people would sit and enjoy the breezes from the ocean. There was a garden around the house with low shrubs, plants and trees planted for their shade and beauty; steps cut into the rock face of the cliff led to a private beach where the children would play. There was one place which was particularly pleasurable, it was a stretch of beach where small boats were moored and where the family would take the children some half mile off shore to fish and to swim in the sea around the boat. They were not allowed to go without an adult accompanying them. It was extremely beautiful, very quiet and peaceful. Besides a place to tie up the small boats that were used for local fishing, there was a small port just around the bay where were moored the larger boats which would bring the family from the mainland. There were also workshops where the boats would be repaired if they had been damaged in a storm or simply for attending to their general wear and tear. That area was out of sight of the house. Both you and Yeshua enjoyed the freedom in Cyprus which was not occupied by the Romans* for it was always difficult for the freedom loving people of Jerusalem to accept the occupation. Friends of Joseph in Greece gave him a small piece of land there and when he needed to stay on business he would occasionally take the children, especially the two boys, so that they could enjoy the classical beauty of that part of the world."

"So the time of growing up was both joyous and studious, both you and your brother received private tuition at home in basic studies. When you were older you were taken to the Temple in Jerusalem and there you were taught important historic facts and the ancient Torah which was so important in the life of Joseph. One of the elders of the temple, a teacher called Ezekiel, (not to be confused with the Old Testament prophet Ezekiel) was not only very learned in all matters of Jewish belief but very knowledgeable as to what students should learn and how it would help them in their chosen path, both materially and spiritually. Ezekiel would oversee the spiritual education of many of the young men who were contemplating the life of the priesthood. He could recognise if those who were brought to him by their parents would be truly suitable for this role or whether they were better fitted for other things and it took usually less than a year of communication with these young people to be able to decide their future potential. It was Joseph's wish that you entered the Sanhedrin to continue the family tradition. From very early childhood Joseph desired to devote himself to the service of God despite his father's opposition and it was because of this that he realised the devastating influence a parent can have over a child's spiritual growth and personality. Therefore Joseph always endeavoured to allow his children freedom of expression and choice and it was initially to his sadness that you did not truly believe or understand much of the truths that you were taught both within the family and in school. So Joseph accepted the desires of his son and the recommendation of the teacher who could see that the talents and the energies of both the sons should be directed in a different way than Joseph himself.

"There was a very brief time when you looked favourably upon the daughter of Ezekiel, but as is often the way it was a passing phase - a young man aware of his manhood.

"There were visits to small synagogues on feast days when the whole family would be together. Although it was only the men who

---

* Cyprus was of course ruled from Rome in the same way as Palestine, but there was no occupying Roman army. Cyprus was free from restraint as long as those who dwelt on the island and had ruling powers there conformed to certain rules and regulations laid down by Rome. As there were no uprisings there was freedom of speech, of movement and a state of wellbeing amongst the inhabitants.

could take part in the different rituals they would share what took place with vivid descriptions and all enjoyed the beautiful decoration in the Temple and synagogues at these times. Yeshua would also be there with His two younger brothers and also the older brothers from His father's first marriage. They would all discuss not only the many forms of teaching and beliefs but other religious beliefs and ways of life. Narrowness was actively discouraged and friendships with other peoples was encouraged. The servants were more friends than servants and would serve well and loyally because they were aware of the love and the responsibility that was given to them. Many of these have reincarnated and we have spoken to them so that they are aware of the part they played during that important time.

"There were times when you were young that Joseph would go into the desert and camp there for several days. There would be burning heat by day and severe chill by night and you would pull your blanket around you and desire to return to the warmth of your home. Your father would say to you "warmth and chill are an attitude of mind, imagine that the sun glows within your blanket and you will be warm" You would then sleep contentedly for your imagination was strong when you were young.

"Joseph himself particularly loved the desert therefore he did not spend much time in Cyprus, but his family would spend many months there especially during the intense heat of the summer. Where they lived in Jerusalem it was extremely hot and dusty and difficult to relax there and gain any real refreshment ,even though there was a beautiful garden which had been made at the side of the house and extended towards an olive grove and beyond to the hillside. The children as they grew would love to wander in that garden."

Josephes - a personal profile.

"In height and build Josephes was like yourself, but perhaps a little less tall. He had the 'Arimathean blue eyes' - every member of the family had similar coloured eyes - olive skin, with very black straight hair and jet black eyebrows, high cheekbones and a fairly short and pointed beard. His strong mouth could easily laugh and be joyous. The hands were strong, and yet gentle to touch and he loved to mould and change that which he touched. They were healing hands which could bring quietness and peace to a fevered brow. His favourite clothing was brown in colour and underneath it would be a simple white garment of cotton or silk but the cloak that he wore around his shoulders would be brown. On his head would often be a bright colour chosen from the variety of patterns of silks which were his father's joy. He too loved the desert and the peace that it represented and when he laughed it was deep and true and unyielding. He was extremely loyal to the family and especially to his cousin Yeshua, but some of that loyalty was misplaced. He was inclined to submerge his personality in those that he admired. He felt a lesser person If he could not be the same as they and emulate what they did. He did not realise that his own personality was fine, mature and strong. Although he was admired greatly by his wife and children and was the elder son, because he felt his father's position was greater than that which he could achieve, and that other members of the family had greater spiritual purpose, he felt he could not take his place in the society of the family in the way expected. This of course led to the many things which eventually terminated his life.

"You have much the same personality and mental attributes in this life as you did in that one. To think deeply, with great awareness, great sensitivity and a feeling of anger that arises from being deliberately misled: in fact the thought of being deceived raises as much anger in this life as it did then. These are positive attributes and not weakness.

"Your task within this present life is not so arduous as it was at that time and it is of course another aspect of the soul that dwells within you, albeit one that has deep memory and understanding of that time. That aspect within yourself will share and teach and be heightened in awareness regarding the spiritual attributes of living, and this as time passes will be even more relevant than it is today. We leave you now to meditate upon our words."

A deep childhood memory.

As a young boy in Jerusalem 'Josephes' had a clear memory of seeing his mother tending the back of his father Joseph who seemed to have been beaten. When he asked the Master if this memory had any validity the Master replied as follows.

Master: "Part of the doctrine of the Jewish faith did at one time contain an element of scourging. As far as we are aware this practice has been discontinued although in some smaller sects in Jewish communities in some eastern countries such practices may well continue. Certain questions would be asked of those entering the Sanhedrin or synagogues as Rabbis and if the responses were not as decreed by the learned ones - those steeped in the mysticism of the truth as revealed through Moses - then a rope would be brought down upon the bare flesh of the back. The idea was that those that were sincere in their desire to move forward in the teachings should study every aspect of Jewish Law and be proficient in explaining it. Very little licence was allowed to those who could not remember or considered that any part of the law need not be strictly adhered to. The back of Joseph of Arimathea was lashed three times during his initiation and we feel it is this incident that has evoked the memory that you describe."

Jealousies between Josephes and his brother.

"Although Josephes was the elder son he always felt that the younger son held the first place in his father's heart. The younger son (Eliazar) was a visionary and someone who, if his father could have chosen differently would have been emulated by Joseph. Eliazar had an innocent belief in life and spiritual things which Joseph could not believe in because of his upbringing and the rigid discipline in his life. It was the same with Josephes who had been born as the result of an arranged marriage and not one of love. However there was great respect between the parents and had Josephes paused to reflect he would have realised that respect is worthier than passion.

"Although Eliazar was the typical visionary of that family Josephes had his moments of vision and inner depth. His father recognised how insecure his elder son was when faced with issues in life that made it difficult for him either to turn away from his responsibilities or accept them in the way that was expected of him. Had the roles of the brothers been interchangeable from a hereditary viewpoint, as well as their personalities it is possible that Eliazar would have accepted the yoke of family responsibilities with all its pressures with more enthusiasm than did Josephes.

"There was very often sibling jealousy between the two brothers. It was not true that Eliazar was the favourite son and as he grew older his very fine delicate qualities became more in line with the realities of the life he led, and when he aligned himself to the Zealots it was as if he accepted his ascetic nature because of the things that occurred in his life.

"Josephes was much more the son of his father, a similar dedication, loyalty and desire to give to those who were dependent on him everything that he could to establish their security. It was only extreme anguish with its fear and disillusionment that led him to take his life, almost with a lack of awareness that he also bore with him his child. To those that have not gone through these traumas it is not easy to understand, but if he had overcome that sense of desertion and fear and realised the extenuating circumstances that encircled every action in the scenario then of course much of the life of the family would have been quite different."

Josephes relationship with Yeshua.

"Your relationship with Yeshua's family was similar to many other Jewish families, very close and united. Each member belonged to the greater family, so cousins and brothers and sisters were virtually one. Each were as acceptable in the house of their relations as they were in their own and would obey the instructions and parental discipline of their aunts and uncles as they would their mothers and fathers. At that time the Gentile families were much more separate units. The Jews often incorporated an immense family life, with mother and father figures outside their own natural parentage, and this ensured that a child who was orphaned would be as greatly loved as if he or she was with their natural parents. So it was not so strange that you, as Josephes, and the young Yeshua were so close. You were of a similar age and you both enjoyed the same things in nature, swimming and all the childish delights of life. Living so closely together and being so often in each other's homes was the most natural thing in the world. In fact you were closer to Yeshua than to Eliazar, for when there is both a difference in age and nature a younger brother does not generally play the role of a confidant. This you enjoyed with Yeshua who had great wisdom. However you had strength, will power and vision and He would lean upon you. You were able to communicate well and would often spend many hours, in the tranquil countryside around Jerusalem, discussing your ideas.

"Joseph's family were protected - in a spiritual sense - by their membership and strong belief in the Essenes. The children were influenced by the classical Essene beliefs and dependency one upon another.

"As there was in that life, so in this one, there is a great deal of the strength and purpose of the Christ within you. To say that Yeshua was a rebel is not quite an accurate portrayal of a young man who demanded more of himself than others would accept at that stage in life. In addition there was foreknowledge of His death at a time when most men would be looking forward to fruition of their labours and a gradual winding down of the more difficult aspects of life. As a close cousin of Yeshua you shared His idealism and desired greatly to be part of His life and His ministry and to share His gifts, which you did not. Episodes in your life showed you the almost jealous way you had of wanting to be able to prove yourself in the same way as He did as He matured. You felt that you did not have His advantages because you had a strong father who desired the best from his children while seeming to give them the liberty to decide for themselves. On the other hand Yeshua's father was much older and had relinquished his responsibilities to the younger Arimathean for he had recognised in Joseph one who had the strength and ability to guard and protect His son.

"In this present life, especially at this time, there is still within you a great deal of Josephes' knowledge of Christ and His dual character of strength and sensitivity which you have learned in this life to handle extremely well. You admired Yeshua so much that there was sometimes a little conflict between you. He had a much more advanced Higher-Self, largely through His mother's previous lives- (His father was not part of His Higher-Self) and His Christing in maturity. He had therefore that sense of the deep understanding of the needs of others which you have never quite achieved."

Josephes and Mary Magdalene.

"You may have wondered if you actually met Mary Magdalene and if you were aware of her relationship with your brother and also her ministering to Jesus. She was indeed one of His followers and most devout. At that time she did not know that they were cousins for she was simply aware of Him as a teacher and a man of great strength and ability and His setting aside of orthodox beliefs appealed to her nature. She had been brought to Jerusalem apparently as the wife of a Roman officer and was indeed very popular. There were many in the area who admired her and sought her as a friend but there were also those who, more rigid in principle, disapproved of her marrying one of the occupying force. So there were those who were her genuine friends and those who wished to stab her in the back given the opportunity. She had a fairly enjoyable social life as did many others who lived in the vicinity. There were many opportunities to meet socially particularly at weddings and on one occasion she had been invited to a marriage of a woman friend with a man who was known to the Arimathean family. It was usual for the whole family to attend such celebrations and you travelled from Cyprus with your wife and child. It was there that you met but you were not involved with her, however there was a vague feeling of kinship and recognition expressed in her gestures and looks, for with her dark skin she was very like her father; her mother being much fairer. It was shortly after that her husband was sent back to Rome and your brother became unwittingly involved with her, but that is another story."

Josephes and Simon Peter.

"Jewish families were often interrelated, this was because of their mode of life and the limitations they imposed as to whom they were allowed to marry. The families of Yeshua, the Arimathean and Simon Peter were all related. In addition Yeshua shared the same Higher-Self as Simon Peter, the latter being the masculine element and Yeshua being the feminine - the more gentle element of that soul. Both were extremely close to one another and yet there could be antagonism and fear between them. There was a similar situation between yourself and Yeshua because when Yeshua did not share something with you He would share it with Peter and your nature was such that to share Him, for whom you had an intense love and understanding, was as a physical pain. You admired the great stature and strength of Simon Peter and even his coarseness of spirit - for he was a fisherman. So there was certainly admiration and not a little in the way of personal jealousy."

Josephes' anger and frustration.

"You were still quite young and one of your children was but a few months old. You had a great love for that child and had decided to dedicate the life of that child not only to Judaism, which was of course your inheritance, but to the frank and open teachings of your cousin Yeshua and to the meaning of life that He portrayed. You felt that the one thing you wanted to give to this child was your openness to the reality of these teachings. When you learnt that Yeshua had been crucified you blamed your father totally for this action for you had no knowledge that Joseph had been detained at the house of Caiaphas and was not in the Sanhedrin to offer his dissent to the decision of the elders. In any case Joseph could not have altered the tide of events however much he desired to do so and of course he had the knowledge of Yeshua's death and the part that it would play in the development of mankind for thousands of years to come. Joseph had not shared this with his family, or indeed with any one else, for if he had shared it with you it might have made a difference to your actions and your anger and desire for self destruction. For you felt that if you could not be with Yeshua and share His life and teachings you would rather be with Him in death. This clouded anger you portrayed to your father who with his own grief, his own self condemnation of not being able to persuade the elders of the Sanhedrin to withhold their judgment of Yeshua took refuge in the desert. You then decided to teach him the ultimate lesson by destroying not only yourself but your beloved son.

"It was because you felt that not enough had been done to procure the pardon and release of your cousin Yeshua that produced the great emotion and feeling of inadequacy. It is not only anger but helplessness in situations that cause people to do unwise things. Certainly with both brothers there was anger because there was also helplessness. The feeling that your father had not done more affected your own lives. It was to Joseph's great sadness that he could not speak to his sons to reassure them and to prevent them taking headstrong action which in both cases ended young and vibrant lives. Joseph loved his family deeply: his sons, daughters and grandchildren as they grew all had a place in his heart which can never truly be described. Each one was led along their path, was guided and uplifted by his strength. In some cases this lasted till their lives were completed, but in others it was not to be. Joseph's life was not an easy one but few truly spiritual lives are."

Josephes untimely death - was it really suicide?

"...that action may not have been entirely a death wish, it could have been a walking into water with the idea of cleansing, of purification, of allowing the self to be rid of the dark thoughts, fears, anger and anguish, but as so often happens Josephes got out of his depth and those waters can be very strong. Also the shore is notoriously rocky and uneven and it is easy to take a false step thus going deeper then intended; the water would then quickly close above the head, and remember you were carrying your young child so it would not have been easy to regain your balance. We do not feel, although we cannot be certain, that it was your intention to take your life or that of your son. There are many actions which lead eventually to a form of reconciliation in one way and condemnation in another, so do not dwell too harshly upon that aspect of that life.

"The bodies of both Josephes and his child were recovered and the usual period of mourning among Jewish families began. Their bodies were laid to rest in the tomb where Yeshua had been laid after the crucifixion. In Joseph of Arimathea's most troubled moments in his life he had never visualised that so soon after losing a beloved nephew he would lose a son.

"We have already mentioned (Chapter 9) that there was a very small secluded garden around the entrance of the tomb, it was indeed a quiet oasis of total beauty within the noisy often polluted area of Jerusalem. The utter calmness and peace of an area used for prayer and for healing. It was green, cool and peaceful and the grieving family would often go there to pray. There was a shrub very close to the door of the tomb which in the night air was heavy with perfume; at that time of the year it was in flower and added to the mystical feeling."

Ruth, the wife of Josephes.
In December 1991 a Colombian woman was given the following past life.

Master: "Josephes, the elder son of Joseph of Arimathea, was a rather unwilling partner to his father, just as Joseph had been to his own father. In his case he desired above all else the priesthood and to be a teacher and an Elder, but he had been an obedient son and he expected some of that obedience from his elder son. Josephes travelled widely with him and when his cousin and close associate Yeshua visited India Josephes went to Cyprus to manage the business there. He lived on the big estate which was run by many servants who were the friends and companions of Joseph. During his time there, of his own freewill and desire, he met the daughter of a business associate, a merchant man who in his own life had desired riches with power and responsibility without due thought of those who worked for him and with him. Now this man had two daughters. The soul of one of those daughters is an aspect of your own soul therefore your knowledge of her is within your total soul and will thus be remembered as we speak.

"As was the way with the Jewish families at that time, similar to many of the Cypriots and Greeks and other members of eastern countries, you had been betrothed at birth to the son of another business associate in order that the riches of the families would be enhanced and would go forth in time and prosper. You had reached puberty. Your wedding would soon be arranged and as was the way at that time would take many days before the nuptials would take place. You were already prepared for this event. You had never met him to whom you were to be espoused but you had met Josephes.

Instantly there was love between you and great desire. Josephes began to court you and you returned his feelings. You went to your father and pleaded that the marriage between you and the son of his business associate be cancelled. So great was his anger that you were imprisoned in your room and told that this marriage must take place. You did not realise what was entailed at that time, what great riches your father could lose through allowing you to break the alliance and had you known you would not have cared for your heart reached out to Josephes. You loved him deeply and had already given yourself to him. You were not aware of it but you were already with child.

"The nuptials took place and then when the marriage was to be consummated your husband realised he had been cheated. So great was his anger that he left the house and went straight to your father and put a knife through his heart. Your father was virtually innocent, he had no way of knowing what had passed between you and Josephes, although as a man of knowledge and intellect he should have been aware of your great love. However men at that time seldom listened to the women within the family for they were but chattels.

"Joseph of Arimathea went speedily to Cyprus to be with his son and to protect his family from any other repercussions, but none were to come. You had remained silent. You had admitted union, with your agreement and desire. In many areas of the world such an act of infamy would be followed by death but your husband had taken his revenge on your father therefore he desired revenge no more. The marriage was immediately annulled and you were sent away. Naturally Josephes sought you, brought you back to the estate where you gave birth to a son and eventually became betrothed to and married Josephes.

"Your life together was not a very long one but during that time you were very happy with Josephes and bore him another son and these children were much loved and revered by Joseph as his grandchildren as were the children of his other offspring. When the trial of Yeshua took place and he was first scourged and then condemned to death upon the cross Joseph went to plead for His release and was detained by Caiaphas, who would not allow his release in case he brought pressure to bear to prevent the crucifixion. Josephes was in Cyprus at the time and heard of the crucifixion but only heard that his father had seemingly played no part in the prevention of this heinous crime. He brought you and the children to Jerusalem and there he confronted his father with rage and anger.

"Already the resurrection had taken place. The etheric body of Jesus had manifested and He was thus able to continue His work before the Ascension. Again Josephes was not aware of this. In his great grief and anger he committed suicide by allowing himself to be drowned in the Sea of Galilee. You were taken into the home of Joseph and there protected, loved, guarded and your children brought up as the other children and grandchildren of Joseph.

"All the family of Joseph have reincarnated in this life. They have been born in many areas of the world that they may learn through progress in the present life the continuance of the soul itself, but it is also part of their heritage that they should know the part played and the love that surrounded Jesus as well as all the other families that were so close and so in harmony together. But the life that you lead now has its own particular purpose. It is greatly needed for your soul that you may be stronger and have greater clarity in your understanding of yourself. It is in the overcoming that progress occurs, in being able to accept those things in life which are sent to destroy, transforming them to allow them to be of beauty. This is the resurrection of the soul, the transforming of seeming death into the reality of life and this will be yours. The turning point is now. When you go forth from this place it will be with renewed energy, renewed determination to overcome that which has sought to destroy you and failed. Hold on to this; realise the truth of what we say. It has failed, it has allowed the determination within you to grow stronger."

Note: This last paragraph, a part of a very personal message relevant to her life today, has been included to give an idea of the true purpose of these trance sessions. The fact that we do not know what is being referred to is irrelevant. It should be remembered that in all these talks the Master is essentially speaking to the soul.

Eliazar, the second son - nicknamed Eli.
In June 1991 the following past life was given to an Austrian.

Master: "You already have awareness through your deep understanding of many things that took place at the time of Christ and we can confirm that you, as our younger son, were indeed he whom you feel you were. We referred to you by the nickname Eli - the diminutive. Several in the family bore the name Eliazar. It was indeed a family name on your mother's side. It was the way of Jewish families at that time to name the first born with the father's family name. Therefore your elder brother was called Josephes and you were called Eliazar after your maternal grandfather, a man of importance both intellectually and spiritually and a one - time leader of the law of the Sanhedrin.

"Joseph loved both his sons greatly. Josephes was strong both of intellect and body and would do his bidding. But you were a visionary - very similar to yourself in this life. As a young child you were so dreamy, so unable to relate to that taking place in the surroundings of your home, so deeply moved by the division between your father and mother with a desire within to be a peacemaker and to bring together those whom you loved most dearly.
Yet karma, as well as circumstances chose the path of all concerned both individually and as a family. The true division came not from the alliance between the father Joseph and Mary of Magdala but as a result of your birth. Your soul nearly returned to spirit and so did that of your mother. For a long while Joseph's strength kept him at the side of his family with undivided love but flesh is human, as you have found out. This cannot be denied and is part of life's experience. Who is Man to judge whom to love or not love when the heart is involved and when desire is deep and flaming within each?

"Your childhood was as gentle as your nature demanded. You would travel with your father to the desert, you would listen to the words of the Essenes and they fired great hope and longing within your breast. You listened also to the words of John the Baptist so that your faith might be cemented in both mind and soul. It was the one united action within the family that brought blessings to all. Your mother had become divided within her intent and her mind had become clouded with her fears and anxieties. Yet she was protected and greatly cherished, but women at that time were so indoctrinated with that which they should and must do which society demanded of them that it could become a mental trauma, especially if the partner in life had understanding and sympathy for the feelings of the person. Joseph, your father, always had gentleness within his passion.

"At the time of puberty - as indeed at the time of all youths when they reached that point in life where responsibilities would be placed upon their shoulders - you were ordered to leave home, as indeed were all boys, in order to prove your strength and reliability. We use the word "ordered" advisedly. Because of your gentleness of spirit, your vision, your gentleness, you had evaded responsibilities and also evaded being apart from your parents, brothers and sister for long periods of time. Even when with the Essenes you would long to return. You would wait for your father to appear on the skyline and would run to meet him. You were already into manhood and it was imperative that you should be strengthened in order to survive . To walk into the desert with barely sufficient sustenance for the journey was decided by yourself - no one sent you. In communion with your Higher Self you felt strong enough for the journey and it was upon that journey that you first met Sarah who would become your wife.

"During times of absence while much was occurring within Sarah you were indeed about your father's business, becoming more aware of your responsibilities and your growing strength, yet still retaining that gentleness and understanding within you which were your heritage. Chivalry also - you were your father's son - and in the same way that your father had cared for and nurtured both his affianced wife and Mary of Magdala so you too would remain faithful to Sarah and also to one other whom you also loved. That was a fleeting relationship and again came at a time of pressure, anxiety and fear. There are often times when the burdens of life are so great that those who are the closest cannot be the best companions. It is at these times that another enters life, with the shoulder upon which to weep, the bosom as the pillow and the body as the calming culmination of love. You were, and are, no different from other men, so do not look backwards or forward but live in the now and understand that which is of the heart can only be Truth.

"For many years you were a man devoted to your family and then came a time of great trauma within the land, as has indeed been reflected at this time, so similar in many ways to conflict between one tribe and another and one race and another. Such great desire for the homeland, for the vision of Judea within the heart and the great desire that indeed the Maitreya may come, find calming peace within a warring nation and bring the words of God in strength and majesty to the people of Zion. It cannot be so in life. Freewill denies it and even those blessed with the Christos are of flesh and thereby have weakness of the flesh, desires of the body, great visions, great purpose but they are mortal, they cannot survive the knife-thrust, the gallows and death. We will not tell you of the manner of your death but simply that you joined those Zealots who had great love and heart and power for that which they felt was good. You became separated from your family. Your father Joseph never ceased to sorrow at the loss of his dearly beloved son for indeed you perished as many others perished in the cause of Light. This is the story, hold it close within you. Eli is close within your Higher Self and many of your actions reflect his guidance and his help. He learned through experience, as so many do, and his influence is good within your soul. We see this reflected in not only your thoughts, your speech, your actions but also in your appearance - never more so than now - but you might well in the future be tempted to give your life for that which you feel is Truth; only if you do, listen well to the soul of Eli and turn away. It is not your way within this life to sacrifice."

Sarah - the wife of Eliazar.
In May 1991 an Englishwoman was given the following past life.

Master: "You were born in a very small hamlet called Urca in Palestine. Everyone there was related one to another. Vast areas of land made them secluded within themselves. A building, which served as a hermitage, stood a short distance away upon a natural hill of stones and rock. So small was this dwelling, that only one Holy Man could live in it, using it to sleep, to pray and to do all the natural healing work for all who passed by. Aeons of time ago it had been a road that travellers used to go from one area of Palestine to another. It was a place of refuge, with a natural spring with constantly flowing water, shelter from the sun and gentle, loving hands over the ages to cure, to bring light and peace to the troubled and to the sick. As one Holy Man would reach the fulfilment of his years another, multi-lingual man would be brought to that place and would live there constantly looking within for light, speaking only when a traveller would pass. Below this natural rock formation was a deep pit and beyond that four or five small dwellings also of rock and stone simple to the point of barely existing as homes, one open room, mats upon the floor, a place to cook just outside in the open and yet the coolness of those dwellings which stood facing away from the sun cannot be described. As the children were born and as they grew so more dwellings were built until at the time of your birth there were about twelve such dwellings clustered around bringing refuge and peace to those who looked upon them and each person had their own purpose. They would go forth daily to look into the distance from the top of the hill and see if anyone ailed upon the road and if they saw a sick person dying from thirst or hunger or exposure several would go forth. They would bring back that person and first they would be taken to the small refuge or hermitage, whatever name you desire to give, and there once resuscitated would be taken in to a dwelling and gradually rehabilitated into life before continuing on their journey.

"You were born a female child, the only child of your parents who had already lived many years. Your mother was considered barren and rejoiced when knowing that she was with child, then full of fear that it might perhaps be an illusion because of the depth of her need but when she came to her full time and you were born the whole community rejoiced. You were taken to the Holy man and blessed and you were given the name of Sarah. You grew to a young woman never having gone beyond the tall hill overlooking the plains. Several times as a young child you would return speaking of a traveller who was exhausted and likely to walk into the desert where he might die. And the men would go forth and would return. Not all of these people were ailing or ill some just weary with their travel.

"You were affianced to one of the young men within the group. There had been no intimacy between you - you were still too young but it was understood that he would partner you and you were content. One day you saw a traveller. The steps were coming very slowly and there was a place upon that plain where many were overtaken by the heat and the lack of water, perhaps for days and instead of walking straight would begin to walk in a circle. You and others would watch for this and as this person approached you ran back and the rescue party went forward.

"He was quite a young man. He was not yet fully bearded, slim in frame and his skin was quite dark. His eyes were brilliant and yet tired. He held on to the men who half supported him and then carried him the last few yards to the refuge. For several days he was ill with fever. It was then the duty of the women to sponge him down and press between the lips such moisture as could be taken. At one time he was near to death but he recovered and in due course was taken into your simple dwelling where your parents administered to him and where you continued to help and talk with him. He was a young man acquainted with several dialects and soon you found together the right mode of speech that you could understand one another and you felt a deep stirring within you, a response to his need. When the time came for him to continue upon his journey there were tears. It was hard for him as well as for you.

"Two years passed and you had come to the full ripening of your beauty. The nuptials were arranged, a time of rejoicing for the wedding breakfast would be held, a new home had been built and you and your partner would be taken to this place and left together to know each other and be fulfilled. But you dreaded this moment for your heart was filled with love for the young traveller. Your mind called to him wherever he was to return and to give voice to his feelings that you might know whether you might hope or not, or whether you must take your fate and live with the man chosen to be your partner, with whom you did not share the same ideals, the same feeling of oneness as you felt you had experienced with the traveller.

"On the very eve of the nuptials he returned. He had grown. He was barely recognisable for the youth who had passed that way before. He did not need to return along that road. His planned journey would have brought him back to Jerusalem on an alternative route. He had with him several animals that bore many bales of silk and other things for trade. Many he distributed with love in his heart to the small community for he had originally come without his purse. But he returned with his purse full and he was told that the wedding that would take place was planned for the early hours before the heat of the day. You looked together one upon the other. Your eyes pleaded. He spoke with your parents of the love that he had felt within his heart for the young girl throughout the many months when he had been growing into manhood while travelling and being about his father's business of trade, that his father was one who had not believed in his son's love so young before emotions could be well formed. His father however was an enlightened man and much loved by those who served with and beneath him.

"Your parents were appalled for they felt that which was planned must take place. The young man went across the divide of the deep pit and up the rock face to the temple and spent many hours with the Holy Man. You feared greatly that he would not return that he would pass by on his route back to Jerusalem without even a wave; but he did return. You had very few belongings. That which you needed you put in a sack on the back of his donkey. You were lifted upon it and the sorrowing community silently watched you leave. The young man whom you should have wed left the community and was not seen again. His pride had been severely hurt. He could not raise his head in the community with their beliefs and their rigid principles. He too saw the Holy Man, received his instructions and then departed.

"You were taken by the traveller on the long weary route to Jerusalem. Several nights were spent in the open, sheltered only by the cloths which he carried and by the warm bodies of the animals. There was rejoicing when you arrived at the place where his family lived. Without question you were welcomed and immediately preparations for the nuptials were set in motion. You were introduced to the brother of the traveller, so totally unlike the man you now loved so deeply, but who had held you in respect for your youth and your virginity until he had the blessing of his family.

"The wedding took place and for a long while you lived in the home of the family. It was a large house with many rooms. The elder brother and his wife lived in one part, the father who at that time dwelt alone lived in another. His wife of many years, respected but not loved, dwelt with her daughter who had not yet chosen who she desired to wed (for indeed the father had an open mind and was in many ways a rebel in his society believing in the free will of man in its totality). You were wondrously happy. The first child that you bore was a son and there was great rejoicing. The second child lived but a few hours and the whole family mourned for her. Your husband's father went into the desert. He was there many days praying to Jehovah for the soul of the child and he also communed with an angel and realised even more deeply the love and the light that was to come eventually to the world. You had another child and he grew to fruition and they both brought great light and love into the home. As they grew they would mix with other members of the family, among them Yeshua their cousin.

"It remains to tell you that the traveller - your husband - was the younger son, Eliazar, of Joseph of Arimathea."

The affair with Mary Magdalene.

In the life of Eliazar the Master mentions "one other whom you also loved." This refers to Eliazar's love affair with Mary Magdalene, and in August 1993 the Master was asked if he would reveal the events leading up to the separation of Sarah and Eliazar.

Master: "As we have already stated initially there was happiness and peace between them. They enjoyed greatly the life that was provided for them by the father - the patriarch - Joseph of Arimathea. They lived under his guidance, he greatly loved his family and provided for them well and Sarah was very content with this. Content also with the children that she bore and their radiance and light, which added much to the dimension of your life. However Eliazar was of a different character, of a brooding nature, always aware of what lay ahead and yet feeling his inadequacy to move towards it and be fulfilled. In many ways he resented what his father gave so willingly, he envied him that which he had inherited and felt he was able to give because he had the abundance and affluence which he, Eliazar, desired to acquire, so that he too could share it and allow his family to be independent - to lead a separate existence. Josephes again was of a different nature. He accepted what was given gladly, but also used his gifts in order to be individual and separate in his life. The two brothers shared a great love for their father, but they were quite different in their nature - Josephes being more joyous and Eliazar feeling that as the youngest in the family others had been chosen before him. It was this trait in his nature that began to erode the closeness between you two. He even became jealous of his children, their closeness with their mother and with the other children in the family as they were born, and became desperate to seek his own individuality, his own ability. He tried to be successful in the family work but it was not what he desired to do, therefore his abilities fell short of perfection.

"It was at this time that he became interested in the work and life of John the Baptist, always close to the family, except for a period when he was travelling. Eliazar admired John's fire, his exuberance, his magnetic personality. Although he was somewhat wild - looking, John the Baptist had a personality that was unparalleled and when he spoke, those who idolised him sat spellbound. Often Eliazar would go and listen to messages that were as of hell fire, that fell from the lips of his cousin. Although he deeply loved Yeshua he felt that Yeshua missed many opportunities, that His more gentle and subdued nature - although when this flowed it could be just as dramatic - was not closely akin to that of John. Eventually he went to live in John's house. John felt he had potential to continue his work and taught him how to baptise and cleanse sins. Both were aware of John the Baptist's purpose and how eventually when Yeshua returned from India He would be Christed by John in Baptism. Eliazar desired greatly to be present at this also, but at this time his father felt that he needed again to be at home for he depended upon him in many ways.

"It was with reluctance that Eliazar returned home. At that time the chasm between you and Joseph started to grow and you began to live your own life with the other women of the household and your children. Then Eliazar turned for comfort in other directions about which you have been told. He did not however at any time until he was told by his father realise the closeness of the family bond between himself and Mary Magdalene whom he had grown to love. This was the final straw to Eliazar. He felt he could stand no more, that so much had been withheld from him, which if he had known and understood would have added to his strength. He thought that he could have been his father's confidant and perhaps have taken some of his burden had Joseph been more open with him. It was with this anger Eliazar left home and returned to the house of John the Baptist who at that time was banding together a group of Zealots whom he hoped would go forth and continue his own teachings. But because of events of that time in the Roman Empire, these Zealots formed their own group to fight for the rights of the Jews instead of spreading the teaching of light - the teaching of the Way as planned and desired by John."

"A final question Master, was I, as Sarah, particularly close to any one member of Joseph's family?"

Master: "You had a warm loving relationship with Eliazar's mother. Her nature was of one of great gentleness, and understanding of the grief that can arise in the heart of a woman when she feels, for whatever reason, she is misunderstood or even spurned, and with the memory of her own marriage was able to guide her own daughter and daughter-in-law extremely well. You were also close to the wife of Josephes whenever you were together. You were very much alike and you enjoyed your children together. These children, of course, mixed freely with the children of Mary and Joseph. The family did not make distinctions between those born within the Family and those that were of the greater family. They would all mix and dwell in whichever home they were staying and often you and your children would stay with Mary - the Holy Mother - whom you loved and esteemed."

Rachel.
In 1991 an Englishwoman was given a past life as the daughter of Joseph. The revelations included her life in the Arimathean's family, her marriage and details of her son. Permission to reproduce these tapes has not been given.

A Grandchild.
Amos - the first born son of Josephes and Ruth.
In April 1992 the following past life was given to an Anglo-Danish man.

Master: "You were the eldest son of Eliazar and his wife Sarah born when they had not long been wed and were very happy together. For much of their married life they lived in one of the houses that Joseph lived in and owned. As a very young child the life of Amos was very little different from any other child born and raised in Palestine except that it was more sheltered. The family home was shared by the daughter and two sons of Joseph and Miriam. There was not independent living accommodation at that time and in a Jewish household the family was a unit and if the father had status in the community, like Joseph, the family would remain together possibly for the whole of their lives interrupted only by the older members returning to spirit. There were three homes but the one in Jerusalem was less inhabited and often Joseph was there on his own while the family was in Arimathea or Cyprus.

"The children of the Arimathean were educated firstly at home by individual teachers and tutors, then in the settlement of the Essenes at Qumran and ultimately in the Temple in Jerusalem. The grandchildren's education in the Temple stopped when Joseph resigned from the Sanhedrin after the crucifixion. However from the age of about six or seven you would have been at Qumran. The Essenes were of course an important institution and they wrote on Scrolls the history of Palestine as it took place. Famous figures like Caesar, Herod and Caiaphas would also write of what was happening and this was ultimately taken to Qumran where it was collated and stored. Most of the Scrolls that are decipherable are kept in the Vatican in Rome and are very gradually being translated and produced in book form. You learnt the Ancient Hebrew that was not used any more in Jerusalem. Aramaic was the language most used and most members of the family could speak Hebrew as it was then. You also had some knowledge of Greek and you studied the history of the Jewish nation and Jewish law and other forms of spiritual teaching not just that to do with your own inheritance, but from all beliefs. It was considered important that all mankind who had a common belief in God should understand each other's particular spiritual values, and Joseph above all other teachers felt this was of great importance.

"When you finished your education you returned to Cyprus and continued to live again in the family home with your mother. After your parents separated you continued to live there with your mother but from time to time the family would unite in Palestine particularly for spiritual functions. The very large estate in Cyprus which covered many miles of forest and coast and included a large dwelling has already been referred to. It served both as a holiday home for relaxation and a haven for safety especially at the time of the death of Christ when members of the family were being sought for revenge.

"You worked often because you enjoyed being on the estate amongst the trees, helping others to fashion furniture and other utilities from the fallen timber. This had to be done regularly in order to keep the forest land from being over-crowded and from the death of many trees due to that over-crowding. You were an artist who enjoyed taking timber and fashioning it in artifacts of ornament as well as toys for children. You have to bear in mind that this was two thousand years ago. The toys that you are aware of were not in existence and yet young children still had to enjoy and educate themselves and very often this would be through toys. You loved carving, and as a direct result of Yeshua's death made in His memory little wooden crosses that people could carry.

"You knew Yeshua when you were very young and He was already adult but He always loved to talk to children. He would teach them in His own way the simple truths of God's love, of creation and the purpose of life. There were times when He also would come to Cyprus. The whole family would meet there very often and spend a few months. It was cooler there than in Palestine. In the height of the hot weather in Palestine many would leave and go to a cooler clime and many of Joseph's family would meet in their home in Cyprus. Yeshua loved to go there also and He often went there before He began His studies in India and occasionally your other uncle and aunt would be there. It was sad that your mother and father soon began to have differences of opinion. You felt more in agreement with your father than you did with your mother in that life. You understood his frustrations. He always felt that he was the younger son and did not have the same responsibilities and possibilities as his elder brother - Josephes and he often felt that Josephes was more favoured by his father than he was. This was actually not true for Joseph loved his sons equally and his daughter-s also (see chapter 16). He tried to be a fair and a just man. He had several grandchildren; one who was mentally defective he loved greatly, would have given much for him to be normal and wept greatly when he reached the end of his life and passed to spirit.

"You also had a younger brother and two sisters on of whom died within a few hours of being born, but you always felt you had a special place in your father's heart and he would take you on journeys into the desert where you would learn of nature and would feel very close to him. There were times you would also go into the desert with your grandfather Joseph and he would teach you how to keep warm under the stars whether the weather was bitterly cold or whether it was hot, to adjust to different climatic conditions, to take care of yourself and he would teach you the ancient rites of Judaism. Of course when Joseph left to go and live in Britain you did not see him again, but you cared for your mother for your father had perished with the Zealots. Your mother's health was not good and she needed your support. While she was still middle aged she became weaker and died and when you became adult, you returned after her death to Palestine. You followed in the same footsteps as your grandfather Joseph of Arimathea, by entering the priesthood within the temple. You became a rabbi and then a teacher and for the remainder of your life you were attached to the Temple and taught students in the same way as your grandfather had done before you. You were in your fifties when a sudden illness beset you and you passed to spirit.'

Ruth - a daughter of Eliazar and Sarah.
The past life of Ruth, a sister to Amos, was given to a Brazilian woman in November 1994. In that life she married a teacher at the Essene centre in Qumran.

Chapter 16

The Mary of Magdala Affair

In April 1991 a French woman was given a past life as Mary of Magdala.

Master: "You had indeed a past life at the time of Christ. Your name was Mary and you came from Magdala. A woman of great beauty; it could be said you were a temptress, and yet the word is too harsh. Your husband did not recognise your qualities of gentleness and strength and he turned away from you. There were other women in his life and there was a great sadness in your heart for you desired above all else a child and that side of your relationship no longer existed. Women at that time were not encouraged in learning. They were encouraged to care for their children and their home. Most could not read nor write and had no desire to do so, for if they outshone other women they were disregarded as friends and often had intensely lonely lives. You had a lonely life because of your beauty which was recognised by many as a threat to the sanctity of the home, for men would turn and look on you with lust. You held yourself aloof, fully aware of the effect that you created, but fear held you apart. You knew the violence in your husband's nature and that your beauty could be seriously marred. But you were a woman of passion and great desire and you decided to sublimate this in learning. Your parents were of noble birth and you had brothers who had entered the Sanhedrin and learnt many languages; one was a rabbi and the other a counsellor to those who needed interpretation of Roman Law. This second brother was a hard man, one whom you could not admire even though he was strong and had great knowledge. You were very like this brother for you were twins. However you disparaged each other's learning and knowledge, and he looked upon you as a woman of no education and no ability. This was the way in many homes in that part of the world where women were not educated and were there as the property of men. A very similar situation exists in that region today for it has changed little throughout the Age.

"You disguised yourself as a man; it was difficult. You had, as we have said, great beauty and charisma, but this disguise gave you pleasure for you saw the different attitude of people towards you when you walked the streets. You approached the temple of learning and produced authenticity of your noble birth and made yourself out to be a brother who had not approached the Sanhedrin before having been away in Syria. Your credentials were accepted and you entered the temple of learning. You were taken into the care of Joseph of Arimathea who recognised an ability to learn and to excel in those subjects that you had chosen, for you were quick to learn Hebrew and to write in Sanskrit. Joseph was a very young member of the Sanhedrin and had reached his position because of his heritage. He had a great desire and need for learning and wished also to become a rabbi and to teach, counsel and protect. Joseph ceased travelling with his father and entered the Sanhedrin permanently and soon became their youngest elder. This is the background of how you met him. For a long while he taught you and then you became careless. The ochres that you used to darken and coarsen your skin were not applied so evenly. The cloth that you wrapped around your head to disguise your beautiful tresses was not so firmly positioned and your hands were not the hands of a man. Joseph began to look beneath the disguise and realised that you were a woman. This was a great surprise to him, but being a man of character and some humour he allowed you to continue your deception. Joseph's marriage had been an arranged one, his wife had born him three children and although he admired her for her strength of character he felt little desire for her; but he began to have a great passion for you. At first, he did not realise you were married, for he would not have condoned adultery. Many have reported him as an adulterer, but he was ignorant of your marriage status when he took you to himself. A child was conceived and born.

"You went to live in Magdala, a province away from Jerusalem, in order to bear the child. Your husband was led to believe that you had met with an accident and died and so little did he care that he did not check this story. You were visited occasionally by Joseph who had been badly shaken by the revelation of your marital status. However he greatly loved his child - the young Mary Magdalene - but could not claim her as his own. As a man of discipline and a candidate for the high priesthood in the temple he was too proud to permit a scandal of this kind. A lesson here may be learnt that pride goes before a fall, a lesson he was to learn throughout that life on earth. A vote was taken in the Sanhedrin and three names were put forward for the position of High priest. One member who had discovered the existence of yourself whispered among the other members that Joseph was not as upright and respecting the spirit of the law as many had supposed. Thus history was changed and Caiaphas became High priest. You appreciate the significance of this, for it was Caiaphas who condemned Christ to death. If Joseph the Arimathean had held that position his nephew would not have been crucified. And yet it was written that it must be so for Christ was born to die in a manner which would help to save the souls and lives of many. So ultimately all that occurs in life occurs for a purpose and must be so. We think we have total freewill to live our lives as we choose but there is guidance from Spirit - from the Higher Self."

In answer to some specific questions, asked In August 1991, the Master gave the following additional details about their relationship.

Master: "Eventually you became very aware of the family situation in Joseph's home and his commitment and loyalty to his family. Initially the liaison between yourselves was one of total sexual attraction and need which deepened into enduring and lasting love. There was never any question but that Mary of Magdala was the woman of his choice - the woman whom he would have wished to become married and loyal to for the whole of his life - but as we have said he had been affianced very young to his wife, as was indeed the custom. Because neither his wife nor he had deep love for each other they decided that their children would be brought up more liberally to make their own choice. Unfortunately in the society in which they lived this was not the right decision. It meant that Joseph's daughter married late in life and very unsuitably and that his daughter by Mary of Magdala had the same fate.

"There was antagonism to Mary of Magdala from those around - and you must remember society of that time would stone a wanton woman to death - so you were taken to a place of safety. You were protected by Joseph who visited you whenever possible and initially he was active in bringing up the child. However responsibilities to his family, the business and to the Sanhedrin meant that these visits were indeed spaced widely although you never doubted his love. You did not accompany the party to Britain for the same reasons. It was difficult enough for Joseph to admit to the party his relationship to his natural daughter but if he had attempted to take his now aging mistress as well, there probably would have been no journey. Looking back upon all the circumstances, you can see the importance this journey had both for Britain and for other areas of the world where the disciples travelled and two or three of them were initially in a boat which was large but still very crowded. The journey itself proved to be difficult and arduous.

"You were comfortable and left well provided for. There was one who was left as your protector who ensured that the remainder of your days were pleasant, well coordinated and comfortable. This separation broke the heart of more than one, but this so often happens in life."

Chapter 17

Joseph's extended family

In February 1992 an English woman was given a past life as Mary Magdalene.

Master: "Mary had an olive skin and beautiful red-gold hair. Slim and small she was a woman many men desired and earlier in her life she would submit to them, for that was her personality. As she matured she became more aware of other needs and spiritually profound. As a child she had great vivacity and in this way was like her mother, although she had not experienced the hardships her mother had been through at the same age. For obvious reasons she took her mother's family name, but she was also called Ruth. Later Joseph officially proclaimed her his daughter and heir, for his other children had either died or been provided for. Only her mother called her Ruth and when she was first introduced into Joseph's household he quietly greeted her by that name and she realised that here was a person with some intimate knowledge of her. However it was not until the journey to Britain began that Joseph revealed to her that he was her father and by that time she had had begun to suspect that there was a relationship between them. Both had very similar skin and hair colouring whereas her mother was much lighter skinned and fairer.

"We have already outlined her personality and when she became more independent there was an underlying bitterness mainly because of the problems that ensued when the man she loved - a Centurion - by whom she had children, returned to Rome to resume a relationship that he had left some years before. The two children were not strong and died early, one when still a baby and the other soon after the father left. This increased her bitterness profoundly, but when she became a follower of Christ she then realised that all these phases in her life had indeed been guided, that she might herself be fulfilled in the role that she was cast for by her very birth. Both her children were boys and perhaps it was as well that they did not survive, for to be aware of their mother's downfall would have caused great pain. We would like to make clear that in no way was she romantically associated with Yeshua although we understand that many writings have alluded to this.'

At a later date the Master was asked why it was that it was generally accepted that Mary Magdalene was a loose woman for nowhere in the the Bible does it mention this.

Master: "She was not a prostitute in the way understood today. When she was first deserted by the man she loved, it was a very difficult time for she was pregnant and already had one small child. There was no way that she was able to maintain herself and the child. Like many women who loved their children and did not want to see them perish from hunger and neglect she had to sell herself for money. She also had to bear the humiliation of being deserted and face those around her when they realised that she was not legally married. It was very difficult at that time for women to evade punishment by their own kind. There were also many jealousies. She was stoned on one occasion because she was seen coming out of a dwelling where she had sold herself in order to buy food. There were those who hated her for her beauty and they instigated the stoning. This was in front of the child. It was horrendous, but the child had the intelligence to run and beg for help that his mother might not be killed. This came about and she was saved, but the child she was carrying was born prematurely and only lived a matter of weeks being so young and frail. It was at this time that Joseph of Arimathea found out that his daughter was living in Jerusalem. He had not been in touch with either the mother or his daughter for some time because of the great difficulties facing Jesus. Joseph always provided sustenance for her mother but when he heard what had happened to his daughter he immediately resolved to provide for her so that she should not be forced to prostitute herself in order to live. He sent his younger son Eliazar to her house with food and money and it was because of these visits that a relationship developed. Eliazar did not realise at that time she was related to him, because for obvious reasons Joseph had not told his son of this. Eventually they found they cared for each other and became lovers.

"Once more Joseph found himself involved for he realised more and more the difficulties that his relationship of many years before had brought upon his family. He realised also that the belief of the Jews that the sins of the fathers should be visited upon the children for many generations was indeed true. Mary had not been betrothed and she had been bitter in her youth and this is why she lived first with a man of her choice who was unable to wed her because of his religious beliefs, his nationality and his marriage to a woman in his own country. Her bitterness rankled very deeply and led her eventually to promiscuity. However she was drawn to Yeshua, to His gentleness, His love towards all, His lack of condemnation won her heart and her loyalty and she turned from the way she had followed. She had hated being a servant, but she became His. No deed was too servile although He did not desire either a slave or yet a servant, for women to Him were friends as well as companions. But so great was the love in her heart for Him that she changed her ways totally.

"First, Joseph had to explain to his son that Mary was his daughter. Eliazar was very angry yet full of remorse and fear and he left the family home. He had already allied himself to the cause of the Zealots and now decided to travel with them totally. He left home disparaging his father and full of loathing for himself, desiring only his own death, for he was a man of principle who had till then trodden the straight and narrow path and felt that he had been seduced away from it by the beauty of a woman. Then having discovered that she was his sister, his self disgust and hate for his father and for the woman were strong. Mary also,when she was told later, was full of hatred for Joseph although this gradually abated. Joseph took her in his care and a child was eventually born. It was not long after, that Eliazar died with the Zealots not having been reconciled either to his father or to Mary Magdalene.

"Joseph did not reveal that he was Mary's father until the crisis came when Mary the Mother of Jesus and many others were forced to flee. They were condemned to death for believing in the name of the new truth and religion for they were regarded as traitors to their Jewish inheritance and hence must die. Joseph decided to take them to the safe haven of Britain. Mary Magdalene refused to go until she was told who her father was and eventually accompanied him in gratitude and pleasure. Up to that time she had not known that Joseph was her father although she had been aware of him as an elder in the Sanhedrin for he played a very important part in the life of Jerusalem as well as Arimathea."

A Grandchild.
Abram - the first born son of Mary Magdalene.

In April 1992 the following past life was given to a Swiss woman.

Master: "You were the son of a woman from Palestine and a soldier from Rome. You lived but a short while and although it was at first a rather lonely life you were greatly loved. Alliances between alien countries were discouraged. Local woman from Palestine were often tortured, or stoned, or derided because they loved someone from a race that had taken arms against Palestine and then occupied it and yet there are good and bad in all peoples; they cannot all be gathered together and called evil, or all called divine.

"Your mother in that life considered that she was betrothed, that is to say almost married to this soldier. She had lived with her own mother in comparative solitude for fifteen years and had met and loved greatly the young soldier who was so keen to bring harmony to his people and those of the occupied state. She pleaded with her mother to allow her to accompany this soldier to Jerusalem and eventually because she loved her daughter greatly and understood her temperament the mother agreed.

"You, her son, lived in a small whitewashed dwelling which was just outside the busy area where the markets were in Jerusalem, in the shadow of the Temple. You knew nothing of the background of your parents, you were sheltered and seldom left the four walls of the garden which surrounded the dwelling of your childhood. Only a woman came and brought food, cleaned the house and spent much time speaking with your mother. One or two children from neighbouring houses would be allowed in to play in the garden which had many trees which kept the hot sun from your heads and bodies and allowed you to play in comfort.

"One day you realised that your normally contented and happy mother was in a state of great distress. The tears were flowing down her cheeks and she held you to her in great anguish. You looked upon the figure of your father standing disconsolately looking at his family, tears also in his eyes, and gradually you realised that he was to leave you. He was returning with his unit to Rome. Your mother went to the authorities and begged that she also might travel; but she was refused, at first with no explanation and then reluctantly the Roman officer told her that the man she loved and dwelt with was indeed married to a woman in Rome and that only those that were truly married were allowed to accompany their husbands to that country. By the time you returned to your dwelling your father had left.

"Your mother was much concerned with helping a group of people who were called the Essenes. They would meet in the quiet places of the hills surrounding Jerusalem. Those that taught them had great knowledge and wisdom, but they were also strict, almost as strict as the Druids who could be extremely cruel and mete out punishments which were hideous in the extreme. In many ways the Essenes, although more spiritual, could also be exceptionally strict and cruel to those who evaded their responsibilities. Your mother was very much aware of the Holy Family. She knew of Yeshua, had seen Him many times when He returned from His travels in India and had seen also His mother and her tragedy when the Father of Yeshua died and she was left alone. There were times when Yeshua was present at Essene meetings for He had a powerful position among them. He who speaks to you, Joseph of Arimathea, was the paranymphos (guardian) of Mary the Mother. He was also the spiritual guardian of Yeshua for many years allowing Him only to travel under his auspices or guarded and protected by those he sent personally. If the occasion warranted it Joseph would even travel with the young Yeshua himself.

"There were also times when your mother would go to Galilee. Many of the disciples who followed Yeshua would be there. One called Peter would play with you, would tousle your hair and run and hide until you found him, he was a big rough man with a long, full beard and laughing eyes. He had children of his own whom he seldom saw because he travelled so greatly with His Master and when they met together in an upstairs room to speak to Jesus and be taught by Him, you then had to be alone in the yard and would sit quietly with the children of the owner of the inn who would wait upon the group. Your mother also would wait upon them and she would care for those who were hot and tired from the journeys. You would fetch a bowl with clean spring water in it and she would use this to bathe the feet of The Master and to oil them and to care for Him in whatever way she was able. When the meal was finished you would travel home with her. You knew that she carried another child, and you were saddened because your father was no longer with you.

"Then one day she was taken from your home and was bound and held by others who lived near and who regarded her as a fallen woman. They mocked her because she had thought she was betrothed and yet was not, and they called her a whore, tied her to a rock and threw stones at her until she was near to death, and you ran screaming and crying to the home of Peter who dwelt near for it was his turn to guard The Master while He slept. Peter came and chased away those who were throwing the stones and untied your mother and carried her unconscious into his house where she was looked after and cared for, but the child she was carrying was born early and it lived but a short while and then was taken back to spirit.

"You did not live yourself beyond your seventh year for you were not strong and often did not eat nourishing food. Your health deteriorated and you developed a fever and passed to spirit. You looked upon the face of your mother, her beautiful red-gold hair, her olive skinned features and her eyes so full of love and tenderness for you. You did not understand, few children do, about the lives and tragedies of parents, the things that encircle them which form their karma and the events which often they hide from the young that they be not disturbed and saddened.

"Your mother was Mary Magdalene. Your father, a Centurion in the army of Rome, was never advised either of the death of the woman he loved, when she eventually died, many, many years later in Britain, nor yet of the fate of his two children whose advent he had looked forward to so greatly. His karma was great, he knew that he had done wrong in taking a woman when he already had one that belonged to him. That which afflicts the parents afflicts also the children, for their lives are affected because of their parents actions. In more enlightened times it is better known that to protect children against these disasters and these problems in life is to do them a disservice rather than to serve them well, to speak with them, to enable them to understand right from wrong; but two thousand years have passed and the world is a very different place."

Part IV

Joseph of Arimathea's Ministry

Chapter 18

The end of the beginning

It is difficult to imagine the scene in Jerusalem immediately after the crucifixion.

Master: "The effect on the general community was not great. The rabble, as they were then known, were easily led. They were always stirred into rebellion by a handful of coins. They would do exactly as they were told. Saul, (later to become St. Paul), led the rabble away by distributing money. Among those who followed Jesus and His teachings there was great sorrow. Reported sightings of His risen body were faithfully given to all those in power both Roman and Jewish. This added to the great fear of retribution from on High, but many of the concepts of the God of the Jews began a radical change after the crucifixion. Nothing of this nature had ever been witnessed or perpetrated before yet there had been some horrific trials and killings during the history of the Jews."

One thing is sure, life for many of those who had been in positions of authority was never the same again.

Master: "When Caiaphas realised that his actions and words had resulted in such a heinous crime he was so overwrought, and full of fear of condemnation and of retribution from God, that he resigned almost immediately from the high priesthood. He felt that by so doing the retribution would pass over him leaving him virtually without blame. This was an accepted teaching of the Jews. For a very long time those in power felt they could, when the results of their actions were obviously miscalculated and misconceived, evade responsibility by removing themselves from high office. For quite a while there was no true High Priest for the turmoil was such within the body of the Sanhedrin that the suitability of a replacement and whether indeed it would be allowed by the Roman governor was not clear. Where the organisation of the temple and the ideology behind the teaching was concerned it was a time of great emptiness, but this is not recorded in the Gospels. All that was recorded found its way to Qumran where it was officially documented by the Essenes and the scrolls are virtually a verbatim record of all that happened during that dramatic time. Words written by those in power could not at any time be destroyed and copies of these were also sent to Rome.

"During the trial Joseph went to plead the case for his nephew and he was detained at the Palace to prevent him obtaining Jesus' release. It was not an imprisonment as such but he was placed under guard and could not leave. As he paced to and fro on the balcony looking out over the greenswards he could see in the distance the Mount of Olives, his own home and the hill of Golgotha and he became acutely aware of the preparations being made for the scourging of the one he loved so greatly. It was all he could bear, and many things went through his mind - of his family and how it could have been one of them - the loyalty and love of his wife and children, the many thoughts, many resolves that had been broken, much heartache, much bitterness. Eventually he was given his freedom only to find his family berated him because the action they expected of him had not taken place. They would not listen, they would not accept that he had been placed under guard, that he had been helpless despite the position of power he held in the Temple, He had been helpless against such opposition - the combined power of hatred by the Sanhedrin and the Roman forces.

"He believed by this time that his work in the Sanhedrin must cease for he felt that some of his integrity had been lost through his desire to spare the pain and suffering and humiliation that had been inflicted on his nephew through his mode of death. This was the human side of Joseph arising from that which had been pure duty and he had made his views known to Caiaphas. Those who upheld his views such as his great friend Nicodemus, also desired to leave the work in the Temple and leave the country and make a fresh start without the limitations of Roman rule and the desire of those such as Caiaphas to limit their beliefs to those of the governorship of the time. There were many others who felt similarly and so there was, as you might say, a mass exodus from the Temple. Several went to other countries accompanying the Disciples on their journeys. Remember, many of the Disciples were ignorant men and needed those who had greater ability to teach. Many of the words spoken by those that travelled were the words of those that expounded the faith and had knowledge of language. There were limitations to the gift of spirit in allowing many tongues to be understood and spoken, it needed also those who were proficient in languages to accompany the leaders of the expeditions."

Attacks on Joseph.

"Immediately after the crucifixion Joseph became the object of great mistrust and abuse at a time when his family needed him very greatly. Joseph was evading assassination and attacks both from the Sanhedrin -Caiaphas desired his death - and those whom he had thought of as friends and colleagues who turned against him when they found that he was one of the outer circle of disciples who had followed the teachings. They considered that because Jesus' teachings were different from the accepted truth then Joseph must be like minded.

"On more than one occasion Joseph had been molested and beaten. One of these attempts on his life had been horrific and almost successful for one of his hands had been virtually amputated. He had been found by a loyal servant who took him first to his home and then to Cyprus. It took several months for the very painful hand and arm to heal and for the remainder of his life there was very little feeling or use in the wrist and hand which had been almost severed. He did receive healing and at times while asleep was aware of a divine force beside him giving healing. There was a blinding pure white light surrounding him, he could not open his eyes and was aware that if he did so he could well be blinded. He felt intense heat and cried out that this should be taken from him as he could not bear the intensity of the heat and the energy which wracked his body as though in great pain but when he awoke, drenched in perspiration it was to find that the hideous wound on his wrist had virtually healed and much of the nerve responses had been restored. Although this could be termed miraculous and certainly was of divine intervention there is much in the mind of man that repels total healing and those times were no different from the present for many that could be healed are not, because they doubt its success. As time passed

Joseph's healing was never truly successful because he doubted that total feeling could be restored. (All this is recorded on scrolls yet to be found). On recovering from his injuries he made the decision that he would have to take his family to safety.

"Joseph was responsible not only for his own family but, as already mentioned, for Mary the mother of Jesus. After the tragic deaths of Josephes and his son, Ruth, with their other children were taken to a place of safety - to the estate in Cyprus. It was Joseph's great sadness that he was unable to allow Mary of Magdala the mother of his child Mary Magdalene to accompany his family. Those with an understanding of Jewish Law, Jewish custom and Jewish family life would recognise that this would have been outside the bounds of possibility. She was adequately cared for in Magdala, the place of her birth, and was surrounded by many friends. It was the same for the daughter Mary Magdalene for she could not be taken to Cyprus initially. After the announcement of Josephes' untimely death there was of course a long period of mourning and anguish. Very gradually other members of the family were taken there and because of the unrest and fear that prevailed this had to be done under the cover of darkness and over a period of many months. By this time Eliazar had left Jerusalem and sought a life with the young men who were disrupting the way of life of those who wished to establish a correct and strict code of conduct, but Sarah and their children also settled in Cyprus. So eventually Joseph's wife, daughter, sons wives and grandchildren were all in Cyprus, where they were looked after by trusted servants and also friends who would visit them from time to time."

The fate of the family.
"For at least one year after the Crucifixion there was doubt as to what would happen to the family as a whole. Joseph spent much time in prayer seeking guidance and help as to how he could guarantee the safety of his family and also continue the work which he had sworn he would do. He received yet another visitation from the angel Gabriel. He was told his future role was to continue the ministry of the Christ so as to allow mankind to be aware of the Truth of life in its fullness and not its narrowness. Joseph also received a visit from the etheric body of Jesus and a long discussion ensued regarding the future and how the aspects of teaching should be continued in other areas of the world.

Joseph had realised for a long while that his days were numbered in the land of his birth and he made a plan to take as many of the family to Britain as possible. Because he had inherited some mines in the western part of the island He knew many of those who ruled in different areas, and one in particular King Arviragus offered him, and any of those whom he wished to take with him sanctuary. Thus they would be free from the harassing situation in Palestine and the unrest which was already spreading to Greece and Cyprus. Although Britain was a land well known for the love it showed to strangers Joseph did not wish to live there for the remainder of his life but he gradually realised that having once left Palestine he could no longer return.

"In this plan Joseph had however not reckoned on the failing health of his wife, the inability of his daughter to face the extensive sea voyage and the youth of the grandchildren. At that time the journey was extremely hazardous in the open boats available. There was also to be considered sanctuary for the disciples staying in Cyprus. In addition the lives of some of Joseph's servants were being threatened and he gave them, as it were, a pension for long service and in recognition of the love that they had shown to the family. By now the faithful servant (Simon Zelotes) who had rescued Joseph after his near fatal attack had been able to bring safely to Cyprus all those that would eventually travel to Britain. Among the eleven who accompanied Joseph there was Lazarus, his wife and his sisters Mary and Martha. Also Mary the mother of Jesus, Mary Magdalene and two of the disciples and Simon Zelotes who had been guarding them and keeping them away from the authorities until they could be rowed to the safety of the large boat that would make the journey to Britain. Joseph was now about 70 years old and he realised that when he left Palestine he could no longer return and he would never see his family again. This was the biggest decision of his life and the most agonising, but Joseph realised that he had to fulfil his purpose and that his own personal feelings must not stand in the way."

Those left behind.

As already stated Ruth and Sarah, the wives of Joseph's two sons, and their children lived out their lives in Cyprus except Amos who went to Jerusalem after his mother's death.

Regarding Joseph's wife
"Indeed there was great emotion, great sadness; it was as sad for Joseph to leave as it was for Miriam to be left."

About his wife Miriam.
"You remained because of your health, you had extreme fatigue, were very anxious with a great fear of what lay outside the home. There had been such brutality in the land not fully appreciated even by historians. Your daughter Rachel loving you greatly and already separated from a brutal husband decided of her own freewill that she would remain with you. So with a loyal servant and several others who were able to protect you and Joseph's wealth you eventually left Jerusalem and returned to the home in Arimathea and there you remained the rest of your life. It was always Joseph's wish that you should all be together. But after he arrived in Britain he realised that you would not have survived the terrible privations endured on the long sea journey to Britain. Then there were the dreadful conditions endured when they began to build their settlement. Those who were older did not live very long. It was those younger, stronger and fitter in every way that managed to build the settlement and also uphold Joseph.

"During your life time Joseph had regular news of you. After your death he desired to bring his daughter to join him, but she would not embark upon the journey - also being fearful."

The Master discounts certain stories about the journey.
Master: "There are indeed many fables written regarding that time which are untrue. It has been stated that Joseph, with others were set afloat from Palestine and banished from the country by the authorities. This is not true - this mysterious 'being set a sail without oars' has no foundation."

Chapter 19

Joseph's flight to Britain with Mary and others

The terrible sea journey to Britain is told through the past lives of two people Simon Ben Zoteh and Japhet*. Both played an essential role in ensuring the survival of most of the twelve in the party, but without the assistance of Simon Ben Zoteh it is doubtful if any would have survived. He had also an interesting life before that journey and we start with him. The following past life was given to an Englishman in October 1991.

Master: "In that life as now you were born a male. Your father died while you were still an infant and you had to work to support your mother and sister.

At this time you had barely reached puberty and you sought work in the Temple. It was a time of crisis for many. Christ had returned from India to Jerusalem and was seeking Joseph of Arimathea and He entered the Temple while you were present. The work that you had been given was that of cleaning but He saw within you that which the Elders had not seen - not through blindness, but through lack of caring and lack of desire to be aware. He saw a light which shone around you and saw your potential. He led you to Joseph and asked that you be taught. Joseph being one of the Elders, although still quite young, did not need to seek consent either of the priests nor yet of the High Priest, but he knew that if this uneducated child was permitted to sit and learn there would be comment. At that time Joseph wished to play an obscure part within the Temple life due to misdemeanours in his own private life, but when Jesus made such a request no-one refused.

"For at least a year you were taken away from your normal duties and at Joseph's expense you sat at the feet of the teachers including Joseph himself. You grew rapidly in strength and stature; you had the

---

* The spelling of Japhet does not follow the traditional Jewish form, that is it does not have the final 'h'- as in Japheth - the second son of Josephes and Ruth. The Master advised that this should be so because of Japhet's background.

capacity to learn and to teach but this was forbidden for you were a half caste. Your father was of the Jewish race but your mother was Nubian and this was frowned upon by many in society. Nubian children were given the same opportunities for work and education according to their status but those of mixed race were not. They were considered not to be a caste that was worth educating and many remarks were passed concerning your presence and certain forms of work was forbidden to you because of your heritage.

"At this time Joseph's grandchildren needed education in their home. We have already explained that the house in Jerusalem was built upon a rock and that Joseph had arranged that a tomb would be hewn from this rock. The workman had hollowed out the rock and Joseph had drawn plans showing an inner chamber to contain three stone-wrought benches where the corpses would be laid and an outer chamber where mourners could pray and wail for the deceased.

"It was beginning to be difficult to continue your education so you were taken into Joseph's home where you shared your knowledge with the young grandchildren until the time when they too could enter the Temple for a more formal education. But your primary task was to oversee the construction of the inner and outer tomb, so when you were not with the young ones you were overseeing the workmen to ensure that the ideas and principles of Joseph's plan were adhered to.

"As we have already explained it was a time of great trauma after the crucifixion and both the Roman government and the Jewish hierarchy, especially Caiaphas, desired the death of Joseph, his family and the Holy Family. There were traitors within the Temple, ones that Joseph had trusted with secrets. A boat was needed. If one of Joseph's fleet had been used it would soon have been missed so you hired a boat for fishing but in reality to take a small group safely to Cyprus. And later Joseph himself followed after the near fatal assassination attempt.

"The journey to Britain was indeed hazardous, there were storms and the substantial supplies of food in the boat had been ruined by the sea. When eventually the group reached the shore they were starving and dehydrated. Mary the Mother, always a fragile gentle woman, was desperately ill and near to death. Others were severely ill from seasickness and from drinking salt water. Not far from the shore of the west country in Britain there was a great storm which overturned the boat. Two were drowned, others clung to the wreckage and were rescued largely by Simon who was a strong swimmer and able to right the boat. Already many on the shore had seen the accident and had pushed out rafts and small boats and took them safely to the shore. You gave your life that others might be saved. You did not die immediately as a result of the journey, but within two years you became very ill. You gradually became weaker and although nursed by the women in the party, you were unable to regain your vigour or your mental state. You had been severely bitten by a fish and the poisoning that resulted entered your brain as well as the bloodstream and you eventually became mad. But you were nursed well with gentleness and care and laid to rest in the tomb that Joseph had prepared for his family beneath what eventually was to become Glastonbury Abbey although at that time only a rough wooden church had been erected. Mary the Mother was already buried there having survived the journey only a short while, and certain others also.

"There were some who returned to Cyprus and two of the men travelled widely in France and even Greece. These men took up the cause and the teaching, becoming Apostles in their own right. Many were buried in that sanctified ground of Glastonbury and the bones remain undisturbed and untouched. Centuries later there were those who feared the desecration of the grave of Joseph of Arimathea and Mary the Mother and they were removed to safety, but those from earlier burials were neither found nor disturbed. All those who played their individual part in the history of that time have returned to Earth that the Truth, the understanding of spirituality in its true form might again be recognised and shared and that their gifts might be spread world-wide and mankind healed in mind and in body, understanding that life itself is eternal and there is indeed no death."

The part played by Japhet.

The past life given to a Danish woman in September 1990 is of an aspect of her soul who was a man called Japhet. This life takes up the story of what happened to the travellers from Palestine after they reached the beach on the south west coast of Britain. The life is told in full because it is such a good example of reincarnation and Karma.

Master: "You had two lives in quick succession. You were born at the same time as Christ but died a few years later. You desired to achieve things which at the time were the prerogative of a male dominated world and you were a female. A sense of frustration and lack of achievement led you to return to spirit. You did not take your life but did little towards staying alive. At such times much counselling goes on in spirit and in your particular case it was decided that, as your soul needed to learn from the energies present at the time of the change between the Ages and in particular the energy released through the Christ-light made flesh, you should return soon. And this you did.

"Again you were born in Palestine but of wandering parents. They did not stay very long in any particular area, but desired to move with many others from one encampment to another gleaning what they could from the earth for sustenance and working at whatever seemed feasible in order to earn their way through many countries. You would have been perhaps between your eighteenth and twentieth year when the opportunity came to work on a boat that was sailing to another country. You were fascinated with water and this would enable you to travel upon it, and see if it was true that other islands and countries did really exist.

"At the same time we ourselves were leaving Palestine. As we have already indicated there had been a great deal of persecution after the crucifixion including certain of our number who were taken, under torture they told the authorities the whereabouts of Mary the Mother's home and where other members including two of the Disciples were hidden, waiting the right time to flee the country; it was time to be off.

"The boat in which you travelled and worked followed the same route. It was a vessel which carried iron-ore to a country well established in mining - Britain. It had been turned away from the Palestinian port because there was no longer the desire to trade with those parts of Europe where there had been uprisings against Roman tyranny. After our boat was beached we saw a much larger boat a little way along the coast. Some of our number approached the captain of this boat and obtained food. Nourishment of any kind had been difficult to obtain and there were those in our party nigh unto death from thirst as well as from hunger.

"It was at that time you first saw our band of people. You had within you a great compassion for the sick. You had nursed your mother until she closed her eyes and returned to spirit and looking upon one of the women of our number and seeing how fragile and ill she was - how near to death from lack of food and severe thirst your heart was touched.

You made it your task to tend her and care for her, moving her from the inclement weather into an adjacent cave. It was from this cave after many weeks of rest that we eventually continued upon our way. It was the help given by you and the captain that had enabled us to stay alive. Even so there was one who died due to the rigours and extremes of the journey. The captain gave you the opportunity to travel with us as you were able - bodied and by now deeply attached to the young woman whose life you had helped to save. You helped in a very positive way, nursing, waiting and serving all those who needed your aid. Later you helped in the establishment of our simple church and accompanied Joseph when he travelled to the far north - now Scotland - to meet the Druids and encourage their help and cooperation in establishing the link with the one Truth. You were present in the role of a servant, although it was never considered such. You continued to be the constant companion of Joseph after other members of the group had been laid to rest. As we have said Mary the Mother of Christ died first and Mary Magdalene while still in her middle years largely through the arduous life that she had endured during the difficult times in Palestine, but she also found the quite severe weather conditions in Britain difficult for her constitution. You married someone who worked with you in the church group and you had two children one of whom died in infancy. When Joseph died you continued the teaching and passed to spirit as a relatively old man. There were others that worked with you, descendants of the original people who had come from Palestine and also those that were incorporated into the work from various parts of Britain. They were loyal always to the Teaching of the Way and demonstrated in their personalities and their way of living the true Christ aspect."

Chapter 20

The Wattle Church

After Joseph and his followers had recovered from being shipwrecked they began to put into operation the plans for "the de-paganisation of a very important and already spiritual land".

'De-paganisation' is the Master's word for he avoids at all times the word Christianity which he points out "...arose not because of the connotation of Christ with the teaching but with the commencement of the churches for they took on certain teachings of their own".

Master: "Most of Britain was under the jurisdiction of what might be called Kings. They controlled different areas and there were probably ten or twelve such rulers one of whom was Arviragus who controlled an area roughly from the Home Counties westwards. He was one of the greatest of the kings showing mercy to those that paid their taxes to him for his protection and for his wisdom. Joseph had stayed with him as a child on his visits to Britain with his own father and had grown to respect him very greatly. In fact the two families had at one time become closely involved when Joseph's elder daughter had been betrothed to the son of Arviragus."

It will be recalled that Joseph desired that his children should not be betrothed early in life but should have free choice. His own marriage had not been of the happiest because he and his wife did not share the same understanding that many who marry through love now enjoy. Therefore they both agreed that where possible their own children would have a choice. The betrothal was never consummated and eventually the daughter was betrothed to another.

Master: "Joseph and the others had been taken to the home of Arviragus and stayed there for many months before any felt strong enough to commence work. Arviragus bestowed upon Joseph twelve hides of land in the area now known as Glastonbury. There they could build as they wished and start a communal life."

"Arviragus was one who had great warmth and love for those who brought the word of Truth and Light and he made every effort to bring comfort and peace to them. At first, when it was mooted that a wattle church and buildings should be erected the king was full of horror that gentle people, as he considered them, should be allowed to experience the hardships of the winters in Britain, which were at that time extremely cold and the summers more inclined to heat than they are in this century. Joseph was however intent upon his mission and he felt that the humble people of the area would be more inclined to come to a simple structure than they would to one which resembled a temple such as that in Jerusalem.

"It was called a wattle church because of the weaving of the branches which supplied its main strength. It took a long while for the building to be erected. Men came from far and wide and brought different kinds of timber from the extensive forest lands. Britain was at that time an extremely beautiful island and many different kinds of trees grew there; the forests covered two-thirds of the land mass and in many instances grew to within a few feet of the beaches.

"At last the simple structure was completed. It could hold, at any one time, no more than twenty people. Gradually more and more people sought the Truth and the door was left open during the mild weather which allowed many, many more to sit outside and listen to those who taught. Eventually the building became too small and Joseph had erected outside a platform upon which he would stand and address the multitude. It reminded those whom he had brought from Palestine, of the days when Yeshua himself would stand upon a mountainside, a tall hill, a cliff or even a boat on the water and how His voice would ring around all those present who would hear each word so clearly and to whom no language was a barrier.

"Joseph would often go to the home of Arviragus and take bread with him and his family and use the opportunity to teach and share his resolve to turn Britain from a pagan land into one with beliefs in the world to come.

Joseph had made a number of visits to Britain in the past and had previously shared his beliefs and views with the king who was among the first to accept that way of life. Arviragus thus became the first 'Christian' king in Britain.

Note: It is worth recording that The Domesday Book contains an entry - folio p249 b - which states that The Church of Glastonbury has in its own ville twelve hides of land which have never paid tax.

"The wood from which the little wattle church was built was not very durable and before very long a larger and stronger church was built. Much harder wood was used and this came by way of rivers and roads from the Midlands where another ruler dwelt. Joseph taught in this church which had a capacity of about one hundred people. In much later times the much larger Abbey was built - the one now in ruins. We feel that subsequent structures have been built over the original church."

Glastonbury - The Crystal Isle.

"Joseph had the ability when necessary to materialise objects. it could be the transformation of a simple pebble taken from among thousands on the beach or an awakening of energy as a rushing wind and a great light. When the wind departed and the light dimmed there would be a stone of great size and beauty. On occasions Joseph felt the need to demonstrate, to those he wished to convert, the power of God within the universe and to do this he would raise the staff that he always carried over the ground. The staff would glow with energy and he would manifest some attractive object, nearly always a beautiful crystal. Sometimes this would be done to obtain a crystal with some special healing abilities. In these instances Joseph was using mystical rites, including alchemy.

"There was one such special object which he manifested in this way. It was a pure, clear quartz crystal some three or four feet high, terminating at one end in a very fine point with seven facets. Totally symmetrical and beautiful It stood on the ground on its broad firm base with the point uppermost. It took three men to lift it and place it in the centre of the original little wattle church. There its radiance would pour forth and those on nearby hills who were praying and communicating with spirit would swear that they saw light emanating through the loosely tied single branches of wood that comprised this church. The structure had to be erected in such a way as to withstand the great storms which were prevalent especially at the time of the equinoxes.

"The crystal remained in the church when Joseph went on his travels, but he took with him small crystals that he had also manifested to help in healing. The crystal survived until Joseph's death and then it dematerialised, it simply ceased to exist. There are those that doubt alchemy, and well they might, for so very few have that gift, just as few can effect total healing, but there are still some that can when the gift is awakened in them.

"A great deal of work was done within the twelve hides of land which included the whole of the Glastonbury area and a little beyond (an alternative name for Glastonbury was Ynys-witrin that is the Isle of Glass, or crystal). Each group worked together to create the kind of life that would bring the greatest sanctity, the greatest love, especially to those who suffered ill health or were impoverished due to many different reasons."

Chapter 21

Joseph's travels

Joseph lived to be over one hundred years old and travelled widely during the thirty years of his ministry.

Master: "The work of Joseph and his followers at Glastonbury was initially slow but gained the confidence of both those who ruled and the population. It was through the invitation of the different ruling bodies that Joseph travelled to other areas of Britain crossing the sea more than once to teach in Ireland and France. He also went to Wales but had the greatest affinity with those in Scotland. It was his great joy to visit that area and certain parts of the Highlands which he felt reflected his beloved Palestine and the desert area to which he related so greatly throughout the early days of his life. The moorland, the craggy hills, the beautiful lakes were to him a manifestation of spirit upon the Earth. He shared the beliefs and the work of those to whom he spoke, particularly the Druids. In many ways he enabled them to have a broader and more spiritual understanding of rites other than the magical rites that were part of their heritage. So he helped them to come very gradually towards the teachings of Jesus, some of which were already part of their practices and to accept that certain of their behavioural patterns would not help mankind but would hinder their progress.

"In the beginning there was this mixture of pagan beliefs and some of the teachings of Christ. If that mixture of the beauty and power of nature together with the power of spirit manifesting Man's loyalty had remained, most of the hideous religious wars coming down through the centuries would never have happened. Man however makes his own laws and through this comes death and destruction, but from death and destruction arises birth and rebirth - the two cycles of existence - the negative and positive in all aspects of life."

The Druids.
Master: "The main source of spiritual understanding and teaching came through the Druids. There were many encampments of these good men throughout England, Wales, Scotland and Ireland. Their influence was great yet they instilled fear into many. Unless there is an element of fear many feel that there will not be obedience or enlightenment; the

Druids ruled by fear. They did not believe in one of the most important principles that we desired to establish, that the spirit within each one is also part of God.

"The Druids were in complete harmony with the countryside and at one with nature, but many of them were ignorant of the truth of creation and those who were not did not seek the Druids' way of life. It is well known that not all that the Druids did was spiritual. There were indeed times of sacrifice both of their young and of animals which they considered very profound. As indeed was the sacrifice Abraham was prepared to make of his son Isaac, for it was the Jewish belief that if you sacrificed something that meant a great deal to you it would bring you joy and prosperity. One of the tasks of Joseph was to enlighten the Druid community of the Truth of spirit as had been revealed by Christ."

A time of drought.

Master: "At one time there was a great drought throughout the whole of Britain. Many were dying. People sought water in all the places where springs had been, they dug deep into the soil but could find no trace of water. A well supplying constant water had already been made at Joseph's command for those that dwelt in Glastonbury. At that time Joseph had travelled to Scotland with a small group of teachers and while there some of them had died and others had had a fever. Seeking water was not something that Joseph undertook lightly. There were days of meditation and prayer and he requested the power to find a spring.

"The Druids had formed a circle. They had chosen a place where the design and beauty of the corn growing there showed its spirituality - that it was blessed - that the energies which had disturbed the growth indicated a place where water might be found. Already they had erected stones and a group of Druids desperately endeavoured to bring forth rain but however hard they tried - and there were many days of words and actions - there was no rain. It was a time of mysticism, of incantations, of power and desire, much of which Joseph discouraged, knowing the awareness of the certainty of prayer which had been taught to him by Yeshua, but not always the certainty of incantations. Joseph himself had considerable power. One of these powers was to find in the ground a spring of water, often lifesaving to those dying of thirst. But he had as hosts the Druids and there was no way he would show his strong power to them without their bidding it. Although they had prayers and incantations and many spells that they would weave in order to achieve what was needed they did not have that one ingredient which Joseph understood so well - the power of the love of God.

"So he left the group and went some miles away by himself and he divined for water and found it. He returned and there were many who came with him and dug industriously until the water was seen and trapped in a well. Although it was confined to that area it encouraged others with similar gifts to move around the country finding water which responded to their touch. That well is still there. Many seek it for its purity and never has it failed however little rain there has been in that area. There are other such places but they are few.

"At one time Joseph was proclaimed brother to the Druids and they endeavoured to bestow upon him some of the mystical rites that were theirs. But that was not his way. His way was in the path of the Christ. The Christ had many powers but they had been bestowed upon Him through the Divine. Although His mystical powers were recognised they were wrongly attributed to Him being the Son of God, His powers arose simply from His divine nature; many called these mystical creations miracles."

A selection of some past lives illustrate among other things Joseph's great healing powers.

A miracle of life.
The following past life was given to a French woman in March 1992.

"May I ask you if I had a life at the time of Christ?"
Master: "There were those that dwelt in the parts of the World where He travelled, those who heard of His healing and miracles and those who grieved when He died. But there were also those, like yourself, that were not a part of any of this. You dwelt in that part of Britain which is now known as Scotland - on the border between Scotland and the farthest tip of England. You came from a sheep farming community and your parents had two children. You were the elder and in that life as in this life you were a woman. As you grew you had a great love for very young animals and very young children. You married but you were barren and could not give to your husband the child he craved. He too was a sheep farmer and would bring in the very young lambs to be warmed by the fire and to be cared for by yourself,

to raise them and make them strong before they were put back in the barns and fields.

"It was at the time when the Christ had already been crucified, and had arisen. His disciples were travelling the World bringing the truth of the Way and the Light. He who speaks with you, Joseph of Arimathea had already travelled to Britain with some of the devotees of Christ and created the first Church to the glory of God and Christ. It was part of Joseph's discipleship to travel the length and breadth of Britain bringing the teaching with Him.

"He delighted in the beauty of Scotland which had at that time few inhabitants. The isolation there appealed to him for he was used to the deserts and the peace within them when his Soul was heavy within him. He would travel to Scotland with a companion and often by the wayside he would pause to heal a sick animal or a man who had laboured too long and had great tiredness. He paused at the small home that you shared with your husband and with the animals. He paused for refreshment which you willingly gave as you would to any stranger. He spoke with you of the love that Christ had brought to the World. You had not heard of this love and yet deep within you, you realised that the spiritual aspects of your life did not come just from the countryside or the World in which you lived. You had no awareness at all of other countries, not even that there was an ocean surrounding the country you lived in, for you lived far away from it and had never moved from the place where you were born.

"Joseph spoke many languages and all who spoke with him understood what he said. It was a gift given by Christ to the disciples so that they could be understood by all Mankind and speak to them freely. When Joseph passed on his way, it was with the heartfelt thanks and goodwill of a woman who loved and cared deeply for humankind. But he left also a gift of healing within you, a gift which stirred, for at a given time you gave birth to your first and only child. A miracle of life, a miracle of the love which stirred within a woman's breast for the child she had never been able to conceive. There was great rejoicing among the neighbours and with your husband and it seemed as though even the animals in the field rejoiced with you.

"There are still miracles my child. They did not cease at that time and they are not only given by a great power. They come through the sensitivity of the belief of the Soul in that which lies outside the denseness and heaviness of the Earth plane. If you believe in miracles, they will occur. Positive affirmations help, but always follow the Light and the truth is never far behind."

Joseph visits France.
The following past life was given to an English woman in September 1990.

"Could you tell me whether by any chance I was alive at the time of the Christ, or at a time when you were alive?"

Master: "You were, as were most of those we love who are within the world at this time. The time we speak of was after the Ascension when Joseph of Arimathea and several of the disciples and interested people were then chosen to spread the Teachings throughout the World. One of those countries where the Truth was spread, was France. And it was then a greater area of land than it is now. The people of that country were not barbarians in any way at all. Many accused those in Britain of barbarism, but they too were gentle people who farmed their lands and looked after their animals. They fought hard for that which was their own through the many invasions that came from other lands, but to friends they were greatly welcoming and had much gentleness and love in their hearts. And so too did those in other parts of the continent.

"You were born in France and your family tilled the land and looked after their beasts. But some of your family were fishermen. And one whom you loved greatly was a cousin who built boats - first vessels that would bring in the fish supply for the neighbourhood and then larger boats, the ships which sailed from port to port, transporting people and goods to different areas of the world. And you had great love for him and he for you. But you had different beliefs. You followed the beliefs of the Druids. And in the many forms of rites which the Druids performed, you would take part. Their rites and rituals were an essential part of your spiritual development. And your cousin had no belief at all in an afterlife nor in a true reasoning as to why he lived within the World, or why the World had been created. And this was your only point of controversy. Other than that, you were siblings, but siblings that loved passionately. And you dwelt together and you had children. The boys you allowed your cousin to teach his own disbeliefs, but your daughters would clothe themselves in certain attire and when the great meetings were held, would often walk for many days to the places where the rites and rituals were held.

"And then the news of the Christ and what had occurred so many thousands of miles away reached your own country. You heard also that those who had often come as merchant men were again coming to the land, and this time were bringing the teachers and preachers of the new faith with them. And this faith was very akin to Druidism. And there was great happiness and laughter and many who belonged to the cult of which you were part, surged down to the port and met the boat containing one of the disciples, who took up residence within the land. And your partner in life was persuaded to listen to him, for he too was a fisherman. The disciple was practical and knew the hazards and the problems of life and spoke with him as humankind are wont to do. And yet he also spoke of matters of the Soul which provoked your cousin to listen.

"But gradually, it became apparent that as his knowledge grew, it seemed to separate you regarding your desire for each other, for he also felt that he wished to travel with this disciple, to tend to him and to listen even more deeply to his words. And there were certain Druid rituals which would take place at times of the moon, rituals which you had reluctantly taken part in, for you had felt they were not truly right. But it was explained to you that you could win back your lover's love by using certain incantations and words of power. You did this and it was so. But when you evoke that which is of darkness, the darkness dwells within, and you became ill. And in that illness, you were unable to walk. And after some months of this and being nursed by the man you loved, there was another visitor to the shore, Joseph himself. And he made it his business to visit many, and to listen to their interpretation of the Truth and enlighten them further. And he also had the power to heal. And he was taken to you, and he saw immediately that your illness had come about because of what you had done to win back the love of your man. And he spoke to you of his own love for many who practised the faith of the Druids, and how akin to the love of Christ so many of their beliefs were. But as there is the light, there is also the darkness. And if life's desires cannot be achieved by the use of light, then they were not worth achieving.

"And he cast out evil from you and you arose and walked and your allegiance to his beliefs and teachings was strong - and in that way you were reunited with the man you loved. For you did not need the words of power to keep him by you. You needed only to share the Truth which meant so much to you both and to spread it to others who were as yet still ignorant of the true light.

"And that, my child, was how we were united in the past. And it is this recognition which so often occurs when the children of earth meet a Master for maybe many lives or maybe only one. For that recognition is on a level which earthly eyes cannot see."

"Master, was St. John the disciple who first came to France?"

"That is so. You have awareness of this or does it come from deep memory?

"I once read that the Cathars believed St. John brought Christianity to France just as Joseph of Arimathea did to Britain."

"That is so - the Beloved Disciple."

The death of Joseph.

Master: "Joseph was a man who loved solitude, he loved quietness when communication was not possible. Many times throughout the year he would walk up the steep hill on the Isle of Glass and sit and meditate and gaze out upon the estuary and the lands that were partly covered with water. When the tide was high he would look to the distant skyline and occasionally commune with those in spirit, who had no difficulty in again entering into the time scale of the world. The awareness of their love, guidance and help would come to Joseph. He could also commune with Yeshua who could float, so to speak, at will between the realities of the spirit spheres and earth, not being part of either realm. Therefore He could meet with those that he loved and speak quite freely in both worlds. When he wished Joseph could also commune with his son Josephes.

"Often as he aged Joseph would sit and muse on those times in Palestine and see again the young children, in their innocence and beauty, surrounding him. As is the way with all who grow old, their minds consistently return to the time of their youth and to their children, when there was so much beauty to look forward to and plan for before the differences within the family began to destroy the serenity and calm.

"The climate of Britain was not very conducive to the health of Joseph and there were many occasions, especially in the depth of winter, when he would experience a great ache in his bones. Even his ability and awareness of self-healing did not always assuage the pain. He ceased travelling during the last few years of his life and no longer lived in the more primitive dwellings that had been built when the family first arrived, but lived in a house that had been solidly built and was more like the home that he had in Arimathea where he could muse on the things that had given him so much pleasure in his youth.

"Joseph was over a century old when he died and his death was very private. He requested that only those whom he loved greatly should be present; his passing was very peaceful. His soul was received by his Higher Self and went to the sphere of light that had been earned through the many incarnations culminating with the life of Joseph himself. At this level he has established the teaching rhythms which are needed by the Earth for Man to go forward and be linked with his spirituality and his ancestry, which is important to his incarnations and soul's progress. Each one to whom Joseph speaks is linked within the network of past, present and future."

Chapter 22

The Epilogue -
under Roman occupation

In the first chapter the Master commented that "...the Truth which Jesus brought is still hidden within the Church archives. This truth is relevant for it would bring spiritual freedom to everyone."
Examples of this are the release from the concept of original sin and the belief that only certain sects after death will go to a place where the soul lives - but the soul only knows life!

It is hoped that the reader will now feel that the main objectives of this book have been fulfilled and in particular the Master's comment about "...a greater understanding of the opposition Jesus encountered in endeavouring to speak out in a land that was occupied by a pagan force and where the Jews felt threatened by any talk of one supreme power."

The Master explained that "The belief in the heart of the Jews was that the true Messiah whom they had begun to visualise as a divine being was not as a man with failings, joys and despair."
Even a man prepared to die physically for His beliefs did not match the ideology in the Jewish race of a Messiah representing God in all its facets. Therefore they could not accept that one born of woman, one who came through life from childhood to manhood experiencing all that others experienced, the temptations, the delights, the fears, could indeed be one who was divine. So there was a misconception of what is divine.

Master: "Remember that to ancient people God was represented as outside themselves. They had no concept of the soul as spiritually enlightened people now have, that concept of the divine or of creative discipline within the self. So they could not imagine one who would become a king or a leader and thus usurp the authority of the governing power.

"They feared the Romans who had great power and great authority. The Sanhedrin was only allowed to exist while it accepted the authority of Rome. As soon as there were those Elders such as Nicodemus and the Arimathean, who moved outside that discipline there was immediate threat to human life. The leaders at that time also feared reprisals. They feared that a way of life which had been sacrosanct for so long would indeed be threatened. This was their fear and it was this that motivated the actions and the reactions of that time. The reason that the great vote went toward the destruction of Jesus was to show to the masses that His humanity and His ability to suffer proved that there was nothing of the divine within Him. They also tried to provoke Him into claiming the throne of David so that those who understood the great power of Rome could indeed sanction His death in order to maintain peace."

It was no accident that Jesus was born at that particular time and in that part of the world. The influence of the Roman occupation played a great part in many aspects of Jesus' life. It was, of course, the Romans who introduced crucifixion as a means of death for criminals, thus providing a very large public spectacle which created the maximum impact for the resurrection.

After Jesus' death the magnificent network of roads throughout the Roman Empire contributed much to the rapid spread of Christ's teachings as did the widely dispersed Jewish communities.

The inclusion of many individual past lives should have given a fairly vivid picture of the way of life of ordinary people at that time and hence a better appreciation of that particular age and also the part played by reincarnation and karma in all our lives.

The Master commented that it is interesting to note that 2000 years ago "...maturity came very early, many young men were betrothed at an age when today they would be considered still children. Twelve or thirteen years of age would see them fathering their children and girls as young as eleven would conceive and bear their first child. There was often a difference in age of only fifteen to twenty years between generations and even less in some cases."

The important role of the Arimathean in the life of Jesus.
Master: "All children need guidance and the mother of Jesus was extremely young and inexperienced in all things. His father was elderly and had little interest in the upbringing of his younger children by his second marriage. His two sons by his first wife were already adults and while Joseph (the carpenter) enjoyed his work and enjoyed being among the Essenes he could not really understand Jesus' talents, which were far beyond his conception of how a child should be.

"The upbringing of Joseph of Arimathea was far more intellectual and he was inspired at an early age to understand that he would play a great part in the education and the upbringing of his great nephew, which he did. He travelled with Him, he taught Him in the Sanhedrin, he arranged that He should go to the Essenic school at Qumran, he arranged for Jesus' tuition in his home so that He would be conversant with the Jewish Law, the Hebrew language and to be fluent in Sanskrit. When it was apparent that Jesus would travel widely before beginning at a later age His true mission in Palestine, he arranged that he should learn the language of the countries where He would travel. Jesus learnt Greek and three Indian dialects when it was apparent that He would be staying and conversing with the spiritual teachers in India. Joseph was far more active in the life of the young Jesus and the growing young man than His parents. Jesus also loved greatly the son (Josephes) of the Arimathean and they were as brothers together, while the step brothers of Jesus were much older in years and different in aspiration. Without the Arimathean and his family Jesus would have been impoverished intellectually and spiritually in His younger years. It was Joseph of Arimathea who after the crucifixion and resurrection - of the Christ as He had then become through baptism and through the light which God the Father had placed in Him - was the pioneer in bringing the Teachings of the Way and the Truth to Britain. He was also responsible for the travelling of the Disciples to different areas of the world. He had great influence and therefore used that influence so that the life's work of His nephew would never, never diminish but would grow as the centuries passed.

"Not a great deal in the Gospels is based upon the scrolls, but the church having the entire scrolls distinguished between what they wished mankind to learn and read and those which would give early man too much knowledge, too much freewill and growth of intellect. The church felt that they were the propagators of truth and therefore they limited what would go into the Holy Book. The Old Testament is, of course, a record of Jewish life and that is complete, but as we have said only the shortened version is in the New Testament. When all these scrolls are released and published, even if only slowly then readers will see the part that many have played in the propagation of truth and the furtherance of the teachings.

"The inclusion of the Arimathean's family helps to show not only life at that time, but also what kind of man Jesus was and that much of His teaching was in the strict understanding of the Jewish community and especially that of the Essenes. As we have already said it is the Church that created Christianity not Jesus, for He created a way of life based on Essenic teaching which was ancient and very profound. He was first an Essene, secondly a Jew, and thirdly a teacher and prophet, and in that order He taught."

Some details both of Jesus' boyhood and young manhood before He was Christed fill an important gap in the Gospels and some details in the Holy Book which are not accurate have been mentioned.

Above all the Master set out (see Part I) "To widen the horizon of the Gospels and to show that there was nothing magical or mystical that could not occur today. While much of what is revealed in the Gospels is largely true there is the illusion that much of what took place was superficially illogical. The events which revolved around Christ do not mean that He was above scientific reasoning which is always within Universal Law. The reader should also be left in no doubt that the heart and soul of every human being can be linked to the total soul - the Higher Self."

The part played by religion.

Master: "It must be borne in mind that religions arise from ignorance and not from Truth. It is the identity of God which has caused Man to hesitate concerning his beliefs. The man Jesus brought with Him a light, a purpose and a way forward to enable mankind to accept that there is but one universal light which can be called by any name, but still it is the Yahweh, the Jehovah, the Creator, the Light which gave birth to the world. Even Christ's mission was doomed, not to failure but misinterpretation, and throughout the last two thousand years it has become another religion, to divide and subdivide mankind. All this must cease.

"The Truth is not always portrayed in the Gospels for they were written long after Christ's death. They are not written in the words of those who were with Him, loved Him and cared for Him. The spoken word is seldom recorded accurately when written down and certainly not when there has been a long while between the events portrayed and the writing, for the memory becomes clouded.

"Because of the Christ those that followed Him were called 'of the

Christos' and then eventually 'Christians'. The term 'Christianity' was used later due largely to the teachings of Paul and to the church which arose around those teachings. But Christ's teachings were virtually the same, they showed the light and love possible in man and his ability to give hope and understanding to his fellow creatures: also man's ability to listen to the voice of God and be led in the same way as Abraham and Isaac and those who led their people throughout the lands. For they too could speak to God in their hearts and hear Him within their minds.

"Unfortunately in more recent times Christianity's real impact and purpose have changed. There is too much dogma and there are the many different creeds to which Mankind adheres doggedly and with determination. Our purpose at this time is to release Man from this bondage, to redirect him to the inner spiritual activities of the soul and to relearn within his consciousness the Truth which Christ spread.

"Some people have the gift of understanding. They make up their minds about what to believe in and what to lay aside as fictitious. However many who are brought up in the Catholic faith adhere rigidly through fear to the teachings given by the priests. It is fear that prevents people from acknowledging the Truth.

"It should however be remembered that everyone sees the Truth according to their own progress through life and that they must have the right to accept what they believe, even if this is not the full Truth or reality of what occurred. In our teachings we endeavour to portray the Truth to those who listen and read."

The House of David.

Master: "Jesus, His mother, Father and Joseph of Arimathea were all descended from the House of David. From the time when David ruled it was the understanding of that Tribe that their lives were governed by purpose and sacrifice. This led to the misunderstanding both of the Magi, who thought that Jesus was destined to become a king, and also of the rulers of Rome as to the majesty and purpose of Christ when He stated that He was king, for of course He was not king of the land but of the universal kingdom of God the Father - the Creator."

Why was Jesus born a Jew?

The reader may have wondered why Jesus was born into the Jewish faith and why in that particular culture. Was the Jewish understanding of God at that time more accurate than that of other faiths?

The Master was asked that question and he replied:

"The simple answer is not so much yes or no but a blend between that which Jesus taught and that which His soul needed to give to His Higher Self - that particular flow of energies. Not every Higher Self has the same basic structure any more than a child is the exact replica of only one of its two parents, it is a blend of both. The parents are of course a blend of their own parents and this goes back to when Man first received an intelligent response to his request for life, that is when the soul, totally aware of all existence, entered into Man to guide and help him forward.* The question is of far greater complexity than appears at first. Within this blending the freewill aspect is of paramount importance to each member of society for if it is used in the correct manner there should be a balance which brings about peace. Peace is not in fact possible because not only do individuals not relate to that truth in the soul's knowledge but also they do not know how to blend it with the essential truth in others.

"The inherent belief of the Jews is that their fatherhood is in Jehovah - their name for the God force - the creative energy which brought forth existence. The Jews were able to immerse themselves in the concept of an all-embracing God and live their lives completely within the framework of understanding of this one truth. This is so near the ultimate Truth that it was considered an excellent background for Jesus to enter into life and to absorb as His earliest awareness of what is beyond the material world. If He had been born in a different place it could well have been the teaching of the Buddha which would have entered His consciousness, both from an historical viewpoint and from what was happening around Him. But of course He would then have been born in a different part of the world and to parents who had around them the influence of the Buddha. We use this purely as an example.

---

* Up to three and a half million years ago the soul in developing Man was a group soul very similar to that of animals, but much more highly developed. Collectively this soul asked the Creator to be allowed the potential for much greater development. This was granted and soul burst into thousands of millions of fragments - the so called big bang - which scientists wrongly believe to refer to the creation of the universe, which has always existed in one form or another and always will. Thus in answering Man's prayer for greater development, the much greater need of Soul to have a means of development was also fulfilled, for Man is very nearly the perfect vehicle for this, the personality being, if you like, the animal part of Man's nature.

"Initially Jesus accepted the Judaic faith as laid down by Abraham in all its strict principles, but then he became aware within Himself of the release from that strict religious bond into a more realistic way of life, accepting the principles of other major beliefs and the way that they changed the outlook of mankind as a whole."

The Essenic Teachings.
Master: "The Essenes had a wonderfully clear concept of the Truth and this was very important to Jesus in clarifying His own ideas. His own conscious beliefs were very strong and went beyond those He inherited from his parents for they stemmed from the source of all Truth. This is why He was able to teach so clearly those who were ignorant of anything but the indoctrination they had received. He often spoke in parables so that He could reach a far wider audience who understood those stories, whether they comprehended advanced teaching from the Torah or had only awareness of their basic needs of life, often not met.

"Virtually every teaching Yeshua gave was a teaching based upon Essenic principles - the brotherhood of Man, the Fatherhood of God and because of his intelligence the ability of Man to survive above the animal world and the world of nature. All is within the principles that the Essenes taught their students, to be truly aware of the role of science and spirit entwined together to bring forth a greater knowledge in humankind of the principles of life. Life itself is a scientific force, it is those who follow the principles of science to the exclusion of the principles of spirit that are at fault, not science itself which is based on the principle of creation and also the ability of the intelligence of Man to link with the forces of light for expression and unity."

The Essenes, Masons and Druids.
Master: "The Essenes and the Masons were linked together very closely in fundamental knowledge and behaviour although the Masons began some five thousand years before the time of Christ and were linked through the building of Solomon's Temple, which is when they became fully established in their craft and its principles. When the Essenes were formed they were linked to the same principles, but the use of craft was on a more scientific level than the Masons who were very practical and used their skills as carpenters and masons to fulfil the great plan of Earth for evolving Man. Joseph, the father of Yeshua, was a Mason as well as

being an Essene and he would speak on both principles when he was asked to undertake the important function of speaker at the rituals which regularly took place. At one time only men were allowed in the Essenic temples and the Masonic meetings. Nowadays most of the Masons are still men although there are groups of women who fulfil a similar role, albeit not yet acknowledged by the Masons, but their rituals are very similar.

"The Essenic rituals also involved the use of fire, earth and water and those within the circles had certain procedures to follow, certain teachings to learn by heart and certain words which they had to commit to memory in order to be part of the ruling body of the group. Gradually women became more and more involved with the Essenic groups. Even the root of the word is very similar and many of those who were involved in the Essenic rituals were also aware of the Masonic rituals which they incorporated. The one linking force was the Fatherhood of God, the Creative Force which indeed was the Great Mason Himself - the Builder - He whom they acknowledged had all knowledge, all ability and from whom originated, at the beginning of time, the blueprint for the Earth. In believing in the Fatherhood of God they also believed in the Brotherhood of Man. They formed perfectly symmetric circles in which they sat, in the centre of which was the symbol which both Masons and Essenes worshipped. This we are not permitted to reveal but certainly that which was acknowledged by all forces in the two groups played a very important part in the moral aspects of both, and in the principle of their spiritual and economic growth.

"In this age it is sometimes said that secret societies are against mankind in general, but the good that is done by them must never be overlooked. There is good and bad in all societies and in all groups of endeavour. To look toward the righteous is to ensure that the path forward is fully understood and kept as the steps proceed. Most Essenes were Jewish and much of the ritual which took place in their homes was also followed in the Essenic temples.

"Those of the order of Druids used the same symbol for they followed the same principles, but without the strict spiritual factors and the worshipping of God without power and without brutality that other sects followed. Very gradually however the Druids also accepted these principles and adhered to them, and (as we have seen in a previous chapter) mostly through the teachings of Joseph of Arimathea and those that were with him in his spiritual group in Britain. Other Druids in other countries were taught by the Disciples and others who had surrounded Yeshua. He was as the hub of a wheel, the Disciples around Him forming a circle with streams of light from each one centring into His own God force."

The important lesson of discipline.

Master: "The lesson of discipline is indeed one which brings together in the life of the soul a great need for advancement in whatever way is chosen. It is a hard taskmaster. So often there are those who have lived successfully through many lives, some very difficult, learning the lessons that are appropriate at that time, for that generation. When they return to the Higher Self (as already explained in the first chapter) all this knowledge is shared equally within the structure of the soul. Many lessons are repeated time and time again, especially those relevant to the Age in which the soul has decided to return, and none is truly easy. The very fact of living on the Earth and being aware of freewill negates any simplicity in life. This was shown by Yeshua when within His incarnation He accepted the role of Christ. Many things were demanded of Him which with clarity of mind and understanding of all His past He felt were unwarranted, for the nature of His role should have allowed Him to be excused many of the difficult stages of His life. But discipline makes no allowance for the ascension of the soul or its knowledge.

"Discipline is needed continuously through earthly life so as to place in perspective all aspects of life including returning again to spirit and then once more descending to the Earth. Discipline is the rule of law which guides each personality forward, makes life a worthwhile opportunity for expansion so that spiritual development may unfold, and the awareness of this be absorbed into the personality. Recollection of the past does not always help the individual along the specific path he has chosen. Very often those with absolute unawareness of any life before find the positive aspect of life much easier to tolerate and to accept than those who have made a study of the past and the possible future. Simplicity helps very greatly the lesson of discipline. Complications, especially that of reasoning and the power of the mind, which is in intelligent Man, make the acceptance of these lessons more arduous.

"The personal effect of discipline in life affects the choice. Only humanity is given the choice as to how they act. However seemingly intelligent the animal world may have become, especially in domesticated animals, they do not have a choice for they work by instinct; this is their guiding rule and they must accept it. If humankind accepted that their instinct is a good guide, not so many mistakes would then be made as life unfolds and maturity is reached. The soul being the Higher Self expressed in the reality of living. Those people who are able to accept that there is a rule in life which mankind generally agrees gives an acceptable life for the majority, it is because the Higher Self has managed to convince the personalities they represent, that living a God-fearing life and not causing destruction, pain or anxiety to others allows a greater unfolding of purpose in the self. Those who live a life of turmoil and unease will often fall into a pit of depression, anxiety, and severe illness because they suppress the voice which helps to guide them. As the lessons of discipline become more apparent the resentment of these troubled minds deepens."

God's purpose within the life of Man.
Master: "There are two aspects of life - life in its spiritual sense in the realms of light, and life as it has become through the trials and tribulations of mankind upon the Earth itself. Primitive Man had no knowledge of any law be it Divine Universal Law or a law made by Man for the preservation of Man. He had purely and simply instinct, but as he grew through applying that instinct with more intelligence than animal life is able to do, he began to be guided inwardly by soul which by that time had entered his deep subconscious mind which guides and fulfils life even if belief is not present. The many different forms of belief, once they began to ensure the progress of humankind, formed creeds and faiths which were established in the world, but now are beginning to wane. The world exists in spirals and as a spiral reaches a peak so it takes the knowledge gained within it, transmutes it and begins over again. Analysing what it has learned throughout the centuries it takes instructions from the inner self regarding the transformation and analysis of those truths. Thus Man can continue to profit from what he has learned and gain even greater understanding through Universal Law.

"Light signifies the presence of God. Saint Paul himself decided that monotheism (belief in one God) was the greatest of the truths for it allowed all mankind to relate to the God within and to the purpose of the soul. The true comprehension of the purpose of Man is realised through meditation and visualisation of each in his own way according to his own understanding. God's purpose in the life of Man is to bring together that which is certain, that which never changes in the spiritual realms which are so close to the Earth and yet because of their faster rhythm are so very far from Man's freewill. A great step forward occurred in the teachings when Paul had his vision and temporarily became blinded by the magnificence of seeing the One God in His true form. Paul was a man of great intelligence, born to a father who had knowledge beyond his time and who had fostered in his son a belief in the ability of the self. The transformation of that self enabled Paul to be aware of situations outside the limitation of Man himself. Paul was, of course, totally aware of the beliefs of his own race, but he also realised, by that flash of pure brilliant light, that he had been allowed to enter into a different realm. This occurred at a time when paganism had reached its peak in the life of Man, who was already evolving towards a greater understanding, a greater need in life. Polytheism (belief in many gods) was beginning to fail in the world of knowledge, the world of belief, however ancient, and Man was seeking the understanding of the one God force which could unite him and fellow Man with a purpose. Paul therefore moved in this stream of light which became part of his own soul and its purpose. He was literally transformed from the Man that he had been - intolerant, unable to accept the views of others, a Man hesitant because of his own lack of stature and apparent vision, although it merely needed the trigger to bring him enlightenment. He was thus able to cast aside the beliefs of his own people and began to embrace the teachings of Christ, that he had once followed avidly and angrily, even though he would not allow this to be known to those to whom he conversed. His own feeling was that it was the Christ light that had appeared before him. Adhering to this, he felt also it was a protection and that as Christ Himself had done he would be able to endure with fortitude all that might be presented to him, unto death itself.

"Paul was inspired by the combined energy of God within the Christos. God, the First Cause, is the Christos, the meaning of all life, the I AM. Jesus was the manifestation of that Being in the flesh, so as to bring the teaching to mankind in a way that they could understand through seeing, hearing and relating to another human being like themselves. Only those who took on the mantle of a prophet were able to interpret the energies of God when He appeared in the way of Light, but Jesus using the Christos in Himself was able to project the ultimate truth towards those who wished to listen and learn, and this marked the beginning of change in the existence of Man. Paul, was unaware of Jesus as a person and did not follow Him during His life, but was instrumental in continuing that philosophy and teaching throughout his life. As also, it must be understood, were Peter and John and others among the chosen ones who had first-hand knowledge and acceptance of these teachings, even though at first they were not clear to them.

"We said at the beginning that what is within the world must be and will continue to be. Remember however that Man's increasing understanding of life through repeated re-incarnations, where aspects of the soul returning at the end of that life share what has occurred with the entire soul - or Higher Self, so enriches it that further intelligence and understanding of belief can take place. If the Higher Self did not move forward there could be no purpose to creation at all. To stay still and not partake of that ever increasing spiral of existence is to lay aside the true purpose of Man, to allow him to be clothed in flesh and to bring about changes not just in consciousness but in action"

Was the karma of the Jewish nation during the last 2000 years due to their failure to spread their beliefs?
Master: "Very largely this is so although of course the Biblical 'Promised land' was not in fact actual territory but a vision of the future. Much of the interpretation which Moses placed upon understanding the Word of God was due to his inability to see clearly the future of his race. He misinterpreted it to the extent that he led his people on a search for actual territory instead of concentrating on the teaching which would have led them to greater understanding. Much of this, many centuries later, Paul himself with greater intelligence was able to reason and to teach, but that which is given at one stage of life is only suitable for those who have reached exactly that point in their development. That which is beyond the now is not yet acceptable to the intelligence of Man.

"Although Man has now reached a great peak in his awareness and ability to live and use science as he does, he cannot possibly relate to that which will take place during the twenty first century. Then an even greater epoch will begin in which Man's ability to relate to the spiritual realm while still in the flesh will be realised. Prophecy can only be given in a very narrow range for a short while ahead. Man's intellect cannot express nor yet accept that which has not yet been seen or heard, so Man's movement forward takes place as the shifting of the Earth towards those spiritual realms slowly and inexorably takes place."

Man's life on Earth.

Master: "Future life upon Earth is unknown because that which is created on a day to day level of learning produces the future. Certain things must be so because they are part of a karmic link within the world itself. But mankind has the power to learn only through action. He can link with past events at his time of meditation and feel deeper awareness of the contentment of being in the world. Even the present can be changed, though the past cannot, for it is cemented in the present, but the future emerges from the thoughts and the actions of the past and present. It is interwoven with every soul incarnate and of course there are theories that the realities of the past, present and future are as one. It is important to live life in the now, to be aware that the actions of the present mould the future, so that with greater knowledge mankind can produce a worthwhile future and an upward pathway towards perfection engendered by spirit teaching. If man is a fatalist - if he believes too greatly in fate, and thinks that which he does in the now is of no importance, then alas the world will perish. But as little by little he realises his true place in life and how the unfolding of his purpose can give dimension to the future, the world itself will have a greater understanding of how to survive and to achieve."

A final word from the Master on the importance of love.

"...A time for planning, a time for being at peace within yourself and finding peace with your neighbours, finding a way to live together, to have harmony one with another when arguments beset you and where differences in your spiritual beliefs lead to warfare or a disintegration of love. Without love the world cannot survive. The love vibration began the world, gave it life and encouraged the soul to desire to live individually upon the planet. Love, closeness, harmony, upliftment, compassion, healing - they all stem from the God force which is love."

Genealogical Charts

The House of David

This genealogical table clearly shows the relationship between Jesus, John the Baptist and Joseph of Arimathea, all descended from the line of David.

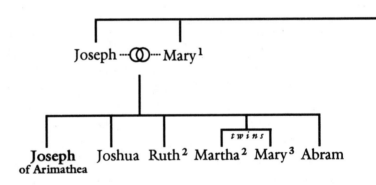

1 *The three half sisters bore the name of 'Mary' (a common Jewish name) linked to the family name of their respective fathers, for their mother had had three husbands.*

2 *Died in childhood*

3 *Still born*

4 *Died in infancy*

5 *Sex unknown*

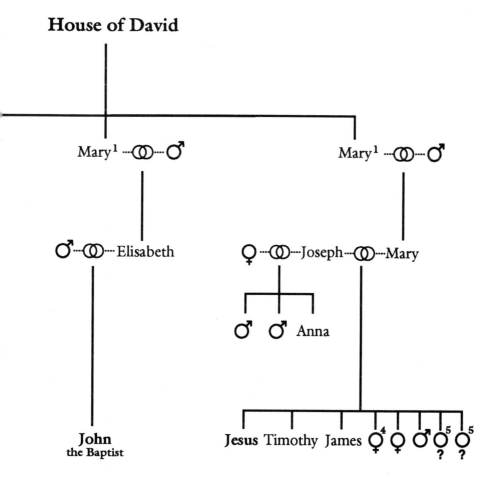

House of David

Joseph of Arimathea's Family

1 *Non-Jewish*

2 *Died within a few months*

3 *Died soon after birth*

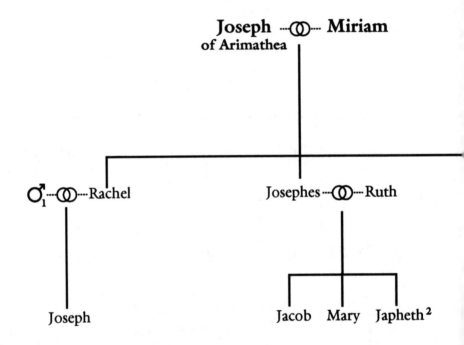

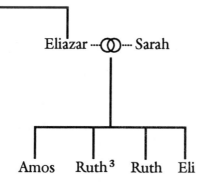

The extended family of Joseph of Arimathea

1 *Died at 1 week*

2 *Died at age 12*

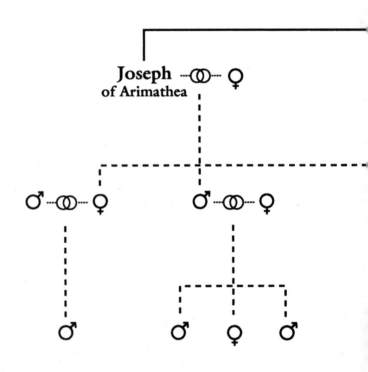